HISTORY OF MOVIE MUSICALS

HISTORY OF MOVIE MUSICALS

THOMAS G. AYLESWORTH

GALLERY BOOKS
An imprint of W.H. Smith Publishers Inc.
112 Madison Avenue
New York, New York 10016

A Bison Book

Published by Gallery Books
A Division of W H Smith Publishers Inc.
112 Madison Avenue
New York, New York 10016

Produced by
Bison Books Corp.
17 Sherwood Place
Greenwich, CT 06830
USA

Printed in Hong Kong

Previous pages
Page 1: Judy Garland in *The Wizard of Oz* (1939).
Page 2, top left to right: Julie Andrews in *Star!* (1968); Marilyn Monroe in *Gentlemen Prefer Blondes* (1953); Rita Hayworth. *Center:* Yul Brynner and Deborah Kerr in *The King and I* (1956). *Below left to right:* Barbra Streisand in *Funny Girl* (1968); Gene Kelly in *Singin' in the Rain* (1952); Cyd Charisse.
Page 3: Fred Astaire in *Royal Wedding* (1951). *Above:* Busby Berkeley's 'By a Waterfall' number from *Footlight Parade* (1933).

CONTENTS

Introduction	6
The Early Years	10
The Berkeley Years	24
Fred, Ginger, Shirley and the Rest	38
The Operettas	72
The Extravaganzas	86
The War Years	98
After the War	132
Stage to Screen	168
The Recent Past	218
The Box Office Winners	239
Filmography	241
Index	252
Acknowledgments and Credits	256

Rex Harrison in *My Fair Lady* (1964).

Dick Van Dyke and Julie Andrews in *Mary Poppins* (1964).

Ray Bolger and Judy Garland in *The Wizard of Oz* (1939).

Judy Garland in *Summer Stock* (1950).

INTRODUCTION

Movie musicals. You either love them or you hate them. And there is nothing anyone can say to you that will make you change your mind. Most people can be found in one of two groups—those who go to movies for escape from reality and for pure entertainment, and those who go to movies to learn, to appreciate, to think. For the first group, most movie musicals represent the ultimate—the dream of escapism. For the second group, movie musicals represent a debasement of the film art form. The two views are irreconcilable.

What slapstick comedy was to the silent screen, the musical cinema is to film fans and movie-makers today. As it was in the case of the slapsticks, the plot in a musical might mean something, but more often than not, it got lost and stayed lost. But audiences love them, and even the most sophisticated film viewer is captured by musicals because most of them are fundamentally so innocent. Many musicals are about show business, and what could be more fun than making a movie about one's own lifework? Besides, musicals often give the producer, director and writer a chance to bring back the old songs and corn of vanished theater, film and vaudeville days and polish them up for a new audience.

Students of the movies often say that the Europeans are best at making art films and Americans are best with

Barbra Streisand in *Hello Dolly!* (1969).

Christopher Plummer and Julie Andrews in *The Sound of Music* (1965).

Chorus line from *Forty-Second Street* (1933).

Snow White and the Seven Dwarfs (1938).

the more escapist types of movies. The Dream Factory in California excelled in making thrillers, Westerns and especially musicals, because musicals are the most escapist films of all. After all, America has a huge diversity of traditions, probably the largest cadre of songwriters and lyricists, and certainly the greatest reservoir of material and talent from the musical stage.

But what is a musical? It isn't a movie with an occasional musical interlude, although *The Jazz Singer* (1927)—a film that most people call the first musical—can be defined as that type of picture. No one would ever say that *Casablanca* (1942) was a musical, even with Dooley Wilson bursting into song from time to time, especially with the classic 'As Time Goes By.' Most Marx Brothers movies paused a couple of times to let Chico hold forth on the piano and to give Harpo a showcase number on his harp. But those are not musicals.

Forty-second Street (1933) is a musical, as are *Singin' in the Rain* (1952), *The Music Man* (1962), *1776* (1972) and even *Saturday Night Fever* (1977). These films have one thing in common—they rise and fall on the success of their musical scores. Without the music, there would be no movie.

To most people, the very word 'musical' conjures up a picture of something light and frothy, bubbling with wit and foolishness, something that surely has no message. That is because the word 'musical' and the word 'comedy' seem to go together. People referred to 'musical comedy' long before they shortened it to 'musical.' But some musicals don't fit into this mold. Who can deny that there was a message—a serious message—in *West Side Story* (1961), *Jesus Christ, Superstar* (1973), *Godspell* (1973) and even *South Pacific* (1958)?

The musical can illuminate the talents of huge numbers of performers, as in *That's Entertainment* (1974), or it can showcase a single person, like Judy Garland in *A Star Is Born* (1954). It can be happy, as is *Good News* (1974), or sad, as is *Carousel* (1956).

Without the musical, we might never have heard of such child stars as Judy Garland, Mickey Rooney, Shirley Temple or Deanna Durbin. And, in addition to giving kids a break, the

Mitzi Gaynor and Rossano Brazzi in *South Pacific* (1958).

Eleanor Powell and Fred Astaire in *Broadway Melody of 1940* (1940).

Gene Kelly, Debbie Reynolds and Donald O'Connor in *Singin' in the Rain* (1952).

musicals gave us a chance to get acquainted with such minority-group talents as Bill Robinson ('Mr Bojangles'), Ethel Waters, Lena Horne, Nancy Kwan, Chita Rivera and Rita Moreno.

The history of the movie musical has been a history of famous stars, composers and directors—Fred Astaire and Ginger Rogers, Jeanette MacDonald and Nelson Eddy, Shirley Temple, Judy Garland, Barbra Streisand, Julie Andrews, Doris Day, Cyd Charisse, Mickey Rooney, Bing Crosby, Frank Sinatra, Gene Kelly, Cole Porter, Harold Arlen, Irving Berlin, Richard Rodgers, Jerome Kern, George Gershwin, Ernst Lubitsch, Rouben Mamoulian, Vincente Minelli and many more.

Make no mistake about it: the musical may be a success because of the star, because of the director, because of the material used. But it is more likely that it succeeds through a precarious balance of many ingredients, and that film-making ability is not a guarantee. Look at the great film-makers who have tried musicals and not quite captured the magic—Carol Reed and *Oliver!* (1968), Josh Logan and *Camelot* (1967), William Wyler and *Funny Girl* (1968), George Cukor and *My Fair Lady* (1964), John Huston and *Annie* (1982).

What makes a musical great? It isn't necessary to have the songs growing naturally out of the story, as is the case with grand opera. The Astaire-Rogers musicals usually didn't have this quality and they were great; Fred Zinnemann's *Oklahoma!* (1955) did, and it was not great. A musical doesn't have to be original to be exceptional. *The Wizard of Oz* (1939) was an original and was a blockbuster, but who remembers another original, *Where Do We Go from Here?* (1945) with Kurt Weill's music, Ira Gershwin's lyrics and Fred MacMurray's talent? A great musical doesn't have to be an import from Broadway. *On the Town* (1949) and *Cabaret* (1972) were classic adaptations, but *West Side Story* (1961) was a poor imitation of the original. Emphasizing dancing over singing or singing over dancing does not spell success, either. Who can say that Ginger Rogers was better than Barbra Streisand, or vice-versa?

As the film critic William Bayer once said: '. . . The criteria for a great musical are among the most elusive of things, for though it is obvious that a musical must work, that its diverse elements must come together in some way, this "way" remains mysterious and seems to depend on something called "chemistry," which is a word used to describe a phenomenon that people recognize but can't rationally explain. Still and all, a great musical gives pleasure because of its lightness and artistry and the ebullience of its fantasy, because, like the Fabergé egg, or a trompe l'oeil ceiling, it is "right." And that, admittedly, is as dubious and subjective a standard as one can employ.'

The whole thing began with the Jolson Revolution that exploded like a bombshell on Friday night, 6 October 1927. The movies were never to be the same again.

A caricature of Al Jolson in blackface that was used on a promotional poster for *The Jazz Singer* (1927).

THE EARLY YEARS

The movie box office had sagged in the middle of the 1920s. For some reason or other, people were staying home, and Hollywood was worried. Theater owners started adding novelties, such as vaudeville acts, live condensed operas and musical comedies on stage to drag the people in. Things piled up until the featured movie itself seemed in danger of getting lost in these live shows.

But a thing called the Vitaphone (recording discs synchronized with the film) was available to the movie-makers. It had been developed by technicians at the Bell Telephone Company—who had been working on it since the time when Thomas A Edison was interested in movies. Unfortunately, the people who ran the movie studios rejected it. All, that is, except the Warner Brothers. It wasn't that Harry, Jack, Sam and Albert Warner were so daring, it was that they were having business problems. They had been involved with films for a long time, ever since the Nickelodeon days, and had worked themselves up the ladder until they became producers.

The problem was that they had invested all their capital, plus all they could borrow, in their studio. So strapped were they that they could not pay to get access to the first-run theaters because they were beaten out by their more well-heeled competitors. And of course they didn't have the money to buy theaters of their own. They were at the bottom of the barrel, and it took a while before the people in charge of Vitaphone came to see them.

The Warner Brothers were desperate, and contracted for the exclusive use of the Vitaphone device, not knowing whether or not they could use it. They had to produce enough sound films to carry them through until the time when their silents were no longer making money. But they plunged ahead.

The Jazz Singer (1927) was not the first Vitaphone production—it was merely the first full-length movie to use the process. The first Vitaphone program was held at the Manhattan Opera House in New York City on 6 August 1926. It had short subjects in sound, featuring musical stars like violinist Mischa Elman and tenor Giovanni Martinelli, followed by a silent film, *Don Juan* (1926), starring John Barrymore. It was a silent, but Warner's production chief Darryl F Zanuck (who had started his career in the early 1920s writing scripts for Rin Tin Tin movies) hired the New York Philharmonic to record background music for the film.

The gimmick didn't work. The music seemed to be coming from behind the screen rather than from the orchestra pit, but that wasn't the real problem. Theater owners resisted buying the expensive equipment necessary for that little innovation. So for a year after *Don Juan*, only a few theaters were equipped with the system and all they had to show were those 'Vitaphone Shorts.'

Then came *The Jazz Singer*. Al Jolson was an established star on Broadway and he asked a lot of money for this experimental film. Warner Brothers didn't have all that much money, so they offered him stock in their company instead. Had Jolson accepted, he would have received a fortune, but he refused, and the Warner Brothers somehow got enough money together to hire him.

The Jazz Singer was not really the first musical or the first sound motion picture—it was a melodrama that highlighted seven songs sung by Jolson, plus a few lines of dialogue that he reputedly ad-libbed on the set and that were allowed to remain. Those included his patented 'You ain't heard nothin' yet' and a speech to his screen mother, played by Eugenie Besserer.

But the songs were sensational. Among them were such Jolson trademarks as 'Toot Toot Tootsie Goodbye' and 'Mammy,' plus 'My Gal Sal,' 'Waiting for the Robert E Lee,' 'Dirty Hands, Dirty Face,' 'Mother, I Still Have You' and the reverent 'Kol Nidre,' sung in synagogues on the eve of the Day of Atonement. 'Mother, I Still Have You' was the first song ever written for use in a film.

The film was not great. It was a mediocre movie with a shopworn story. Running for 88 minutes, it told the tale of young Jakie Rabinowitz (Jolson) who alienated his father (played by Warner Oland, who went on to play the title roles in 16 Charlie Chan films) by abandoning a future as a cantor and following a career in jazz singing that eventually took him to stardom. Sam Warner, who was primarily responsible for the movie and

Opposite: Jolson in blackface.

Above: Jolson as Jakie Rabinowitz and May McAvoy as Mary Dale, the showgirl who loves him in *The Jazz Singer* (1927).

Jolson came back in *The Singing Fool* (1928). It was a tear-jerker that was best remembered for the song 'Sonny Boy.'

this revolution in film-making, died under the pressure, just 24 hours before the grand opening.

The audience was enchanted. There were bursts of applause after every number, and a standing ovation at the end of the film. It was a Warner Brothers triumph. They had given birth to the movie musical and convinced other producers that sound was here to stay—all in one evening. The next day they took out an ad in *The New York Times*:

> We apologize to the thousands who were turned away from last night's premiere. If the WARNER THEATRE were as large as Madison Square Garden, we still would not have been able to accommodate the crowds that clamored for admission. There will be two performances daily at 2:45 & 8:45, and we respectfully suggest that you purchase tickets well in advance.

The revolution had happened. Manufacturers of the sound equipment were swamped with orders from exhibitors. By the end of the year even the most confirmed skeptics realized that any sound film was attracting large crowds to any theater that showed it. By the spring of 1928, the worst sound film would outdraw the best silent movie in any town. And there were some strange talkies. *Our Dancing Daughters* (1928) starred Joan Crawford; it was a silent movie with some sound effects thrown in. When *Showboat*, starring Laura La Plante and Joseph Schildkraut, was released in 1929, some incidental music had been added.

There were problems with the new sound systems. Early recording equipment was so sensitive that it even picked up sounds made by fabrics. Therefore taffeta could not be used at all, and petticoats had to be made of felt and wool rather than silk; shoes had to be soled with felt and rubber. The Vitaphone camera had to be enclosed in a soundproof booth so that the whirring of the camera itself would not be recorded. And it was hot in the booth. Without air conditioning, the temperature inside would rise to the point where cameramen could stay inside for only a few minutes at a time.

By the middle of 1928, all the Hollywood studios had to face three new problems with the sound film. They had to re-equip with sound devices. They had to figure out what to do with their backstock of silent films. They had to do something with their contract actors and actresses whose voices were not up to the primitive recording equipment of the day.

Panic was the order of the times, and many of the pictures suffered. Gone was the free-flowing action and continuity of the silent movie. In was a

A dance number from *The Broadway Melody* (1929). It was a loosely disguised biopic of the vaudevillian Duncan Sisters.

static, stagelike technique caused by the fact that the microphone was immovable and all action had to be centered around the spot where the mike was. Cameras, in their booths, could no longer be moved around freely. The director could no longer give audible suggestions as a scene was being photographed.

Jolson returned to the screen in 1928 in *The Singing Fool*. The plot was so melodramatic that the theaters must have been awash in tears—of either sympathy or laughter. It was a dismal tear-jerker about a brash entertainer who comes to his senses when his little boy dies, memorable only because Jolson sang 'Sonny Boy' in it. *The Singing Fool* was followed by three other Jolson musicals, *Say It with Songs* (1929), *Mammy* (1930) and *Big Boy* (1930). None of these attained *The Jazz Singer*'s box office take, although they were popular.

Hollywood went music crazy in 1929: stars of stage musical comedy, vaudeville hoofers, ukelele artists, ballerinas and low comedians descended on Southern California by the train-load, and it was said that the only stars who did not take singing or dancing lessons were Greta Garbo and Rin Tin Tin. The song-writing industry established a new headquarters in the film capital. Voice coaches made up a special colony. Antique operettas were dusted off. Studios made pictures featuring their entire roster of stars doing novelty numbers, which meant that every actor or actress was featured in some specialty that he or she wasn't good at.

Then came the first genuine musical picture—the first to handle singing and dancing not simply as novelties, but as integral parts of the story line—*The Broadway Melody* (1929). It was the story of two performers (Bessie Love and Anita Page) and their backstage experiences. This film set the style for all backstage yarns of the 1930s, and won the Academy Award as best picture of 1929.

The Broadway Melody was a sweet story of two sisters seeking fame on New York's Great White Way, and it was MGM's first total talkie. It was slangy, it was creaky, but it had some strong performances, particularly by Charles King, and was a top money-maker. It also set some precedents. The chorus girls were gorgeously clothed. The songs, such as 'You Were Meant for Me' and 'The Wedding of the Painted Doll,' became hits. And Broadway was the place to set a musical story. It also taught movie-makers that musical numbers could be presented as lavish extras rather than arising from the story line itself—the play-within-a-play approach.

Metro-Goldwyn-Mayer later used the title, but not the plot, for *Broadway Melody of 1936* and *Broadway Melody of 1940*. There was to have been a *Broadway Melody of 1944*, but the title was changed to *Broadway Rhythm*.

New faces were the rage in 1929. Many of them were imports from Broadway, others were previous Hollywood unknowns, who, it was discovered, had pleasant voices and tapping toes. Bessie Love came back from her triumph in *The Broadway Melody* to make *Chasing Rainbows* (1929), whose most famous dance routine was 'Everybody Tap' and most popular song was 'Happy Days Are Here Again.'

It's a Great Life (1929) starred the Duncan Sisters, who were famous for their 'Topsy and Eva' act in vaudeville. Apparently it was a consolation prize for their losing the *Broadway Melody* leads to Bessie Love and Anita Page. It had virtually the same backstage plot and several musical numbers like 'Following You,' plus a bit of Technicolor. But it was all to no avail. The sisters' personalities were a bit sugary on the screen.

Fanny Brice came from Broadway to make *My Man* (1928), as did Marilyn Miller to re-create her stage triumph in the Ziegfeld hit *Sally* (1929). Paramount imported France's Maurice Chevalier and cast him with operetta star Jeanette MacDonald in *The Love Parade* (1929). This film, which also starred Lupino Lane and Lillian Roth, was directed by Ernst Lubitsch, and established him as a director of brittle and sophisticated comedy. His style came to be known as 'The Lubitsch Touch.'

Paramount also brought in Helen Morgan for what many film historians have called the most interesting musical of the period—*Applause* (1929)—for its probing of the seamy side of burlesque life.

Two other Broadway imports tried to capitalize on the public's love of Jolson's 'Mammy' songs. George Jessel made *Lucky Boy* in 1929, finishing the picture with a song to his mother, and Morton Downey followed with *Mother's Boy* (1929), going everyone one better by singing to his dying mother. Motherhood was still in, but Sophie Tucker, 'The Last of the Red-Hot Mamas,' pulled a switch when she played a mother in *Honky Tonk* (1929) who was rejected by an ungrateful daughter.

Musicals were so popular in 1929 that one of the main Hollywood musical stars, Joan Blondell, appeared in 32 pictures in 27 months. This was just after the Wall Street crash of 1929, when the studios realized that cheap entertainment during the hard times could become a lucrative business.

The block-buster revue-type film of the year was *The Hollywood Revue of 1929*. It starred every MGM luminary but Greta Garbo. It had no story, but that was on purpose. The cast featured

The wedding scene in *Sally* (1929). The lovely Marilyn Miller (the bride) re-created her Broadway triumph.

Maurice Chevalier (center) and Jeanette MacDonald get the message. *The Love Parade* (1929).

romantic leading man Conrad Nagel and an ex-vaudevillian about to become a major radio star, Jack Benny, serving as masters of ceremonies; Joan Crawford and Marion Davies doing song and dance numbers; and Norma Shearer and John Gilbert playing a scene from *Romeo and Juliet*, at first seriously and then for comedy. Other comedy bits came from Buster Keaton, Laurel and Hardy and Marie Dressler, who played Venus rising from the sea in a burlesque ballet, and, crown askew, flounced about as a boisterous monarch and belted out 'For I'm a Queen.' The film also marked the debut of composer Nacio Herb Brown's classic 'Singin' in the Rain,' which was played by Brown while chorus girls wearing transparent raincoats danced on his piano. The song was also sung by Cliff 'Ukelele Ike' Edwards, a performer who went on to be the voice of Jiminy Cricket in Walt Disney's *Pinocchio*

A production number from *The Hollywood Revue of 1929* (1929). It was closer to a vaudeville show performed in front of a camera than a real film.

A minstrel show chorus line number from *The Hollywood Revue of 1929* (1929).

(1940). In addition to all this, the picture had color sequences.

Warners did an all-star film, *Show of Shows* (1929), assigning it to such diverse talents as Beatrice Lillie, Douglas Fairbanks Jr, Loretta Young, Winnie Lightner, Chester Morris and Harriette Lake. Ms Lake was a sparkling bit player who, four years later, attained star status under her new name, Ann Sothern.

One of the starriest of the all-star revues came out in 1930. *Paramount on Parade* seemed to have something for everyone. It opened with Leon Errol, Skeets Gallagher and Jack Oakie introducing themselves as the masters of ceremonies, followed by Charles 'Buddy' Rogers and Lillian Roth perched on top of a cuckoo clock singing 'Anytime's the Time to Fall in Love.' A terribly unfunny skit followed with Warner Oland (as Fu Manchu), Clive Brooks (as Sherlock Holmes), William Powell (as Philo Vance), Eugene Pallette (as a police sergeant) and Jack Oakie (as a revived corpse). Harry Green sang 'I'm Isadore the Toreador.' Maurice Chevalier and Evelyn Brent performed a very chaste adagio dance-strip tease while having a family argument. Nino Martini sang 'Come Back to Sorrento.' Then came another unfunny hospital sketch with Leon Errol. Jack Oakie and Zelma O'Neal sang 'I'm in Training for You' as Mitzi Mayfair and a chorus danced wearing gym suits. Ruth Chatterton, in one of her oddest performances, pretended to be a French streetwalker in a Paris bistro after the World War I Armistice, and sang 'My Marine' to some soldiers—two of whom were Stuart Erwin and Fredric March.

Chevalier, appearing as a gendarme in a Paris park, sang 'All I Want Is Just One Girl,' which was followed by one of the more tasteless bits in the picture—nine-year-old Mitzi Green singing the same song as it might have been sung by Mack of the Moran and Mack 'Two Black Crows' blackface act. She also imitated Chevalier himself. In a classroom scene, Helen Kane did her poo-poo-pa-doop chorus with the song 'What Did Cleopatra Say?'. Nancy Carroll sang inside a shoe box to the accompaniment of the Abe Lyman Orchestra while Al Norman danced to 'Dancing to Save Your Sole.' A collection of the studio's young players—Jean Arthur, Gary Cooper, Fay Wray (who was due three years later to be screaming at King Kong), Mary Brian, Phillips Holmes, Richard Arlen, James Hall, David Newell, Joan Peers and Virginia Bruce—dutifully made their way through 'Let Us Drink to the Girl of My Dreams.' Clara Bow joined Jack Oakie and an array of sailor-suited chorus boys in a Navy song-and-dance routine, 'I'm True to the Navy Now.' George Bancroft performed in another unfunny sketch about party manners. Chevalier's big number was 'Sweeping the Clouds Away,' in which, dressed as a chimney sweep on a roof, he blithely sang as a chorus line of beautiful female sweeps performed in a Busby Berkeley-style dance. It was quite a film.

Another trend of the times was the operetta and the transformation of Broadway musicals into movie musicals. The Technicolor (though only two-color) filming of the Sigmund Romberg-Oscar Hammerstein II operetta *The Desert Song* (1929) starred John Boles as the Red Shadow and Myrna Loy as the sultry Azuri. *The Desert Song*, with its 'Riff Song' and 'One Alone,' concerned the doings of a romantic bandit and the audiences were reminded more of Valentino than Verdi. Still, it was the first full talking-and-singing operetta to appear on film.

The Vagabond King (1930), Rudolf Friml's popular operetta, starred Jeanette MacDonald and Dennis King. It was the story of France's poet-rebel, François Villon. Also in 1930, Warners brought out a fresh and adorable *No, No, Nanette*, and the Ziegfeld production *Rio Rita* appeared, with Bebe Daniels and John Boles.

There were a few directors who proved themselves to be musical movie geniuses during this era. Probably the most outstanding was the previously mentioned Ernst Lubitsch. In 1929

Chevalier and MacDonald in *The Love Parade* (1929).

Jack Oakie and Zelma O'Neal in their 'I'm in Training for You' number from *Paramount on Parade* (1930).

he was already a famous silent film director and found the new art form of musicals dreadfully stodgy and lifeless. He wanted to bring wit, zest and sexiness to them. He had paired a charming redhead, Jeanette MacDonald, with the great cosmopolitan singing star Maurice Chevalier, casting them in his first talkie, *The Love Parade* (1929), followed by *Monte Carlo* (1930), which teamed MacDonald with Britain's Jack Buchanan. In *The Smiling Lieutenant* (1931), Chevalier divided his time between the charms of Claudette Colbert and Miriam Hopkins and *One Hour With You* (1932) was another MacDonald-Chevalier pairing.

The German-born Lubitsch, a successful stage actor and screen director in Europe before coming to Hollywood to direct Mary Pickford in *Rosita* (1923), was undoubtedly the most impressive of the early musical directors. The fact is, he was impressive in any assignment he took on, whether it was a musical, a drama or a comedy. It was, however, in comedy—and its musical counterpart—that he earned his greatest fame, displaying both a talent for satire and a deft ability for handling sophisticated themes. Like most other directors of the late 1920s, Lubitsch was not experienced with musicals when he first took them on, but, on brushing them with his distinct skill, they emerged as the very best that the early musicals had to offer.

Lubitsch musicals, from the beginning to the end, were delightful risqué puffs of froth. Their main themes were sex and money, with the former being a charming game played by those who had ample of the latter. Always involved were fairy-tale characters—debonair, lavishly uniformed guardsmen with roving eyes who become the love targets of queens and princesses from imaginary little European countries with fanciful names like Flausenthurm. The plots usually concerned marriages that started disastrously but ended happily.

That such characters and locales were selected for the plots was no accident. Lubitsch understood that Americans liked sex and money, but he understood just as well that, should his pictures be given an American setting, the bluenose side of the American character might well surface with annoyance and demand a retribution at the film's end that simply wouldn't work in a happy musical. He was dead right. Coming out of Hollywood at the time was a stream of sexually accented pictures, and not a few scandals. They eventually led to a movie-goer's revolt and to the establishment of the ridiculously strict Will Hays Motion Picture Production Code in 1930.

A brief look at the plot of *The Smiling Lieutenant* is all that is needed to see how Lubitsch mingled the elements. Princess Anna (Miriam Hopkins) of tiny Flausenthurm visits Austria and falls in love with and wants to marry a dashing young lieutenant (Maurice Chevalier) of the Imperial Guard. The lieutenant is a skirt-chasing fellow whose latest love is the very co-operative Franzi (Claudette Colbert), the leader of an all-girl orchestra. So far, so ridiculous.

Despite his liking for the ladies, the lieutenant simply isn't interested in the princess and consents to marrying her only to avoid all sorts of nasty international complications. With such a lack of enthusiasm on his part, the marriage, as anyone can imagine, is in trouble—that is, until Franzi, pretty well over her affair with Chevalier and finding that she likes the princess, teaches the frustrated young woman a few tricks in the womanly art of captivating a man. The advice works, and they all live happily ever after.

Any of the Lubitsch pictures would have worked without music, but the songs were fitted in nicely and were usually an integral part of the plot. For example, playing the eager spinster Queen Louise of Sylvania in *The Love Parade* (1929), Jeanette MacDonald strongly established the character as, wearing a quite revealing negligee, she sings 'Dream Lover' on awakening one morning. Then, in *The Smiling Lieutenant* (1931), Colbert and Hopkins plot the man-baiting campaign with the delightful and risqué piano duet 'Jazz Up Your Lingerie.'

Lubitsch's most adroit use of music, however, is seen in *Monte Carlo* (1930). Here, MacDonald, as a princess fleeing an unhappy marriage, leans out the window of a train and, singing 'Beyond the Blue Horizon,' anticipates the new and, we hope, adventurous life that lies ahead. The train's wheels and whistle form the opening of the song, which is then picked up by peasants working in the nearby fields and echoed back to MacDonald.

Lubitsch's plots were sometimes foolish and a hindrance to his elegant style. But he pointed the way to a subtle low-key kind of musical rather than the brash 'sock 'em with everything' style that tended to dominate the medium in the following decade.

Another major film director who became interested in musicals was King Vidor. Carrying his originality over from silents to talkies, he made *Halleluja* in 1929 with an all-black cast. It was the story of a murderer who becomes a minister, and it involved sex, death and redemption. The film was critically acclaimed but criticized for being overly dramatic in its dialogue. Today, it seems exaggerated, patronizing and sentimental. But it was the first serious treatment of black life to come from Hollywood. Vidor's use of work songs and spirituals plus a couple of Irving Berlin songs ('Waiting at the End of the Road' and 'Swanee Shuffle'), his brilliant sound effects and camera work and the intensity of the film raised it above the ordinary.

Later that year, Rouben Mamoulian took the musical into a more serious direction when he made the previously mentioned *Applause* with Helen Morgan. This also matched music with a story that didn't have a happy ending. Morgan played a burlesque queen abused by an ugly world. Mamoulian never let the camera lie. It was not a pretty movie, although it was innovative in the use of techniques that would later be used in a lot of pretty films—the handling of closeups, for example.

By the end of 1930 the musicals had abruptly died—partly because they had been done to death, partly because audiences found that not even musicals could take their minds off the Great Depression, especially when they were dated operettas featuring unknowns from the stage whose vocal qualifications failed to make up for their visual inadequacies. In 1931 the death knell was sounded by a movie critic, writing about a now-forgotten musical. 'Here is a reminder of the dear dead days that we thought beyond recall. For this is a musical extravaganza, replete with prancing chorines, low comics and "backstage" stuff. The picture must have been long delayed in release, for all its much-touted principals have by now gone back to the obscurity from whence they came.'

Obviously, the infant movie musical had overplayed its hand. The public was fed to the teeth with one partly or fully Technicolor song-and-dance epic after another. With the Depression hitting its depths, movie-goers, carefully doling out their money one coin at a time, decided to spend no more of what little they had for entertainment on a tiresome, over-exposed product. Grosses plunged.

The over-exposure itself was bad enough, but there was something more behind the fall from grace. In its first years, the musical had pulled in audiences because sound was such a novelty. Now the novelty had worn off. The days of indiscrimate ticket-buying were over. Sound was an established fact of life and had to be accompanied up there on the screen by those basic ingredients always needed to draw an audience—well-acted, well-told, well-produced stories. The musical, appearing in one form after another, simply hadn't filled the bill, too often sacrificing plot and character for the singing and dancing, too often sacrificing quality in the rush to get to the market, and too often—no fault of its own, really, in the primitive days of a new technology—coming up with sound that was unacceptable except as a novelty.

With the downfall of the musicals, some great projects were dropped. *Great Day* had gone into production in 1930 with Joan Crawford, Johnny Mack Brown and Cliff Edwards. It featured songs with lyrics by Billy Rose and Edward Eliscu and music by Vincent Youmans. It was scrapped after ten days' shooting. Admittedly, it also flopped in a stage version, but despite its lack of success, three of its songs became standards—'Great Day,' 'More Than You Know' and 'Without a Song.'

Another musical, *The March of Time*, designed as *The Hollywood Revue of 1930*, was given up as hopeless when it was near completion. It was finally finished in 1933 and called *Broadway to Hollywood*. Most of the revue part of the film was tossed out, but that left room for a dramatic story line. Starring were Frank Morgan (later to become the Wizard of Oz), Jackie Cooper, Jimmy Durante, Nelson Eddy (in his debut—he sang one song) and Mickey Rooney. In addition, two Marion Davies musicals were aborted—*The 5 O'Clock Girl* and *Rosalie*.

Matters became so bad in 1932 that some theater owners began making it a point to advertise that their current attractions were not musicals.

Everyone thought that the Depression had killed the movie musicals, but actually the Depression was going to glorify them. Musicals were to rise to dizzying heights, far surpassing what they had been in the beginning. They would become the perfect entertainment medium for hard times—big, bold, brassy and totally un-Lubitsch.

Perhaps the hero of the musical renaissance was a man named Busby Berkeley.

Opposite: The young MacDonald.

Gold Diggers of 1933 (1933). A patented Berkeley shot from the ceiling—violin-playing chorines in 'The Shadow Waltz.'

THE BERKELEY YEARS

If the movie musical were to make a comeback, discipline was needed, and a man named Busby Berkeley emerged to provide that discipline.

Berkeley had come to Hollywood in 1929 from a successful career on Broadway. He started out working on the musical numbers (including 'Making Whoopee' and 'My Baby Just Cares for Me') for Warner Brothers in a film called *Whoopee* (1930), which had previously been a Broadway musical. The two-color Technicolor prints of this film, which starred Eddie Cantor, looked rather washed-out, but it was revamped in 1944 and released as *Up in Arms*, featuring Danny Kaye and Dinah Shore.

His next film was *Kiki* (1931) in which Mary Pickford succumbed to the craze for all-singing, all-talking, all-dancing pictures and appeared in a man's tuxedo in one of the production numbers. This was followed by *Palmy Days* and *Flying High* in 1931. The latter was an odd musical that featured Charlotte Greenwood, Pat O'Brien and Bert Lahr. It was the story of an amateur aviator who made a record long-distance flight because he didn't know how to land his plane.

But most of Berkeley's early films were flops, because no one wanted musicals at the time. It wasn't until 1933, when he considered going back to Broadway, that his ship came in.

Actually, the reincarnation of the musical picture might be credited to Darryl F Zanuck, who was head of the production department at Warner Brothers at the time. His instincts told him that the musical was anything but dead, that nothing more was at work than the end of the musical's first cycle and that what was needed to restore the infant to favor was a solidly good film. He decided to gamble on an extravaganza. Casting his planned effort with such veterans as Warner Baxter, Bebe Daniels and George Brent, plus some talented newcomers, Zanuck went into production with *Forty-Second Street* in the latter half of 1932.

Warner Baxter giving Ruby Keeler a hard time in *Forty-Second Street* (1933). To Baxter's left is Ginger Rogers.

Franklin D Roosevelt had been inaugurated and told the American public that 'The only thing we have to fear is fear itself.' These magic words made 'Confidence' the slogan of the time, and Hollywood raced to do its bit to restore the public's belief in the future by reviving the corpse of the movie musical. Billed as 'A New Deal in Entertainment,' *Forty-Second Street* (1933) was just what the public wanted.

Thanks to Berkeley's direction of the musical numbers and a marvelous cast, the picture was a blockbuster. The film's plot was borrowed from an earlier Warner Brothers picture, *On With the Show* (1929), which was a story about a hatcheck girl who replaces the hard-to-handle lead in a Broadway show and wins instant stardom. In *Forty-Second Street* we see just how much work it is to mount a Broadway musical. Julian Marsh (Warner Baxter), a middle-aged producer, sets out to make what he knows will be his last show. But his female lead (Bebe Daniels) breaks her leg on the night before the opening.

He promotes a talented but inexperienced girl from the chorus line (Ruby Keeler), rehearses her for a day, and with the words 'Sawyer, you're going out a youngster, but you've got to come back a star' (trite now, but dramatic then) sends her on stage. Up to that point, *Forty-Second Street* didn't really look like a musical, but rather a backstage melodrama. Then Berkeley took over.

If one thing was the Busby Berkeley trademark, it was a camera shot from high above the action, showing the dancers and chorus girls moving in marvelous patterns. As he told it, the idea for that shot came to him one day at Warner Brothers when he climbed into the rafters to look at one of his numbers, was impressed with the view and said to himself 'I better bring the audience up here and let them see it.' To do that, he literally had to cut a hole in the roof of the sound stage, but the results fascinated movie audiences and quickly set a style for the whole decade of the 1930s.

Shooting from above, Berkeley had his chorus girls go through precision routines that gave marvelous images of changing patterns, resembling the sights seen through a kaleidoscope. The straight-down camera angle was so popular that it was quickly imitated by many directors who didn't have Berkeley's imagination, so it soon became a laughable cliché. But in its early days, the new camera angle was an eye opener.

It wasn't just the 'top shot' that made Busby Berkeley musicals so spectacular—it was a zany kind of imagination that used the camera as few directors had dared to use it before. In *Forty-Second Street* Berkeley started the big number by showing Ruby Keeler doing a solo dance. As the camera pulled back, the audience saw that she was dancing on top of a taxicab, and that the taxi was parked in the middle of 42nd Street. From that point on, the number is supposed to be part of a Broadway musical, but no stage could hold the spectacular mass of scenery and dancers that Busby Berkeley used.

The production numbers in *Forty-Second Street* were superb. The audiences were treated to the 'Shuffle Off to Buffalo' number featuring a newly-wed couple (Keeler and Clarence Nordstrom) eager to spend their first night together aboard a Niagara Falls-bound train, only to have their Pullman car keep them apart by dividing itself into many berths, all filled with chorus girls who have a thoroughly good time making cynical fun of the honeymooners.

Then there was the 'Young and Healthy' sequence, which began with Dick Powell singing and evolved into a team of chorus girls and boys dancing on a revolving stage and forming that old Berkeley trademark—patterns photographed from overhead.

Then came the previously mentioned finale—the number from which the picture took its title. Intended to portray New York's fast-paced and decadent night life, the sequence began with an evening-gowned Keeler singing 'Forty-Second Street,' after which she drops her long skirt for a tap dance atop a taxicab. To the song's pulsating rhythms, the camera moved up the crowded street, encountered various Broadway types along the way, witnessed an attack on a girl and then a stabbing, staying with these occurrences only an instant as it fell in with columns of chorus girls tap dancing along the street. At last, male dancers joined the girls and together, with painted boards, they formed a rising and almost surreal skyline of New York. The number closed with Keeler and Powell looming above the skyline and waving to the audience.

The superbly choreographed sequences dazzled audiences and established Berkeley as the premiere dance director of the period. But it would be unfair to say that *Forty-Second Street*'s appeal lay in his efforts alone. Even without its extravagant ending, the picture would have had an attraction for audiences of the 1930s. It told a harsh story of struggle and hard work. It told it with bitter wisecracks and with Baxter's excellent aura of exhaustion and disillusionment—his role was one of the outstanding characterizations of his career. It played the story against a tawdry backdrop of chorines' apartments and sweaty rehearsal halls. And, in the midst of the exultation at its close, it sounded a grim note—a hard-faced Baxter looking at the stage and knowing that his life's work is over. In all, the film dealt with tough realities that Depression-era audiences understood and that aroused a definite emotional response in them, and director Lloyd Bacon should be given much of the credit for this. When these realities were blended with Berkeley's escapist production numbers, *Forty-Second Street* became a perfectly but eerily balanced Depression product.

This was the classic 'putting on a show' musical from Hollywood's Golden Age of musicals, combining genuine backstage atmosphere with a caustic script. And what a cast it had. Admittedly, Ruby Keeler had to make a small talent go a long way—but she succeeded. Aside from Baxter and Keeler, the movie had George Brent and Bebe Daniels, both veterans, Dick Powell, who had sung with a band, and an up-and-coming sexy starlet with a peppery personality, appropriately named Ginger. Miss Rogers was destined to become one of the hottest musical stars ever.

The critics went wild. *The New York Times* called it 'The liveliest and one of the most tuneful screen musical comedies that has come out of Hollywood.'

For some reason, Warner Brothers thought that they had to have a live stage show to accompany the opening of *Forty-Second Street* at the Strand Theater in New York City. But none of the stars of the picture was in it. The ads read 'AND . . . IN PERSON brought to you direct from Hollywood on the famous "42nd Street" Special—Joe E Brown, Tom Mix, Bette Davis, Laura La Plante, Glenda Farrell, Lyle Talbot, Leo Carillo, Claire Dodd, Preston Foster, Eleanor Holm.'

William Berkeley Enos, alias Busby Berkeley, was now established in Hollywood. He struck back as the musical director of *Gold Diggers of 1933*, in which he showed girls in a peep-show silhouette scene in a way that suggested nudity—which was not to be seen on screen again until Martine Carol took her famous shower in *Nathalie* (1956). Berkeley seemed to have a license to titillate, and used the stage tradition of the underdressed chorus girl to get away with every breach of Will Hays' Production Code possible and still get the seal of approval.

Gold Diggers of 1933 was loosely based on a Broadway play by Avery Hopwood about a group of girls in search of millionaire husbands. In the film, Berkeley had a number that started with the camera zooming in on a singer whose profile turns into a city skyline. Free-flowing geometric designs formed by neon-lit violins filled the screen during 'The Shadow Waltz.' The one serious note was Joan Blondell's singing 'Remember My Forgotten Man' to a chorus of the unemployed—a reminder that many of the soldiers and sailors who fought in World War I were lucky if they could sell apples in the street during the

The two stars of *Gold Diggers of 1933* (1933)—Ruby Keeler and Dick Powell.

Great Depression-plagued year of 1933.

Ginger Rogers was back in this film, playing a conniving little thing eager to make it big. Her name in the film was Fay Fortune, proving that Hollywood figured subtlety was a waste of time. Joan Blondell provided sparkle and humor to the movie.

Blondell and Dick Powell appeared together for the first time in the picture, but they were to go on together and set a record for the number of times a team co-starred in musical films—ten different movies. This record was later tied by Fred Astaire and Ginger Rogers. Also, little did anyone know that Powell, the crooning juvenile, would later emerge as a tough but likeable leading man in serious non-musicals, a competent director and an ambitious producer—the founder of Four Star Television.

Footlight Parade (1933), another in the Powell-Keeler-Blondell Broadway mold, was important because it gave James Cagney his first singing and dancing role in the movies. Cagney had started his stage career as a song-and-dance man. In the early 1920s, when he was struggling to support his family with the occasional song-and-dance engagement, he got a big break—he landed a job with an up-and-coming vaudeville group. The performer he replaced was a young Englishman named Archibald Leach, who later would gain renown as Cary Grant. In one number in *Footlight Parade* Cagney wore a sailor suit as he danced on a table-top with Keeler—an omen of the scores of Navy musicals that were to come.

Ginger singing 'We're in the Money.'

Again, Berkeley made fireworks with tiers and towers of girls who looked like they were made of spun sugar. For the 'By a Waterfall' number, he built an aquacade that used hydraulic lifts to move one hundred chorus girls and had 20,000 gallons of water pumped per minute as the girls tumbled down into a studio-built lake. This scene was a forerunner of Esther Williams' bathing beauty musicals of the 1940s. Indeed, it was Berkeley who choreographed Williams' biggest hit, *Million Dollar Mermaid* (1952).

Roman Scandals was also released in 1933, starring Eddie Cantor, Ruth

Footlight Parade (1933) gave James Cagney his first singing and dancing role in films. Here he is with Ruby Keeler.

Eddie Cantor, Alan Mowbray and Edward Arnold in *Roman Scandals* (1933).

Etting and Edward Arnold, plus, back in the chorus line, a very young Lucille Ball. It was the story of a dreamer (Cantor) who was transported back to Ancient Rome.

For the 'No More Love' number the setting was a slave market. Berkeley had chained girls draped around each level of a pedestal which, he explained, 'graduated in tiers. I thought it would be a very lovely thing for the top row to be all nudes, with long blonde wigs almost down to their knees. I was going to try to photograph them nude. First I thought I would have to put fleshlings on them of some kind. It made a striking thing with all of them chained to this block. . . I realized that if I wanted to do close-ups, that fleshlings on them would show up as being obvious, so I asked the girls if they would mind being photographed nude provided it was done in a beautiful and artistic manner by dressing their hair over their breasts, etc. They said they would do if if I would close the set and film it only at night to avoid unnecessary visitors.' And so it was done.

In the 'Don't Say Goodnight' number in *Wonder Bar* (1934), he reflected his dancers into infinity with an octagon of giant mirrors. It was a strange musical, set in a Paris nightclub, and included both murder and romance. It starred Al Jolson, Kay

A sexy chorine from *Footlight Parade* (1933).

Francis, Ricardo Cortez and the inevitable Dick Powell.

Fashions of 1934 (1934) starred another Powell—William Powell—and Bette Davis. It was a trivial but enjoyable romp about con-man Powell and designer Davis conquering the Paris fashion world. The show-stopper was the 'Hall of Human Harps' production number in which it appeared that chorus girls were part of the structure of dozens of harps. One critic said, 'The theme song of mothers of stage-struck daughters might well be "I didn't raise my girl to be a human harp." '

Then came *Dames* (1934). It was another Dick Powell-Ruby Keeler-Joan Blondell outing with a plot similar to those that had gone before. But it didn't matter. The movie was an ode to Berkeley's talent. He had Keeler's image multiplied endlessly when chorus girls donned masks of her face in the 'I Only Have Eyes for You' number. And then there was the incredible song 'When You Were a Smile on Your Mother's Lips and a Twinkle in Your Daddy's Eye.' There was also a rather neat joke in the film. Powell is told by a secretary that 'Miss Warren, Miss Dubin and Miss Kelly are outside.' This was a reference to the men who wrote the songs for the picture—Harry Warren and Al Dubin—and the man who designed the costumes—Orry Kelly.

Gold Diggers of 1935 (1935) gave Berkeley a chance to direct an entire movie, not just the musical parts. Still he did not stint when it came to the songs, most of which resembled a

Fred Astaire and Joan Crawford dancing 'Heigh, Ho, the Gang's All Here' in *Dancing Lady* (1933).

from an audience-eye view, thus unconsciously following in the footsteps of Charlie Chaplin. He was given a special Academy Award in 1949 'for his unique artistry and his unique contribution to the techniques of motion pictures.'

Ginger Rogers, born Virginia Katherine McMath in 1911, started life as a child of divorce. Her parents separated and were divorced shortly after her birth, and in a gruesome custody battle, she was twice kidnapped by her father before the courts settled the dispute by awarding custody to her mother, who was a reporter for the *Fort Worth Record* and business manager for the Fort Worth Symphony. Although she had hoped that her child would be a painter, she quit both jobs to become Ginger's manager after Ginger had won the Texas State Charleston Contest in 1925, at the age of 14.

After four years in clubs and in

Top Hat (1935) was a splendid wedding of the talents of Astaire, Rogers and Berlin.

Flying Down to Rio (1933).

Shall We Dance (1937).

The Gay Divorcee (1934).

The Story of Vernon and Irene Castle (1939).

The Barkleys of Broadway (1949).

Follow the Fleet (1936).

Top Hat (1935).

Swing Time (1936).

Fred and Ginger danced in *Flying Down to Rio* (1933), but the stars were Dolores Del Rio and Gene Raymond (center).

vaudeville, Rogers made it to Broadway. Her first film role was in *Young Man in Manhattan* (1930). At 22, she teamed up with Fred Astaire. In 1945 she was the highest-paid performer in Hollywood and had the eighth highest income in the United States with a salary of $292,159. Later in her career she appeared in dramatic roles and won the Academy Award for best actress in 1940 for her role in *Kitty Foyle*.

The initial teaming of Astaire and Rogers in 1933 was, in the main, an accident. Ginger, who by now had several pictures under her belt—films in which she had played tough and wisecracking, yet vulnerable young women—was handed a supporting role in a planned RKO musical because, shades of *Forty-Second Street*, the player originally assigned the job, Dorothy Jordan, withdrew because she had married the head of the studio. Astaire was under contract to RKO and was scheduled for the minor role opposite Rogers.

In addition to the Astaire-Rogers dancing there were fine production numbers in *The Gay Divorcee* (1934).

At the time, RKO was a smallish company struggling to make ends meet in the bottom-of-the-barrel days of the Depression. Its new venture, entitled *Flying Down to Rio* (1933), was intended to cash in on Warner Brothers' success by outdoing the just-released *Forty-Second Street*. The picture was to be set in exotic South America, was to tell the story of a flying band leader (Gene Raymond) and his romance with a Brazilian beauty (Dolores Del Rio), and was to end with a fantastic production number performed by chorus girls on the wings of airplanes high above Rio de Janeiro.

On release (production had lasted only four weeks), the film turned out to be a rather slow-moving piece, with too much time spent on its love story, but nevertheless it was a box-office success for two reasons. First, that climactic airborne production number (a blend of actual flying sequences and studio shots of the wing-dancing chorines) proved to be as fantastic and as fascinating as the company had hoped. Second, in another lively number—'The Carioca'—Astaire and Rogers danced across the screen for the first time.

Actually, Fred Astaire and Ginger Rogers (playing characters named Fred Ayres and Honey Hale) were anything but the centerpieces of the sequence. Performed in a lavish night club setting, it opened with the orchestra playing a new, highly rhythmic ballroom dance, 'The Carioca,' and then turned to a chorus demonstrating how partners must do the dance with their foreheads touching. Suddenly, Astaire and Rogers ran onstage and presented their own version of the dance. In all, they were seen for just a few moments before the chorus took over again. But those few moments struck audiences—and RKO—as something special. Here were two diverse people—one tall and (except when dancing) gangly, the other pert and brash—who, when working together, suddenly produced a magic of their own, magic compounded of grace, intimacy, a seemingly effortless dancing ability and high good humor.

Glowing over their success, RKO gave the couple their first starring vehicle, *The Gay Divorcee* (1934), an adaptation of Fred's earlier triumph on Broadway, *The Gay Divorce*. The change in the title apparently was the result of the studio's fear of intimating that divorces could become happy arrangements. The picture had an empty-headed 'mistaken identity' plot, but that didn't matter. The truth was that no one in the audience cared about the plot. The people went to the theater to see Fred and Ginger dance. The film did have some comedy, too. There was Erik Rhodes as the stage Italian, Eric Blore as the stage English butler, Edward Everett Horton doing his double-takes and a very young Betty Grable.

The choreographer was one Hermes Panagiotopulos, better known under his professional name of Hermes Pan. He worked with Astaire and Rogers in later films and deserved a lot of the credit for their wonderful dance numbers.

The Gay Divorcee set the tone for all of their movies. Fred, alias Guy Holden, sees Ginger and it seems to be love at first glance. He pursues her hither and yon through a glamorous resort hotel. She resists, but all one has to do is see them dance to know that he'll get her. This is no Broadway backstage musical where dances have nothing to do with the story line. It is when Fred and Ginger dance that one sees how they feel about each other. All the sensuality missing in the dialogue comes out when they dance to the Cole Porter songs. The film was a breakthrough for musicals. For the first time, not the songs but the dances conveyed emotion. No wonder Fred and Ginger didn't bother with the obligatory Hollywood romantic kiss. They didn't need it.

They were cast in roles far different from the earthy, slangy types they had played in *Flying Down to Rio*. Now they became the sophisticates that they were to be in the rest of their movies. It was a casting natural for the elegant Astaire, but one that Rogers, until she became competent in it, seemed to bear with some ill ease.

The picture presented them in two extraordinarily good dance numbers—'The Continental' and 'Night and Day.' The former, reflecting 'The Carioca' in that it also involved a new dance step, was a lavish musical offering that won the first Academy Award ever given for a song. But, for the Astaire-Rogers team and for the development of the musical film, 'Night and Day' was a far more significant accomplishment. Danced in an art deco ballroom, it established a dramatic story line—the girl reluctantly beginning to dance with an amorous young man and then eventually surrendering herself to him as the music and their partnership in it flow on—that was to be a hallmark of their best numbers. And, allowing very human emotions to show through a dance routine as it did, it was a theme that, with all the variations that reluctance changed into exultation can achieve, has been used time and time again by musicals through the years since that time. No wonder that Astaire later had his legs insured for a million dollars.

Considering their great audience appeal at the time, and how memorable their combined names remain today, it is surprising to realize that Astaire and Rogers worked together, in all but one of their pictures, for just six years. From *The Gay Divorcee*, they returned to supporting roles in *Roberta* (1935). It was Irene Dunne who had the lead in this adaptation of

Fred in an inventive number from *Roberta* (1935).

the Otto Harbach-Jerome Kern stage show. Fred was Huck Haines; Ginger was Lizzie Gatz (but she liked to call herself the Countess Scharwenka). They stole the picture. Fred, with his thin voice and thinning hair, seemed to pass through a magic transformation when he danced. He became the most attractive, most elegant, most debonair human being on earth. If he had danced with Helen of Troy, it would have been hard to keep one's eyes off him and on her. So, it was a tribute to Ginger Rogers that she not only did not fade from view, but added a tart glamour of her own.

The public liked what it saw, so in 1935 RKO gave them *Top Hat*, the sort of vehicle they needed. It was much more like *The Gay Divorcee* than *Roberta*. With its plot of mistaken identity and accidental confusion, RKO might have resurrected William Shakespeare to write the story line. Edward Everett Horton, Eric Blore and Erik Rhodes were in it. Everyone seemed to have money pouring from every seam of his or her sumptuous wardrobe. Venice looked as if it were built by a Miami Beach developer. Irving Berlin's music was great.

Fred Astaire danced his first solo of the film in the room above Ginger Rogers' suite. The noise bothered her as she lay in a bed that would have embarrassed Mae West. Thus we get off to the usual antagonistic start. In 'Isn't This a Lovely Day' we get a chance to see Ginger dance in a riding habit. We get the banter in the words and the struggle in the dance. 'Cheek to Cheek' gives us the lust and tenderness as the two dance what they really feel. It could be argued that *Top Hat* was the team's best film.

Fred in costume—*Top Hat* (1935).

In addition to the empathy between the two, there is an empathy between the dancers and Irving Berlin. We also find in Astaire's trademark solo—his famous 'Top Hat' number—a summation of the elegance and élan of his screen character.

Astaire and Rogers were genuine stars, so it was appropriate that their films were viewed by producers as 'star vehicles.' It didn't much matter what the story was, as long as it provided opportunities for the pair to dance. The story of *Top Hat* is as forgettable and irrelevant as the story of any other Astaire-Rogers film. A dancer falls for a haughty model and chases her up and down Europe, tap dancing most of the way. The journeyman direction of Mark Sandrich (who directed five of their ten pictures) was appropriate for this material. No mastermind, no Busby Berkeley, he did not manipulate people like pawns. No heavyweight director, no Vincente

Fred was a sailor and Ginger was a dance hall hostess in *Follow the Fleet* (1936).

The only number that Astaire ever performed in blackface was 'Bojangles of Harlem' in *Swing Time* (1936).

Minnelli, he did not impose a fantasy concept or try to impart a strong directorial style. Rather, Sandrich did the only logical thing that a director can do with Fred Astaire and Ginger Rogers—he let them dance. *Top Hat* may be the best of the team's films because, in addition to the songs of Irving Berlin and the excellence of the dances, it is the simplest and most pure. And it was made early enough in the collaboration so that Astaire's and Rogers' elation at the miracle of their chemistry shines through and adds to its prevailing charm. Just check out 'The Piccolino' number.

While shooting the dance number 'Cheek to Cheek,' Ginger's feathered gown began to molt and feathers came down on the set like a snowstorm. The feathers were swept off the set and new ones were glued on again, but the next time the dance started, feathers flew again. More sweeping and glueing. This happened many times before the feathers stayed securely in place. In the final shooting, an occasional feather was still flying, but astute cameramen tried hard to avoid filming them.

Follow the Fleet (1936) came next.

Ginger Rogers in *Shall We Dance* (1937).

There was some comic dancing in this one. Randolph Scott and Harriet Hilliard (later to marry Ozzie Nelson and star with him in the *Ozzie and Harriet* television series) played supporting parts and Betty Grable appeared again. It was a story of a song-and-dance man who joined the Navy when his girl turned him down, and had delightful Irving Berlin songs such as 'Let's Face the Music and Dance,' 'Let Yourself Go' and 'We Saw the Sea.'

Swing Time (1936) was probably a better film. There are those who say it was their best. Astaire, as Lucky Garnett, had lost his money, but not his tuxedo. Ginger, a dance teacher, still had the common touch that made her so endearing. Astaire (Lucky) met Rogers (Penny)—Lucky Penny, how cute—and after the requisite complications that gave them the excuse to dance, there was a happy ending. Astaire did a blackface number, 'Bojangles of Harlem,' wherein he actually danced with shadows of himself, his first use of trick photography. There was the adorably satirical 'Pick Yourself Up' in which Fred pretended that he couldn't dance, and the sweep-

George Burns, Fred Astaire and Gracie Allen in *A Damsel in Distress* (1937).

ingly expressive 'Never Gonna Dance.' Other Dorothy Fields-Jerome Kern songs in the picture were 'A Fine Romance' and the Academy Award-winning 'The Way You Look Tonight.'

Shall We Dance (1937) had a score by George and Ira Gershwin, and one of the most unusual dance routines was performed on roller skates by Fred and Ginger to 'Let's Call the Whole Thing Off.' The plot about a dance team pretending to be married was, as usual, pretty weak, but the film had some classic songs, including 'They All Laughed' and 'They Can't Take That Away from Me.'

In 1937, the team was in difficulty. Though popular, they were suffering declining box-office receipts, as was everyone else, because of the continuing Depression. Also, both of them were growing eager to go their separate ways, not because, as the press reported, there was animosity between them, but because each was becoming increasingly interested in solo work. Astaire had no wish to be identified merely as one half of a dance team, while Rogers, whose performing abilities had grown in recent years, was looking to a straight acting career.

Consequently, they appeared singly in several pictures. Astaire danced with an awkward Joan Fontaine in *A Damsel in Distress* (1937). It was based on the work of that master of humorous fiction P G Wodehouse, and included several fine Gershwin songs, such as 'Nice Work If You Can Get It' and 'A Foggy Day in London Town.' Also in the cast were George Burns and Gracie Allen, both of whom even got to sing and dance.

Rogers had a dramatic role in *Stage Door* (1937), co-starring with Katharine Hepburn and Adolphe Menjou in an adaptation of an Edna Ferber-George S Kaufman play about the residents in a theatrical boarding house. She also appeared in *Having a Wonderful Time* (1938), a comedy with Douglas Fairbanks Jr, Red Skelton and Lucille Ball, and *Vivacious Lady* (1938) with James Stewart.

The couple was back together again in *Carefree* (1938). This film represented a big shift. Although it had music in it, some critics felt that it didn't qualify as a musical. It did have an innovative dance sequence—'Yam.' Then there was 'Change Partners' and the historic 'I Used to Be Color-Blind.' The latter was the final number in the film, and Fred and Ginger kissed for the first time. The dance and the kiss were shot in slow motion, a tantalizing reply to the demands of their fans that the time had come for Fred to kiss Ginger. This kiss was, quite possibly, the logical end to their collaboration. When Astaire and Rogers danced together they achieved a delicate tension between reality and abandonment, infatuation and realization. Astaire was always in pursuit of Rogers and she always pretended that she wasn't interested. In their duets, things usually proceeded to the point where it seemed as though Astaire could sweep her away, that after dealing with her many rebuffs he could carry her away to capitulation. And then, on the verge of oneness, there would occur one of their famous pauses, and Rogers would charmingly pull back.

It was in these heightened moments of pause, when fantasy (his) and earthiness (hers) lay in the balance, that the audience observed the essence of their chemistry. By his seductiveness and her feigned indifference and haughty withdrawals, they enacted a wooing pattern, dancing out the basic duelling between men and women and symbolizing the conflict between romance and sex. Watching them swirl together, people felt them approach a oneness of deep intensity. It was clear that they belonged together —that they fit. But the source of their power to enchant was the tension between them, and once it was re-

The delightful 'Stiff Upper Lip' number from *A Damsel in Distress* (1937).

Opposite: 'Nice Work if You Can Get It.'

BOOKMARK
In all thy ways acknowledge him, and he shall direct thy paths.
Prov. 3: 6.

leased in the kiss at the end of *Carefree*, that power was gone. It had to happen. Their magic was much too delicate a thing to last forever.

After *Carefree*, *The Story of Vernon and Irene Castle* (1939) was a letdown. It told the story of the pre-World War I dance team and, since Vernon had been killed in the war, it had a tear-jerking ending. There was one memorable number—a mixture of ballroom dance steps that sent them happily whirling across a gigantic map of the United States.

Ten years later, the pair was reunited in *The Barkleys of Broadway* (1949), a film about the battles of a theatrical couple when one of them wants to abandon musicals for drama. The reason for the reunion was that Ginger was called in to replace Judy Garland, who was having one of her breakdowns. The low point in the film was Rogers reading 'La Marseillaise,' but there were several high points—a reprise of 'They Can't Take That Away From Me' and Fred's wonderful fantasy-dance 'Shoes With Wings On.' 'Manhattan Downbeat' was the last number the great team ever did together. But despite the careers they pursued when they broke up, most people still think of them together, ever young, dancing in some eternal crystal palace.

Another phenomenon was over at Twentieth Century-Fox. It was an unbelievable story, one that Hollywood would have rejected indignantly if anyone had proposed it as a film script. In the 1930s Hollywood was in the heyday of one of its Golden Eras. The movie industry was awash with some of the greatest personalities in its history—Gable, Garbo, Dietrich, Cooper, Tracy, Hepburn, Cagney, Bogart and dozens more. But sitting atop the heap, the biggest box-office draw on earth, was a curly-haired little girl who was less than four feet tall and had never taken an acting lesson in her life.

The girl was Shirley Temple, and hers was a success story that is still without parallel in Hollywood history. No child star has ever had the impact that Shirley did, before or since. It is true that the story of Mary Pickford, 'America's Sweetheart,' is nearly as spectacular. In the earliest days of Hollywood, the days when film-makers were just discovering that there could be such a thing as a movie star, an actor or actress who could draw people into the theater by the sheer power of a name, Mary Pickford was one of the biggest names there was. But Pickford achieved her greatest success in her teens and even older. Shirley Temple almost literally walked out of a nursery school and into stardom.

The most amazing part of the story is how simple it all seemed to be. Shirley never had to fight for anything that came her way. She was born in Santa Monica, California, within hailing distance of Hollywood, in 1928, the daughter of a bank manager, George Temple, and his wife Gertrude. At the age of three, Shirley went to dancing school for lessons—something that a writer later described as 'similar to Lynn Fontanne going to a dramatic academy to take a course in acting.'

Before she was four years old, Shirley was discovered at the dancing school by Charles Lamont, a director of a second-line studio called Educational Pictures. She was put in a series called *The Baby Burlesks*. They were one-reelers in which she imitated such stars as Marlene Dietrich. Then she moved into another series called *Frolics of Youth*. Her first notable feature film was *Stand Up and Cheer* (1934). She was an immediate hit and signed a seven-year contract with Fox Productions at a salary that seemed immense—$150 a week.

Hollywood stars turned out movies at an assembly-line clip in those days, and Shirley Temple was no exception. She made nine films in 1934, four in 1935, four in 1936 and two in 1937. By then, she was sitting firmly on top of all the box-office popularity charts. She had also received a special Academy Award in 1934 'in grateful recognition of her outstanding contribution to screen entertainment' and for bringing 'more happiness to millions of children and millions of

The Barkleys of Broadway (1949).

The most popular girl in the 1930s—Shirley Temple—in a promotional shot.

Opposite: The Story of Vernon and Irene Castle (1939).

Aldophe Menjou was suspicious and a little afraid of Shirley in *Little Miss Marker* (1934).

grownups than any child of her years in the history of the world.'

It was typical Hollywood talk, but it was probably nothing but the truth. Her original contract had been torn up and she was earning $1500 a week, although she was limited by her parents to an allowance of $4.25 a week. Her salary went up to $300,000 a picture in 1939, at a time when a worker could support a family of four on about $40 per week. Even when Shirley was too young to read the scripts of the movies she acted in—she learned her lines by having her mother read to her at bedtime—she was the center of a remarkable cult.

There were Shirley Temple dolls and Shirley Temple dresses and Shirley Temple plates and dishes and Shirley Temple imitators galore—even a Shirley Temple cocktail, non-alcoholic, of course. Every other studio in Hollywood felt that it had to have a singing, dancing moppet to match Shirley Temple. Literally thousands of kids auditioned for the jobs, but none of them ever had the charm that Shirley Temple had.

The plots of her movies were not noted for their originality. In most of them she was either an orphan who found a happy home with a new family, or the child of a single parent (widowed, of course, since Hollywood did not recognize the existence of divorce in those days) who found a new mate for her father or mother. There was always a pause for a song like 'On the Good Ship Lollipop' or 'Animal Crackers in My Soup' and a dance or two with Bill Robinson or Buddy Ebsen.

The curious thing about the Shirley Temple movies that were so popular at the time is how completely they seem to have vanished today. Shirley worked with some great directors, such as John Ford (for whom she made the Kipling classic *Wee Willie Winkie* in 1937) and some notable actors, such as Adolphe Menjou (with whom she made the Damon Runyon Broadway tale *Little Miss Marker* in 1934). But hardly anyone thinks of showing those films today. One of them will show up now and then on television, but the revival theaters that flourish in some cities usually manage to get along without Shirley Temple. Either the world is ignoring some good movie-making or some good film fun has faded with time.

Even though the studio tried to keep Shirley looking young by having her wear false front teeth when her baby ones fell out, eventually she did grow up. Her story in later life is relatively smooth, but there were bumpy spots along the way. Her contract with Twentieth Century-Fox ended in 1940, and she was cut loose by the studio without much sentimental reminiscing. In the hard world of Hollywood, the people who kept track of the money had noticed that her last few pictures were not nearly as successful as had been her earlier efforts.

Shirley moved over to MGM, where she made just one movie. Her career was not over, however; she signed with David O Selznick and was successful in several films as a teenager: *The Bachelor and the Bobby Soxer* (1947) with Cary Grant, *Fort Apache* (1948) with John Wayne, *Mr Belvedere Goes to College* (1949) with Clifton Webb. At the age of 17 she married John Agar, who had starred with her in *Fort Apache* and whose movie future seemed to be bright. But Agar's acting career fizzled out, and the marriage ended in divorce in 1949.

The next year she married Charles A Black. As Shirley Temple Black she has had a remarkably successful second career in politics and diplomacy. She lost in an effort to be elected to the

Above: The top-billed stars of *Stand Up and Cheer* (1934) were Warner Baxter and Madge Evans.

House of Representatives as a Republican in California, but she was named Ambassador to Ghana in 1974 (after serving in the United States Delegation to the United Nations), and in 1976 she was given the post of Chief of Protocol under President Gerald Ford—the first woman to hold that post.

When Mrs Shirley Temple Black was given the Life Achievement Award of the American Center of Films for Children in 1977, it seemed almost surprising that this poised, beautiful woman of 49 had once been a curly-haired moppet who had tap-danced her way to stardom. Those who had been involved in films at the time were very much aware of what Shirley Temple had meant to the industry, but she herself said briskly, 'I'm not sentimental about the past; the most important moment is now.'

Stand Up and Cheer (1934) was a weak little story about the formation of a presidential commission during Depression times set up to lighten the country's spirits, and starred Warner Baxter, Madge Evans, James Dunne and John Boles. But Shirley Temple stole the show with her song-and-dance production number 'Baby Take a Bow.' Within that same year she was

Shirley Temple starred with Cesar Romero in *Wee Willie Winkie* (1937), based on one of Rudyard Kipling's India tales.

Temple with James Dunne in *Bright Eyes* (1934)—a pilot and an orphan.

Shirley Temple dancing with a young Buddy Ebsen in *Captain January* (1936).

a motion-picture phenomenon and a household word.

Her first starring vehicle was *Little Miss Marker* (1934), opposite Adolphe Menjou. It was taken from the Damon Runyon short story about a little waif who was left in a bookie joint as security for a 20-dollar loan made to her father by the hard-boiled Sorrowful Jones (Menjou), a bookie. When the father does not return (there is a hint of suicide), Sorrowful is put in the strange position of having to care for 'Marky' (Temple). He reads her bedtime stories from the *Daily Racing Form* and makes a bed for her out of chairs. The critics went wild. *The New York Times* raved: 'Tiny Shirley Temple is a joy to behold and her spontaneity and cheer in speaking her lines are nothing short of amazing. . . No more enchanting child has been beheld on the screen.'

The studio initiated an advertising campaign: 'She was an I. O. U. for 20 bucks. . . Hocked to the toughest mugs on Broadway—this million dollar baby carved romance into the hearts of Broadway chiselers. . . Damon Runyon's *Little Miss Marker*, with Shirley Temple, the child wonder star of *Stand Up and Cheer*.' The remake, *Sorrowful Jones* (1949) with Bob Hope, Lucille Ball and Mary Jane Saunders, never came close to the charm of this film.

Bright Eyes (1934) featured juvenile villainy on the part of Jane Withers in the tale of a custody battle over a recently orphaned Shirley. It was not much, but it gave her fans her great number 'On the Good Ship Lollipop.'

Even non-fans enjoyed *The Little Colonel* (1935), in which Shirley starred with Lionel Barrymore as her grandfather. She and Bill 'Bojangles' Robinson made a movie legend by tap-dancing up and down a stairway.

In *Curly Top* (1935), Shirley starred with John Boles and Arthur Treacher and played Cupid again, matching up her sister (played by Rochelle Hudson) and Boles. No one could ever forget her 'Animal Crackers in My Soup' number and her tour de force—the 'When I Grow Up' sequence in which she went from child to teenager to old woman. The title song was nice, too.

She danced again with Bill Robinson in *The Littlest Rebel* (1935), and she also rescued her Confederate-soldier father (John Boles) from Civil War imprisonment by sneaking in to see President Lincoln to ask for his release.

Captain January (1936) featured Shirley and Buddy Ebsen dancing charmingly against a New England fishing village backdrop. Once again, Shirley was an orphan who had been taken in by the kindly lighthouse keeper, Guy Kibbee. And once again, the mean old law was trying to break up their relationship.

Poor Little Rich Girl (1936) starred Shirley with Alice Faye and Jack Haley, and it was one of her best. A story about Temple running away from home and joining the vaudeville team of Haley and Faye and eventually managing to get her father (Michael Whalen) married to Gloria Stuart, its best musical number was Shirley's 'Military Man.'

Dimples (1936) was set in New York's Bowery just before the Civil War and had Shirley practically selling herself to a rich lady to save her poor daddy. Best moments—Temple singing 'Oh Mister Man Up in the Moon' and 'What Did the Bluebird Say?'

Shirley demonstrated her ability to impersonate others when she attached a doll to her toes for a clever Astaire-Rogers number in *Stowaway* (1936). It was a film about a slain Chinese missionary's daughter (Shirley) who

Opposite: The Little Colonel (1935).

stows away on a playboy's yacht and succeeds in solving everyone's problems. She also gave entertaining impressions of Al Jolson and Eddie Cantor in the film.

Rebecca of Sunnybrook Farm (1938) had nothing to do with the famous children's book. In this one, Shirley became a radio star while Randolph Scott and Gloria Stuart romanced, but Temple got to dance again with Bill Robinson.

Shirley starred with Jimmy Durante and George Murphy (the senator-to-be) in *Little Miss Broadway* (1938), in which she livened up a theatrical boarding house. The three outstanding songs were 'Be Optimistic,' 'If All the World Were Paper' and 'Hop Skip and Jump.'

Joel McCrea takes Shirley to the circus in *Our Little Girl* (1935).

Shirley as an orphan again in *Little Miss Broadway* (1938).

Just Around the Corner (1938) had Shirley dancing with Bill Robinson again, but it was a tear-jerker and one of her least successful films. One of her best was *The Little Princess* (1939), about a poor Victorian waif who makes good. It was about this time that the powers that be decided she had had it as a tiny-tot star, and began putting her in pictures as a teenager. She was never to be the same again.

Although Shirley Temple was Fox's premier box-office draw of the 1930s, the studio had a strong adult musical presence in Alice Faye. Born Ann Leppert in 1912, her wry expression tended to limit her roles, but she was a key star of her time and commanded a loyal following. Faye started her professional singing life at age 14 and, a few years later, joined Rudy Vallee's dance band as a vocalist. She came to Fox with Vallee for a minor part in *George White's Scandals* (1935), an idiotic show business story of producer White seeing a beautiful woman singing in a small-town show and bringing her (and her friends) to New York to star in a revue. In a real-life version of the *Forty-Second Street* format, Faye took over the starring role in the movie when the person who was supposed to be the star, Lilian Harvey, walked off the set.

On the picture's release, Faye's blonde looks, contralto voice and somewhat-tough-but-still-vulnerable image appealed to the public. She became a fixture in Fox musicals for the next ten years. One other important thing about the picture—it was Eleanor Powell's screen debut.

At first, Alice Faye was often cast in

Shirley appeared again with Bill Robinson in *Rebecca of Sunnybrook Farm* (1938).

Opposite: Poor Little Rich Girl (1936).

Faye, Vallee, and Durante—*George White's Scandals* (1935).

Shirley Temple movies, but she was given an assignment in a 1938 production that was to set the pattern that the studio's most popular musicals would follow well into the 1940s. The picture was *Alexander's Ragtime Band* (1938), and it covered a span of more than two decades in the lives of three performers—a band leader (Tyrone Power), his pianist (Don Ameche) and a rough-cut but eventually ladylike singer (Alice Faye). It was built around a variety of highly successful tunes that America's most cherished popular composer of the time, Irving Berlin, had fashioned over the years, including 'Now It Can Be Told,' 'My Walking Stick,' 'I'm Marching Along With Time' and 'Alexander's Ragtime Band'—in all, 26 of them.

Taking the threesome, as well as pals Jack Haley and Ethel Merman, from their first engagements to their ultimate stardom, the picture gave Americans a passing glimpse of their country's changing musical tastes and tickled their nostalgic sensitivities with its melodies. In so doing, *Alexander's Ragtime Band* played to huge audiences and inspired the studio to follow up with similar vehicles for Faye.

Once again she was sent back to yesteryear for *Rose of Washington Square* (1939), a picture based on the tempestuous Fanny Brice-Nick Arnstein affair that was later to be chronicled in *Funny Girl* (1968) with Barbra Streisand. Unfortunately for the studio, it was too close for comfort, and Fanny Brice won a settlement in court for the use of her story. The most memorable sequence in the film was Faye's fine torch rendition of 'My Man.'

Hollywood Cavalcade (1940) followed. It was a sort of *Alexander's Ragtime Band* with an early motion-picture setting. Alice Faye then revealed her talents as a dramatic actress in *Lillian Russell* (1940), a somewhat saccharine and more than somewhat fictionalized account of the famous singer's life. Her dramatic talents were to be used effectively in the non-musical melodrama *Fallen Angel* (1945).

Tin Pan Alley (1940) was a tuneful, entertaining film musical that followed the adventures of song pluggers and composers from 1915 to 1918. The highlight was the number 'Sheik of Araby' as rendered by that up-and-coming starlet, Betty Grable. Then came *Hello, Frisco, Hello* (1943), a vaudeville yarn that featured the Academy Award-winning song 'You'll Never Know,' and, again, Faye's new competition at Fox—Betty Grable.

Alice Faye's next-to-last film was the previously mentioned *Fallen Angel*, but she came out of retirement to make *State Fair* (1962). She played the part of Pamela Tiffin's mother in this remake of the Rodgers and Hammerstein film.

Starting in 1937, Fox presented the era's most unusual musical star—the Norwegian-born ice skater Sonja Henie, whose smile glittered as brightly as her skates. She had set world marks in the 1928, 1932 and 1936 Winter Olympics, and was put under contract by Darryl F Zanuck after some months touring with an ice show. This proved to be a wise move, since Henie had a pert and engaging personality that appealed immediately to audiences, as did the novelty and the excitement of seeing production numbers splendidly performed on ice.

Her first movie was *One in a Million*

Faye starred with Don Ameche and Edward Arnold in *Lillian Russell* (1940).

Bari, Payne, Havoc, Oakie, Faye—*Hello, Frisco, Hello* (1943).

Faye and Tom Ewell—*State Fair* (1962).

(1937), a film about a Swiss girl whose father was training her for the Olympics; the love interest was Don Ameche. *My Lucky Star* (1938) was another of the 11 films she made in Hollywood. She played an attractive college girl in this movie that featured

Tyrone Power and Alice Faye in *Alexander's Ragtime Band* (1938), the film that was a tribute to the music of Irving Berlin.

such songs as 'This May Be the Night,' 'The All-American Swing' and 'I've Got a Date with a Dream.'

She teamed with Tyrone Power in *Second Fiddle* (1939) and with Robert Cummings in *Everything Happens at Night* (1939). Her most memorable film may well have been *Sun Valley Serenade* (1941), in which she starred with John Payne and Glenn Miller and his orchestra. She played a war refugee and Payne was her foster parent. The film featured 'It Happened in Sun Valley' and 'Chattanooga Choo-Choo.'

Probably the only important thing in *Iceland* (1942), in which she appeared with John Payne again, was the song 'There Will Never Be Another You.' After three more skating films, her popularity dimmed in the mid-1940s and brought about her retirement. She did try again in a British film, *Hello London* (1958), but it was pretty much a failure. Henie then produced and starred in the highly successful *Hollywood Ice Review* extravaganzas. She died in 1969.

After first venturing into the musical field with *The Broadway Melody* (1929), Metro-Goldwyn-Mayer backed off when the movie musical genre ran into problems in the early 1930s. But on seeing *Forty-Second Street*'s cash triumph, the studio quickly came up with a carbon copy—*Dancing Lady* (1933), an emptiness about a chorus girl (Joan Crawford) being lifted to stardom by a tough dance director (Clark Gable). The picture tried hard at Berkeley-type sequences, but missed the mark. Crawford was panned for her limited song-and-dance talents. The film is chiefly remembered because it marked Fred Astaire's first

Sonja Henie and Don Ameche starred in *One in a Million* (1936)—the Norwegian skater's first film.

Irene Dunne and Randolph Scott were in *High, Wide and Handsome* (1937). The hit song was 'The Folks Who Live on the Hill.'

screen appearance. Playing himself, he served as Crawford's dancing partner. The picture also featured the classic song 'Everything I Have Is Yours.'

By the middle of the 1930s another musical star appeared on the MGM lot—the young, shapely and exuberant tap-dancer, Eleanor Powell. A Broadway performer since the age of 17, she came to Hollywood to do *George White's Scandals* (1935) at Fox, moving then to MGM for *Broadway Melody of 1936* (1935). The discrepancy in dates was explained by the studio publicity department—'So new it's a year ahead.' The original 'Broadway Melody' song began the picture, but this was no sequel. Eleanor Powell became an instant star.

The film also began a long career for Buddy Ebsen. The real stars of the movie were Jack Benny and Frances Langford. Langford sang 'Broadway Rhythm' and 'You Are My Lucky Star.' Other Nacio Herb Brown-Arthur Freed songs were 'Sing Before Breakfast' and 'I Gotta Feelin' You're Foolin'.'

Richard Arlen, Ida Lupino, Jack Benny, Gail Patrick—*Artists and Models* (1937).

Irene Dunne and Randolph Scott were in *High, Wide and Handsome* (1937). The hit song was 'The Folks Who Live on the Hill.'

screen appearance. Playing himself, he served as Crawford's dancing partner. The picture also featured the classic song 'Everything I Have Is Yours.'

By the middle of the 1930s another musical star appeared on the MGM lot—the young, shapely and exuberant tap-dancer, Eleanor Powell. A Broadway performer since the age of 17, she came to Hollywood to do *George White's Scandals* (1935) at Fox, moving then to MGM for *Broadway Melody of 1936* (1935). The discrepancy in dates was explained by the studio publicity department—'So new it's a year ahead.' The original 'Broadway Melody' song began the picture, but this was no sequel. Eleanor Powell became an instant star.

The film also began a long career for Buddy Ebsen. The real stars of the movie were Jack Benny and Frances Langford. Langford sang 'Broadway Rhythm' and 'You Are My Lucky Star.' Other Nacio Herb Brown-Arthur Freed songs were 'Sing Before Breakfast' and 'I Gotta Feelin' You're Foolin'.'

Richard Arlen, Ida Lupino, Jack Benny, Gail Patrick—*Artists and Models* (1937).

Once established as a star, Powell moved tirelessly from one MGM musical to another, working in 11 over a ten-year period. Her pictures featured lavish production numbers often set against art deco backgrounds—the battleship, for instance, in the 'Swingin' the Jinx Away' sequence in *Born to Dance* (1937), one of her best films. She starred with James Stewart, Buddy Ebsen and Frances Langford, and played the understudy of a temperamental revue star whom she replaces at the last minute to save the show. Virginia Bruce played the star. Of course, Powell was a dancer and Bruce was a singer, but that discrepancy was never explained. And who cared, with all those Cole Porter songs like 'Easy to Love' and 'I've Got You Under My Skin.'

Who can forget the luminous New York skyline against which a top-hatted Eleanor Powell and chorus performed the finale in *Broadway Melody of 1938* (1937)? Or the vast stairway with its curlicue side ornaments used for the major production number in *Rosalie* (1938)?

Always a pleasure to watch—leggy, vivacious and superbly talented—Eleanor Powell slipped from popularity in the mid-1940s through no fault of her own. Tap work simply went out of style, as audiences switched their affections to the impressionistic dance and ballet being pioneered in such Broadway productions as the 1943 hit *Oklahoma!*

Paramount spent the 1930s concentrating on its *Big Broadcast* musicals and the talents of an amiable singer named Bing Crosby. Bing, born Harry Lillis Crosby, appeared in *The Big Broadcast* (1932) and it made him a star. Soon after the beginning of the talkies, radio started to cannibalize Hollywood talent. It offered stars huge sum for brief appearances on the air, to the great distress of movie exhibitors who claimed that people would rather stay home and hear their favorites than pay to see them as well as hear them in the movie theater. Soon Hollywood returned the compliment by featuring radio personalities. *The Big Broadcast*, for example, had in its cast, besides Crosby, such radio luminaries as Kate Smith, the Mills Brothers, George Burns and Gracie Allen, Arthur Tracy (the Street Singer), Cab Calloway and his Orchestra and the Boswell Sisters. Crosby made a hit singing 'Please' and 'Here Lies Love.'

Paramount followed this film with three more—*The Big Broadcast of 1936* (1935), in which Crosby sang 'I Wished on the Moon'; *The Big Broadcast of 1937* (1936), with Jack Benny, George Burns and Grace Allen, and Martha Raye, featuring 'La Bomba,' 'Here's Love in Your Eye' and 'Night in Manhattan'; and *The Big Broadcast of 1938* (1938), with W C Fields, Bob Hope and Dorothy Lamour, featuring 'Thanks for the Memory.'

The Big Broadcasts and their glittering assortment of stars were popu-

Above: Frances Langford, Buddy Ebsen, Eleanor Powell, James Stewart, Una Merkel, Sid Silvers in *Born to Dance* (1936).

Opposite: Dancing Lady (1933).

Eleanor Powell in the 'Swingin' the Jinx Away' finale to *Born to Dance* (1936).

Bing Crosby looks on as Stuart Erwin romances Leila Hyams in *The Big Broadcast* (1932). It was Crosby's first featured role, and he got third billing.

lar at the box office, but Paramount's greatest musical attraction of the decade was, hands down, Bing Crosby. As a member of the singing Rhythm Boys, he broke into pictures with Paul Whiteman's Orchestra in *King of Jazz* (1930). He then made several musical shorts crooning for Mack Sennett. He appeared in Southern California night clubs, began making records and landed his part in *The Big Broadcast*. From that point on, Crosby was a Paramount mainstay, appearing in 18 more pictures in the 1930s. He also made two on loan to other studios.

One of them was *Going Hollywood* (1933 for MGM). His co-star was Marion Davies. He was a crooner and she was his biggest fan. Also in the cast were Fifi D'Orsay, Stuart Erwin and Ned Sparks. The big hits from the picture were 'Temptation' and 'We'll Make Hay While the Sun Shines.' *Pennies from Heaven* (1936 for Columbia), about a wandering drifter befriending a penniless waif played by Edith Fellows, was the other. The title song was the most memorable.

With the exception of *Pennies from Heaven*, Crosby's musicals of the decade were all appealing, pleasant affairs, but they were modest efforts when compared to the Warner Brothers and Metro-Goldwyn-Mayer spectacles and the elegant Astaire-Rogers vehicles. They now and again sported ambitious production numbers, but more often than not they limited themselves to plots that enabled Bing to display his easygoing, even flippant, manner, and that invariably placed him in a romantic setting for a quiet but throbbing love song to the heroine. In combination, his casual presence and equally casual voice made him an international favorite for over four decades.

This is not to say that his films were without some startlingly good specialty numbers. A young Martha Raye, for example, scored heavily with her 'Mr Paganini' routine in *Rhythm on the Range* (1936) and did her raucous burlesque stripper bit, 'It's On, It's Off,' in *Double or Nothing* (1937). But it was Crosby's singing that usually brought in the customers. Throughout the decade, he turned a parade of songs into international hits—'The Old Ox Road' (*College Humor*, 1933), 'Temptation' (*Going Hollywood*, 1934), 'It's Easy to Remember' (*Mississippi*, 1935), 'Sweet Lelani' (*Waikiki Wedding*, 1937, a best-song Academy

Carole Lombard and Crosby on a desert island in *We're Not Dressing* (1934).

Opposite: Astaire and Powell.

A potpourri of early Bing Crosby musical pictures.
Below: Crosby starred with Edith Fellows in *Pennies From Heaven* (1936).

Crosby with Ellen Drew in *Sing You Sinners* (1938).

Award winner) and 'Small Fry' (sung with Fred MacMurray and a 13-year-old Donald O'Connor in *Sing You Sinners*, 1938).

In all, Crosby provided audiences with a sometimes brash and sometimes sensitive but always refreshing break from the Depression and its problems. But his best work was yet to come.

Madge Evans, Crosby, Edith Fellows in *Pennies From Heaven* (1936).

Gail Patrick, Crosby, Joan Bennett in *Mississippi* (1935).

With Bob Burns—*Rhythm on the Range* (1936).

Deanna Durbin, Helen Parrish, Nan Grey in *Three Smart Girls Grow Up* (1939).

Deanna Durbin (kneeling) in *First Love* (1939). Helen Parrish sneers. In the film, Deanna got her first screen kiss from Robert Stack.

One Hundred Men and a Girl (1937) with Deanna Durbin and Leopold Stokowski.

The most important musical star at Universal Studios at the time was Deanna Durbin, and she was doubly important in that her pictures had reportedly saved the studio from bankruptcy. Hers was another of those improbable Hollywood success stories. Deanna was born Edna Durbin in Winnipeg, Canada, in 1929, but her life began changing when the family moved to California in 1932. She began taking singing lessons and, in her early teens, was seen by a talent scout and signed to a six-months' MGM contract.

In the meantime, Universal had a script for a film called *Three Smart Girls*, which required a young popular-style girl singer, and the studio asked MGM to loan them Judy Garland for the role. MGM, however, said that Deanna Durbin was available and Judy was not, so the script was re-written to make the girl character a classical singer. *Three Smart Girls* (1936) made Durbin a star at the age of 15, singing 'Someone to Care for Me' and 'My Heart Is Singing.'

She made *One Hundred Men and a Girl* (1937) with conductor Leopold Stokowski and a symphony orchestra (the 100 men). *Mad About Music* (1938) was her third straight box-office hit. Universal, which had been a steady money-loser before Deanna came along, was now a big money-maker. So was Deanna; she went from next to nothing to $1500 a week in less than a year. Deanna was set in a formula as a wholesome teenager, as the titles of her next movies indicated: *First Love* (1939), *It's A Date* (1940) and *Nice Girl* (1941).

Deanna Durbin might have gone on playing teenagers forever, but she decided that it was time to grow up on the screen. It didn't work. Audiences did not want to see a grown-up Deanna, and her box-office draw soon tailed off. In 1949, quite comfortable financially, she retired from movies and went to live in France with her husband, film director Charles David. She received a special Academy Award in 1938 'for bringing to the screen the spirit and personification of youth.'

The British were also busy turning out movie musicals. They produced a string of highly entertaining light pieces, among them *That's a Good Girl* (1935) directed by and starring Jack Buchanan; *London Melody* (1937) with Anna Neagle; *The Show Goes On* (1937), a Gracie Fields vehicle; and *Sailing Along* (1938) with Jessie Matthews, the vivacious British singing and dancing star of light musicals.

Nelson Eddy and Jeanette MacDonald in *Naughty Marietta* (1935)

THE OPERETTAS

After the renaissance of the musical films in the early 1930s, there came an operatic invasion. The American opera singer Grace Moore starred in *One Night of Love* (1934). She was later to be immortalized as the subject of a movie biography in 1953—*So This Is Love*—in which she was played by Kathryn Grayson. The highlight of *One Night of Love* was Moore's singing of the title song as she pelted the populace of Venice with apples while riding through the streets in a car (a car?) with Lyle Talbot. Moore had made her screen debut in 1930 in *A Lady's Morals* (in which she was cast as Jenny Lind), and then came *The New Moon* (1930). But audiences did not like her prim dignity. Determined to conquer the movies, she returned in *One Night of Love*, glamorized and jazzed up, and was a sensation. She went on to make five more films—*Love Me Forever* (1935), *The King Steps Out* (1935), *When You're in Love* (1937), *I'll Take Romance* (1937) and *Louise* (1940).

The French-born coloratura soprano Lily Pons appeared in *I Dream Too Much* (1935). One critic suggested that it be retitled *I Scream Too Much*, but she went on to make several more movie appearances. In *Here's to Romance* (1935), the Italian actor-singer Nino Martini sang a snippet of *Tosca*. As is the case today, operatic scenes on the screen had to be brief if the audience were to tolerate them. Also, in many cases, the lack of acting ability, the less-than-handsome physical appearance—or both—of the opera stars became too obvious when they were presented on the big screen. The American soprano Gladys Swarthout teamed with John Boles in *Rose of the Rancho* (1936). She made four more films in a doomed attempt to become a screen favorite, doomed despite the fact that she was stunningly beautiful and could act, too.

More successful were the British-made operettas of Gilbert and Sullivan, usually starring the famous D'Oyly Carte Company. The most notable was *The Mikado* (1939), which starred Kenny Baker as Nanki-Poo and Martyn Green as Koko.

Actually, by 1930 the operetta had been called officially dead at the box office. The camera emphasized the absurdity of its plots and conventions too cruelly. But in 1934 Stan Laurel and Oliver Hardy starred in the Victor Herbert operetta *Babes in Toyland*. It made a lot of money and is still being shown on television at holiday time.

The big breakthrough, however, came the next year. Irving Thalberg, MGM's boy-wonder producer of the early 1930s, and W S Van Dyke, one of Hollywood's top directors, found a way to naturalize the marriage of sound and plot when they made *Naughty Marietta* (1935), a film that made stars of Jeanette MacDonald and Nelson Eddy.

Jeanette MacDonald, of the perpendicular eyebrows, the rosebud lips and the sparrow voice, was born in Philadelphia. She sang and danced in a series of Broadway musicals in the 1920s, and in 1929 she was Maurice Chevalier's leading lady in the film *The Love Parade*, making her a star her first time out. She starred again with Chevalier in *Love Me Tonight* (1932), a picture that seemed to have 'The Lubitsch Touch,' but that was actually directed by Rouben Mamoulian. It characterized Paris as a place where everybody sings. But the songs were fine—among them 'Mimi' and 'Isn't It Romantic?'. Also in the cast were Myrna Loy, Charles Butterworth and Charlie Ruggles.

Then her career took a plunge when musicals went down in the early 1930s. She began rising to the top again in *The Merry Widow* (1934), after her contract had been purchased from Paramount by MGM. *The Merry Widow* of 1934, based on the Franz Lehar operetta with added lyrics by Gus Kahn and Lorenz Hart, was the second time that the operetta had been filmed. The first was in 1925, a silent with John Gilbert and Mae Murray, directed by Erich von Stroheim. It was later to be filmed in 1953 with

Stan Laurel and Oliver Hardy played the leading comic roles in *Babes in Toyland* (1934).

Jessie Ralph is not disturbed by Grace Moore's swoon in *One Night of Love* (1934).

Elsa Lanchester is concerned as Frank Morgan challenges Nelson Eddy in *Naughty Marietta* (1935).

with lyrics by Paul Francis Webster.

The picture reunited MacDonald, Lubitsch and Chevalier. The film didn't do as well as expected at the box office, but then came the first of the eight pictures she was to make with Nelson Eddy—*Naughty Marietta*. MacDonald was never to get beyond her sugary persona as Eddy's soprano. The mix, however, between these two and their saccharine romantic stories spelled 'gold mine' for Metro-Goldwyn-Mayer.

Marietta was only Eddy's fourth film, but he became a star. He was blond. He sang baritone. And the film made more money for the studio than had any musical up to that time.

Considering *The Merry Widow*'s lukewarm reception and Eddy's lack of screen experience, the venture was a risky one. But *Naughty Marietta* paid handsome dividends when it was released. Somehow, the two disparate singers—MacDonald vivacious and Eddy almost hopelessly wooden (a problem that was to dog him throughout his career)—charmed audiences as a team, perhaps because of their youthful attractiveness (he was 34, she was 28), perhaps because their voices, both so genuinely good, blended close to perfection. They were immediately given the sickly-sweet tag 'The Singing Sweethearts,' and spent much of the next seven years working together.

Naughty Marietta had a splendid score that included 'I'm Falling in Love with Someone,' 'Ah, Sweet Mystery of Life' and 'The Italian Street Song.' The sound engineer, Douglas Shearer (brother of Norma Shearer), won the second of his 12 Academy Awards for the recording of the sound track.

Their next film together was *Rose Marie* (1936). It was an operetta in which most of the songs were by Rudolf Friml and Oscar Hammerstein II, including 'Indian Love Call,' 'Song of the Mounties' and 'Rose Marie, I Love You.' The film had a bigger budget than *Marietta*, so it was more lavish than their previous picture. Indeed, it had a large-scale dance number, 'Totem Tomtom,' that was staged by the master—Busby Berkeley. This was the second go-round for this operetta about the Royal Canadian Mounted Police getting their man. The first was a silent version in 1928 with Joan Crawford, and it was to be remade in 1954 with Ann Blyth and Howard Keel.

It didn't have much of a plot, but no one cared. Marie de Flor (MacDonald) is an opera singer, strictly a high-class lady who goes to the wilds of Canada because her brother is there, having escaped from jail and murdered a Mountie. En route, the fair Marie meets a handsome Mounted Policeman (Eddy) who is tracking down her brother. In this movie everybody wins except the brother. He has to go to jail again.

In *Rose Marie* a young actor in his second picture, was tapped as a future star—he played the brother and was named James Stewart. But another young actor, in his fifth picture, was hardly noticed—David Niven.

For us today it is hard to take

Jeanette MacDonald with Maurice Chevalier in *The Merry Widow* (1934)—the Lehar operetta as jazzed up by Lorenz Hart

Opposite: The Merry Widow (1934).

Maytime (1937).

I Married an Angel (1942).

Bitter Sweet (1940).

New Moon (1940).

Sweethearts (1938).

Bitter Sweet (1940).

Rose Marie (1936).

'Indian Love Call' seriously. But that doesn't make us right and millions of people in 1936 wrong. It just means that styles have changed. 'When I'm calling you-ou-ou-ou-ou-ou-ou' is rather laughable in the 1980s, but it set a lot of hearts pounding in 1936.

Nelson Eddy and Jeanette MacDonald were trained singers. They were supposed to bring culture to the audience. Compared to them, Busby Berkeley, Astaire and Rogers and George White were low-brows. It was also all right to be drippingly romantic in the mid-1930s. People then were not embarrassed by love.

Maytime (1937) was next. Twenty years before, Sigmund Romberg's operetta was so popular that two stage versions ran on Broadway at the same time. The hit song was 'Will You Remember?' The film was a delightfully costumed one that took audiences into a never-never land of the Paris of Louis Napoleon, where a young couple fell in love. Make-believe worlds of the past with their period costumes had had a strong appeal to movie audiences for decades. Critics loved *Maytime*, and Metro-Goldwyn-Mayer raked in a lot of money.

Hollywood spent millions promoting itself in 1938—a slump year. The promotion campaign included an ad with the slogan 'Movies Are Your Best Entertainment.' This was scrapped when people noticed that its acronym was MAYBE.

Despite the slump, Jeanette and Nelson made *The Girl of the Golden West* (1938), a costume operetta in which MacDonald was a mid-1800s saloon owner in the West and Eddy was a romantic bandit. The score was by Sigmund Romberg and Sammy Kahn, with Gounod's 'Ave Maria' thrown in to add some class.

The New Moon (1940) was next. This swashbuckler was a remake of the 1931 *New Moon* that had starred Lawrence Tibbitt and Grace Moore, and it seemed dated even then. But the score by Sigmund Romberg and

Florence Rice, Jeanette, Nelson, Frank Morgan in *Sweethearts* (1938).

Walter Pidgeon being threatened by the good guys in *The Girl of the Golden West* (1938).

Nelson Eddy in an exuberant moment in *I Married an Angel* (1942).

Oscar Hammerstein II was superb, even though most of the songs had nothing to do with the story. Among them were 'One Kiss,' 'Softly As in a Morning Sunrise,' 'Lover Come Back to Me' and 'Stout Hearted Men.' Jeanette had 16 costume changes involving 80 petticoats, and her most elaborate gown was an emerald-green creation (even though this was a black-and-white film) that weighed in at 35 pounds. The movie was pure escapism and the public loved it.

Bitter Sweet, Noel Coward's romantic operetta, had previously been filmed in 1933 with Anna Neagle and Fernand Gravet, and it was remade by MacDonald and Eddy in 1940—this time in color. All the spice in Coward's version was gone. But the Technicolor was beautiful, and the Noel Coward songs—most of them—were there, including 'I'll See You Again,' 'Zigeuner,' 'Ladies of the Town' and 'Tokay.' For some unexplained reason, the wonderful 'If Love Were All' was dropped.

In modern clothes for a change, they made *Sweethearts* in 1940. It was one of their best—a Victor Herbert operetta about two opera stars who never stop fighting offstage. It included 'On Parade' and 'Sweethearts.' Dorothy Parker had been hired to add some acid wit to a sugary plot, and it came out as a pretty good comedy. Legend has it that once, while she was working on the script, Parker leaned out of her window in the writers' building and shouted 'Let me out! I'm as sane as you are!'

Jeanette and Nelson made their final picture together in 1942—*I Married an Angel.* It was a Rodgers and Hart musical fantasy and had a couple of nice songs—the title song and 'Spring Is Here.'

Actually, the public had begun to grow tired of 'The Singing Sweethearts' by 1940. Some of their operettas were going out of date too rapidly, and the stars themselves, looking a bit too old for their innocent lovemaking and suffering from the fact that their acting abilities never matched their singing skills, were beginning to strike movie-goers as funny. It was the birth of an attitude that, today, has come to label the MacDonald-Eddy vehicles as high camp.

Time could be stopped in the movies, but time had passed in real life, and the duo's later movies had begun to show wrinkles. Eddy grew fatter, leading some sneering critics to refer to him as 'The Singing Capon.' MacDonald grew too old to carry off an ingenue role. But they spawned an entire line of romantic operettas set in the past.

MGM made *The Great Waltz* (1938). (Some critics referred to it as *The Great Schmaltz.*) The studio had taken a story about Johann Strauss, along with some of his melodies, added new lyrics by Oscar Hammerstein II, and out came 'I'm in Love with Vienna' and 'One Day When We Were Young,' among others. The film starred Luise Rainer and the great Hungarian soprano Miliza Korjus. But it was not a huge success, and the movie marked both Korjus' screen debut and film farewell in American pictures. Nevertheless, it was remade in 1972 with Horst Buchholz as Strauss.

The film careers of Nelson Eddy and Jeanette MacDonald were not over, however. Even while she was starring with Eddy, MacDonald had been in other pictures. In *San Francisco* (1936) she had starred with Clark Gable and Spencer Tracy in a top-grade entertainment with a lavish production and sensational special effects, including the magnificent earthquake footage.

She appeared in an operetta, *The Firefly* (1937), with Allan Jones. It was a Rudolf Friml show with a silly story about MacDonald as a Spanish

Eddy, Lionel Atwill, Ilona Massey—*Balalaika* (1939). 'I came to fight the Czar's enemies—not his subjects.'

spy during the Napoleonic War of 1808–1812. The score was the only redeeming feature of the movie, whose hammy plot had been written by, among others, Ogden Nash. From the original Broadway show came such numbers as 'Sympathy,' 'Giannina Mia' and 'Love Is Like a Firefly.' Jones sang 'The Donkey Serenade,' which had been taken from one of Rudolf Friml's earlier piano pieces.

One of the few films in which Jeanette MacDonald was permitted to chuck her cloying image and showcase her talents as a comedienne was *Broadway Serenade* (1939); after that she was in a musical-comedy spoof of all those World War II spy films—*Cairo* (1941).

Eddy, too, had other fish to fry. *Rosalie* (1937) teamed him with the great Eleanor Powell. It was a lavish hit. The title-song number was a wild one. It was filmed in an area that covered 60 acres of the Metro-Goldwyn-Mayer lot and used 27 cameras to film some 2000 people singing, dancing, or just standing. The original stage play had music by Sigmund Romberg and some Gershwin numbers. But the movie had a Cole Porter score—one of his best. Probably the classic was 'In the Still of the Night.'

Nelson Eddy made a rather dull

Jeanette MacDonald was a cafe entertainer in *San Francisco* (1936).

Eddy and Rise Stevens in 'My Hero' from *The Chocolate Soldier* (1941).

Jeanette MacDonald and Lew Ayres in *Broadway Serenade* (1939).

operetta, *Balalaika* (1939), with Ilona Massey, the Hungarian-born leading lady whose first name is familiar to every crossword puzzle fan. The pretentious plot ranged from pre-Revolutionary Russia, through the Revolution, to Paris of 1938, and everybody sang such songs as 'Magic of Your Love' and 'At the Balalaika.'

The Chocolate Soldier (1941) was a combination of Ferenc Molnar's *The Guardsman* and Oscar Strauss' operetta *The Chocolate Soldier*, and used music from that score. This might well have been Eddy's finest hour. He starred with Rise Stevens, the American contralto, and everything worked. It turned out that Eddy had a talent for light comedy and Stevens was magnetic. Also, their voices seemed to blend together.

Before their deaths, Jeanette MacDonald and Nelson Eddy went on to other careers. MacDonald had a short stint in Grand Opera (although she had to use a body microphone in such huge auditoriums as Chicago's Civic Opera House), and Eddy charmed millions all over the country in live concerts. No matter how we regard their films today, this team made America and the world aware that the operetta can be wonderful musical entertainment.

Paula Wessely and Willi Forst in *So Endete eine Liebe.*

But surely Germany was the movie operetta capital of the world, and some of the German filmed operettas were milestone films. *Liebeswalzer* (1930), with Willy Fritsch and Lilian Harvey, was the first filmed operetta really to combine the realistic elements of film with the static beauty of the operetta. William Thiele directed it as a film, not a series of arias in which all action stopped. Lilian Harvey, a transplanted English singer, became the first real operetta diva in films. The film was so successful that the operetta was retranslated around the world.

Another breakthrough was the jolly romantic film operetta of 1930, *Die Drei von der Tankstelle (The Three*

Oskar Karlweis, Willy Fritsch and Heinz Rümann in *Die Drei von der Tankstelle.*

Fritsch and Harvey in *Liebeswalzer.*

Willy Fritsch and Lilian Harvey in *Der Kongress Tanzt.*

from the Gas Station), also starring Lilian Harvey. It was the story of three men, inseparable friends, who meet Harvey, who is a regular customer of the station, and was the first really natural operetta on film. They sang, laughed, danced and flirted so that audiences just had to care about them. And for the first time in an operetta, the music was used to further the action of the play.

Ronny (1932) was another monumental operetta, combining all the tricks and nuances of previous films. It featured a doll-like kingdom with rococo figurines in a castle park. The whole thing seemed to have arisen from a child's toy chest.

Lilian Harvey in *Der Kongress Tanzt*.

Jan Kiepura and Marta Eggerth in *Mein Herz Ruft nach Dir*.

Karlweis and Harvey in . . .*Tankstelle*.

Käthe von Nagy and Willy Fritsch in *Ronny*.

Judy Garland, Jack Haley and Ray Bolger in *The Wizard of Oz* (1939).

THE EXTRAVAGANZAS

With the success of the more modest musicals of the early 1930s, Hollywood decided to start pouring a lot of money into extravaganzas. The most mammoth, by far, was Metro-Goldwyn-Mayer's *The Great Ziegfeld* (1936). Produced in the Ziegfeld manner, it ran for a monumental two hours and 56 minutes, and was a fictionalized account of the life of the flamboyant American showman Florenz Ziegfeld.

The Great Ziegfeld starred William Powell in the title role, and, in a chiefly hokey plot line, traced his life from carnival sideshows to his Broadway extravaganzas. Hungarian-born Luise Rainer played his first wife, the singer Anna Held, and won an Academy Award for her performance. The role of Billie Burke, Ziegfeld's second wife, went to Powell's screen partner in the highly successful *Thin Man* series, Myrna Loy.

The picture itself proved episodic and its story line predictable, but MGM poured all its resources into the musical numbers and they were all breathtaking, at times even awesome. Especially imaginative was the sequence atop the New Amsterdam Theater, featuring chorus girls dancing on top of beds moving in rhythm with them. As for sheer awesomeness, the 'A Pretty Girl Is Like a Melody' number has never been equalled.

Seymour Felix won an Academy Award for the dance direction of 'A Pretty Girl Is Like a Melody' in *The Great Ziegfeld* (1936).

William Powell, as Florenz Ziegfeld, and Myrna Loy as his wife, Billie Burke, in *The Great Ziegfeld* (1936).

Featuring the tuneful principal song, a dash of operatic singing, a spicing of ballet, a pinch of George Gershwin's 'Rhapsody in Blue,' a liberal sprinkling of salt-white and pepper-black costumes, and an icing of honest-to-goodness showgirl spectacle, it was performed on a massive set. The centerpiece was a giant pillar circled by a gracefully winding staircase, its edge girdled with pianos for three-quarters of its rising distance. Once seen, the whole number was not easily forgotten. It earned a dance-direction Academy Award for its creator, Seymore Felix.

Ziegfeld himself never spent as much money as MGM did on this picture. It cost about two million dollars, making it the most expensive film from that studio since *Ben Hur* (1926, with Ramon Novarro and Francis X Bushman). It returned double its cost and earned an Academy Award as the best picture of the year.

The 'A Pretty Girl Is Like a Melody' number was sung by Dennis Morgan (at that time called Stanley Morner), but at the last minute his voice was dubbed by Allan Jones. No one knows what caused the shift, because Morgan had an excellent voice.

Showboat (1936), the Jerome Kern and Oscar Hammerstein II musical based on the Edna Ferber novel, was directed by James Whale the year after he directed *The Bride of Frankenstein*, but it was no horror film. Among others, it starred Irene Dunne, Allan Jones and the great Paul Robeson singing 'Old Man River.' It featured such classic songs as 'Why Do I Love You?' and 'Only Make-believe.' The picture had been previously made in 1929 with Laura La Plante and Joseph Schildkraut. But when it was remade in 1951 with Kathryn Grayson, Howard Keel and William Warfield, MGM bought up the rights and prints of the 1936 version so that the new one would have no competition.

Probably the most lavish of the 1938 musicals was *The Goldwyn Follies*. It contained the last music that George Gershwin wrote before he died, most notably the haunting song 'Love Walked In.' The all-star cast featured Adolphe Menjou, the Ritz Brothers, Vera Zorina, Kenny Baker and Edgar Bergen and Charlie McCarthy.

Vera Zorina, a Norwegian dancer born Eva Brigitta Hartwig, coincidentally was married to George Balanchine, the internationally renowned choreographer who had been hired to do the ballets for the film. The combination was a tremendous success, and for years after the film was released, any Hollywood musical with any aspirations had to have the same kind of ballet sequences. Examples are *The Pirate* (1947), *On the Town* (1950), *An American in Paris* (1951), *Singin' in the Rain* (1952) and *The Band Wagon* (1953). This custom died out in the 1950s.

In the film, Edgar Bergen was so convincing in his ventriloquist routines with his dummy Charlie McCarthy that they fooled the movie crew. When they were trying their first scene, no matter how hard he tried, the sound man couldn't get the sound right. It turned out that whenever Charlie started to 'speak,' the sound man turned the microphone away from Edgar Bergen and toward the dummy, Charlie McCarthy.

The script had been a problem. The picture was so monumental that nine writers (including Dorothy Parker and Anita Loos) had been hired to write it. Nothing happened, so Ben Hecht was brought in to pick up the pieces. He wrote the final script in two weeks.

The big tragedy was that George Gershwin died at the age of 38 before the movie was completed.

Probably the greatest extravaganza —and the most unusual film—of 1938 was *Snow White and the Seven Dwarfs*,

Kathryn Grayson as Magnolia, Howard Keel as Ravenal and Ava Gardner as Julie, in *Show Boat* (1951).

Gene Kelly and Leslie Caron were the perfect ballet team in *An American in Paris* (1951).

which was the first full-length animated feature motion picture. The public relations writers had a field day:

> Walt Disney creates a modern miracle. . . The magician whose genius has peopled the world with lovable creatures captures a dream of enchantment . . . in laughter, suspense and fantasy, in exquisite beauty of color and design, his first full length feature is the most inspired, the most human, the most artistic triumph ever to come out of Hollywood.

For once, the flackmen were right. The lovable seven dwarfs, the handsome Snow White and Prince Charming, the frightening evil queen live in everyone's memories. So, also, do the songs—'Whistle While You Work,' 'Some Day My Prince Will Come,' 'I'm Wishing.' The critics were unanimous in their praise. 'It is a classic, as important cinematically as *The Birth of a Nation* or the birth of Mickey Mouse.' 'A picture too beautiful to describe.' Anyone who first saw it as a child will remember the fear that was instilled by the queen disguised as a witch; the tears that came when it was thought that Snow White was dead; the wonderful release when the Prince awakens her with 'Love's First Kiss.'

Things did not run completely smoothly at the Disney Studios when they were planning the film. Deanna Durbin had tried out for the voice of Snow White when she was an unknown, but she was rejected for sounding too old—and she was only 15. They had a terrible time naming the dwarfs—that precisely different group of comedians—Bashful, Sleepy, Grumpy, Sneezy, Happy, Dopey and Doc. An early list of possible names for the dwarfs included Scrappy, Hoppy, Dirty, Dumpy, Hungry, Thrifty, Weepy, Doleful, Awful, Gabby, Flabby, Snoopy, Shifty, Helpful, Crabby, Daffy, Puffy, Chesty, Busy, Biggie and Gaspy. Marge Champion, who was later half of the husband-and-wife Marge and Gower Champion dance team, was the physical model for Snow White and later modeled for the Blue Fairy in *Pinocchio* (1940).

The biggest musical blockbuster of the 1930s was *The Wizard of Oz* (1939), which was the most expensive production in MGM history at that time, costing $3,200,000. It has never been off release since, and for many people it is an all-time favorite. Nothing could match the cinema magic wrought by this filming of L Frank Baum's children's classic. Starring Judy Garland, Ray Bolger, Bert Lahr, Jack Haley, the inimitable Margaret Hamilton (who had once been a kindergarten teacher) as the Wicked Witch of the West and the equally inimitable Frank Morgan as the Wizard, here was a combination of sheer beauty, free-flying imagination and good fun that couldn't help but charm audiences.

Everything about the film had charm—the songs by Harold Arlen and E Y Harburg; the special effects like that marvelous yellow brick road, the Wizard's assorted magical contraptions and the Witch's skywriting; the musical sequences—Garland singing 'Over the Rainbow,' Bolger dancing at his eccentric best as the Scarecrow while trying to keep his straw inside

Opposite: Gene Kelly and Debbie Reynolds. *Above:* Bolger, Garland, Lahr and Haley in *The Wizard of Oz* (1939).

HAUNTED FOREST
WITCHES CASTLE

his body where it belonged and Lahr's Cowardly Lion plaintively growling 'If I Were King of the Forest'; and the characterizations—Jack Haley's lonely and likable Tin Woodman, Margaret Hamilton's evil, screeching Wicked Witch and Frank Morgan's all-stops-out portrayals of various Emerald City residents, among them the Wizard himself.

It was all the stuff of magic and it worked critical and commercial magic for Metro-Goldwyn-Mayer. *The Wizard of Oz*, however, had the misfortune to come out in the same year as *Gone With The Wind* and so did not get the Academy Award for best picture of 1939, an honor that most likely would have come to it in any other year. Its director, Victor Fleming, received the best-director Academy Award that year, but not for *The Wizard*. He got it for his work on *Gone With The Wind*. The 17-year-old Judy Garland, however, received a special Oscar for the year's outstanding performance by a juvenile. An Academy Award went to Herbert Stothart for the picture's musical adaptation, and to Arlen and Harburg for 'Over the Rainbow.'

The Wizard of Oz was the first of a series of musicals produced for MGM by Arthur Freed—musicals that would give that studio dominance in the musical field for many years. Freed, who encouraged and gave free rein to such people as Vincente Minnelli, Gene Kelly and Stanley Donen as directors, and who produced such remarkably fine musicals as *Cabin in the Sky* (1942), *Meet Me in St Louis* (1944), *On the Town* (1950), *Singin' in the Rain* (1952), *It's Always Fair Weather* (1955) and a good 30 more of varying quality but consistent commerciality, harbored a definite conception of what a musical should be.

He thought that it should be an organic whole, an entertainment in which story, songs and dances were integrated and unified by a strong dramatic line. Songs, according to Freed's concept, must flow out of the dramatic material and advance the story, rather than serve merely as intermezzos between action that stops when music begins and resumes when the music has ended. A song, no matter how tuneful or pleasure-giving, that did not advance the story had to be scrapped. Such a number was 'The Jitterbug' in *The Wizard of Oz*, a pretty senseless song and dance done

The frightened friends head toward the haunted forest in *The Wizard of Oz* (1939).

The Wicked Witch (Margaret Hamilton) threatens Dorothy (Judy Garland) in *The Wizard of Oz* (1939).

by Garland, Haley, Bolger and Lahr in the middle of the forest. It was completely out of place. Composer Harold Arlen, however, was lurking behind the scenes with his 16mm movie camera, and preserved the number for posterity. This musical cut was shown on the *Ripley's Believe It or Not* television program in October of 1983, and it would better have been completely forgotten.

The same thing almost happened to the picture's most famous and popular song, 'Over the Rainbow,' which the producer felt did not move the story line along. The idea of *The Wizard of Oz* without 'Over the Rainbow' brings tears to the eyes.

In addition, Freed believed that the transition from dialogue to music should be as smooth as possible, triggered usually by the emotion of the character whose exuberance would make bursting into song a natural thing. *The Wizard of Oz* was the first musical calculatedly fashioned according to this formula.

The film had everything going for it. It had a magnificent score that appealed to both children and adults. It had special architecture, special effects and the distortion of normal space-time. And it had Judy Garland. Her place in the history of the musical is as important as that of Fred Astaire.

Judy was born Frances Gumm in 1922 in Grand Rapids, Minnesota, the daughter of vaudevillians. She and her two older sisters were billed as the Gumm Sisters, a singing group. When the act broke up, Judy continued to sing on her own, ending up in the mid-1930s in Hollywood, where she was signed to a contract by MGM—the only person in the history of that studio who was signed up without a screen test or a sound test.

There were plenty of other child actresses on the MGM lot in those days, and Judy did not jump ahead of the pack instantly. She was put on a strict diet to slim her down (the studio commissary was told to feed her nothing but chicken soup, no matter how much she pleaded for banana splits) and was tried out in a short subject, *Every Sunday* (1936), with another young MGM contract singer, Deanna Durbin, just to see how they would look together on film.

Both of them looked fine, and things began to happen. As mentioned before, Universal Studios had a script called *Three Smart Girls,* which required a popular-style singer, and the studio asked MGM to lend them Judy for the part. MGM said no. The script was rewritten to fit a classical-style singer, and Deanna Durbin got the part—a role that sent her right into star billing. Judy, instead, went into a routine musical called *Pigskin Parade* (1936), in which she appeared with Stuart Erwin, Jack Haley and a young Betty Grable. This football musical was Judy's first feature film, and included such songs as 'It's Love I'm After' and 'You Say the Darndest Things.' The film got her good, but not sensational, reviews.

Then came *Broadway Melody of 1938* (1937). She stole the show from such veteran stars as Robert Taylor, Eleanor Powell, George Murphy, Sophie Tucker, Binnie Barnes and Buddy Ebsen—all of whom were billed above her—by singing 'You Made Me Love You' to a photograph of Clark Gable. She did four more forgettable pictures—*Thoroughbreds Don't Cry* (1937 with Mickey Rooney), *Everybody Sing* (1938 with Allan Jones), *Listen Darling* (1938, in which she sang 'Zing Went the Strings of My Heart') and *Love Finds Andy Hardy* (1938 with Mickey Rooney).

Then came *The Wizard of Oz,* and she got the lead by a fluke. MGM had wanted Shirley Temple, and they were willing to work a trade-off with Twentieth Century-Fox by borrowing Shirley in exchange for Jean Harlow and Clark Gable, who were working on the film *Saratoga* (1937) at the time. When Harlow died during the filming of that picture, the deal fell through and MGM decided to risk everything on Garland (who was making a piddling $300 per week at the time). She was, however, a blossoming 16-year-old when she was assigned the part, so the studio made special caps for her teeth, strapped her into a corset that hid her maturing figure, made her diet even stricter and thereby turned her into 11-year-old Dorothy Gale of Kansas.

The Wizard of Oz began in black and white in a bitterly real America of stern faces and endless plains. Dorothy, the innocent dreamer, was swirled from this place to a Technicolor dreamland 'somewhere over the rainbow.'

Here she eluded evil, overcame enemies and found loving friends. *The Wizard of Oz* is one of those films, like *Snow White and the Seven Dwarfs*, on which people are brought up and which they never forget. Children and parents who see it year after year on television never seem to tire of it.

The special effects, created by Arnold Gillespie, were first-rate. One of the most inventive feats was the making of the tornado in the picture. Gillespie tried many ways of photographing the great whirlwind that takes Dorothy to the land of Oz, but every one looked phoney until he hit upon the ingenious idea of blowing air from a fan through a woman's stocking. The resulting miniature 'Twister' was so realistic that for years Metro-Goldwyn-Mayer used this footage in other movies that happened to have tornadoes in them.

He also used a lot of piano wire. How else to let the flying monkeys and the Wicked Witch get airborne? How else to hold up the Cowardly Lion's tail? There is a Hollywood story, probably apochryphal, about the accountant who received several bills for piano wire during the making of the film. He paid the bills dutifully, but after he saw the movie, he complained that he hadn't seen any piano wire in the picture at all.

At the end of *The Wizard of Oz*, the Wicked Witch of the West has finally captured Dorothy and her friends. Gleefully, the Witch sets fire to the Scarecrow. In an attempt to save her friend, Dorothy picks up a bucket of water and heaves it at him. Much of the water accidentally splashes on the Witch and, emitting a stream of shrieks and curses, the Witch begins melting . . . melting . . . melting . . . until there is nothing left of her but an empty cloak and a hat. Dorothy has saved the day, thanks to a superb piece of special effects.

For this 'melting' effect, Margaret Hamilton stood on a small elevator platform built into the floor of the studio. The hem of her full-length witch's cloak was nailed to the floor of the set around the platform. When Dorothy threw the bucket of water on the Witch, the elevator platform began descending below the floor until it lowered nearly six feet and the Witch had completely disappeared, leaving her clothing in a steamy pile. (Steam was provided courtesy of dry ice hidden in the hem of her cloak).

Another special effect backfired badly. The Witch was made to appear and disappear by means of a trap door through which smoke and flames were sent up just before she made her appearance. The timing was just a little off, and the flames did not disappear completely before Margaret Hamilton came up. The fire melted the green copper-based paint that covered her face, giving her third-degree burns. She was out recuperating for some three months.

Judy was not the only person in the picture who got the role as a second choice. The studio wanted Gale Sondergaard to play the Witch and Ray Bolger to play the Tin Woodman. Sondergaard wasn't available and Bolger talked the casting director into making him the Scarecrow. The second choice for the Tin Woodman was Buddy Ebsen, but after a few scenes were shot he became so allergic to the silver makeup he had to wear that he almost died. So Jack Haley got the role. He also got sick, but, fortunately, he was able to stick it out.

Haley, Bolger and Lahr had another problem while making the film. Because their strange makeup made it difficult for them to eat (Lahr's Lion costume, for example, weighed 40 pounds), they had a run-in with the people at the studio commissary. They were asked to leave because of their terrible table manners and had to eat on the set.

As everyone knows, the result justified all the problems. *The Wizard of Oz* still stands today as one of the legendary pictures of all time.

But in the year that the film was released, war had broken out in Europe. And when World War II began, Hollywood was ready to do its bit.

A rather chubby Judy Garland in *Broadway Melody of 1938* (1937). She was billed as 'That new hot little singing sensation.'

Mickey Rooney plays the cello like a double bass as Judy Garland sings in *Babes in Arms* (1939).

THE WAR YEARS

It was 1939 and war clouds were forming over Europe, but in Hollywood there was to be a new day for the musical film. The cause of the reformation was Arthur Freed—the film executive who had come to the coast to make *The Wizard of Oz*. After that film, he made *Babes in Arms* (1939), the first of many Judy Garland-Mickey Rooney musicals.

Soon he had gathered his own group of top professionals: the Freed Unit was born. During the ensuing years it included Vincente Minnelli, Gene Kelly, Busby Berkeley, Red Skelton, Fred Astaire and Cyd Charisse among its luminaries. Script and song writers like Betty Comden and Adolph Green, Cole Porter, Ira Gershwin, Johnny Mercer and E Y 'Yip' Harburg were part of the group.

MGM and Freed had, in Judy Garland, a new but quite experienced star (she had a half-dozen screen credits by the time of *The Wizard of Oz*) on their hands. She was immediately cast with the studio's other main juvenile talent, 19-year-old Mickey Rooney, in the first of several musicals, *Babes in Arms* (1939). The plots of these musicals often seemed interchangeable—the finale always seemed to be a musical show that Judy and Mickey put on to save the old homestead, the ranch, the theater or anything else that the writers could think of as needing salvation—but the sheer expertise of Judy and Mickey, as well as the wealth of talent available to the studios, made the movies work.

Judy Garland and Mickey Rooney in that exuberant paean to youth—*Strike Up the Band* (1940).

Judy is a legend, but Mickey is a legend of a different kind. He has led the kind of life that they write show-business novels about. This short, aggressively talented performer was born in Brooklyn in 1920 as Joe Yule Jr, the son of vaudevillian parents. Before he was two years old he crawled out on stage during a performance and thereafter was part of the act. He had his first movie role, as a midget, by the age of four. Not long afterward, a studio announced that it was holding auditions for a series to be based on a character named Mickey McGuire, who was in a popular comic strip of the time—'Toonerville Folks.' In the strip, McGuire had black hair. Young Joe was a blonde, but his stage-savvy mother used shoe polish to darken it and tugged him off to the audition. He got the part, and carried the Mickey McGuire series for six years. Largely because of him, the series was one of the few successful imitators of the popular 'Our Gang' (later, on television, to be called 'The Little Rascals') series of shorts.

For a while, his parents thought of changing his name to Mickey McGuire. Instead, they chose Mickey Rooney. That was a good idea, because the McGuire shorts were just the beginning. At an age when some child stars' careers were ending, Mickey Rooney was just moving on to bigger things.

Before he was a teenager, he was starring in big-budget films. Among his odder roles was that of Puck, a blithe spirit, in the film version of Shakespeare's *A Midsummer Night's Dream* (1935). In 1937 MGM had the idea of using Mickey in a film version of a domestic play about a typical American family named Hardy. That first film, entitled *A Family Affair*, was so successful that it led to a long series of Andy Hardy features. Mickey played Andy, who was an almost painfully typical teenager. In *A Family Affair*, Lionel Barrymore played Andy's father, Judge Hardy, and Spring Byington his mother. For the rest of the Andy Hardy series the parents were played by two reliable members of the MGM stock company—Fay Holden was Andy's mother and Lewis Stone played his father, who was always good for a stern but kind lecture when Andy went wrong out of sheer youthful spirits. Set in a typical American town called, believe it or not, Carvel, the Andy Hardy series went through a total of 17 films in more than 20 years, earned $25 million for MGM, and featured, along the way, such talents as Judy Garland, Lana Turner, Esther Williams and Susan Peters. The last Andy Hardy film was made in 1958, when it was clearly evident that Mickey Rooney could no longer pass for a teenager on the screen.

But Andy Hardy wasn't the only part that young Mickey played, by any means. He won a special Academy Award for playing a tough kid in *Boys' Town* (1938); he had the title role in *Young Tom Edison* (1940); he was impressive in the film version of William Saroyan's *The Human Comedy* (1943); he did those musicals with Judy Garland, and much, very much, more.

At the ripe old age of 28, with a quarter-of-a-century of show-business experience behind him, Mickey Rooney left off being a young actor and began being simply an actor. His adult acting career continues to this day. His private life hasn't always been smooth—he is a short man who seemed to have a penchant for marrying tall women—but Mickey has bounded through life with the endless energy that he showed from the start. Appearing in everything from tired comedies (*Francis in the Haunted House*, a 1956 film featuring a talking mule) to serious dramas (*The Bold and the Brave*, another 1956 film, for which he won an Academy Award nomination), Mickey Rooney has always given his audiences a good show.

Rooney and Garland with Tommy Dorsey, his trombone and his orchestra in *Girl Crazy* (1943).

Early in 1978, Mickey told reporters that he was going to retire after he had finished the film that he was then making. His agent told the press, in effect, not to pay any attention. He said that Mickey always talked about retiring when he was in the middle of a film, and always changed his mind when the next movie part came along. Sure enough, after that came his long run on Broadway in *Sugar Babies* and his Emmy Award-winning television performance as *Bill*.

Babes in Arms (1939) was directed by Busby Berkeley, but he didn't use his old Warner Brothers chorus patterns. He did, however, use two huge sprawling production numbers—'Babes in Arms' and 'God's Country.' The movie scrapped most of the score from the Rodgers and Hart Broadway show of 1937, keeping only 'Where or When,' 'The Lady Is a Tramp' and the title song. Astonishingly, the missing songs included 'Johnny One Note,' 'My Funny Valentine' and 'I Wish I Were in Love Again.' Producer Arthur Freed added two of his own songs, 'I Cried for You' and 'Good Morning.' The picture was a financial triumph and it started a whole cycle of 'Come on, kids, let's put on a show' films.

When something works, Hollywood generally uses the same formula again. So Mickey and Judy were back in *Strike Up the Band* (1940). The plot was the same—nice, decent All-American kids were having a hard time through no fault of their own. Rooney was the leader of a high school band competing in Paul Whiteman's nationwide radio contest. There was enough sentimentality and good singing for any musical picture fan. Judy's 'Do the Conga,' 'Nell of New Rochelle' and 'Our Love Affair' were tremendous.

Babes on Broadway (1941) was probably the biggest and best of the 'Let's put on a show' flicks, and it was directed by Busby Berkeley. Mickey Rooney stole the show with his acting and musical versatility. The big hit was 'How About You?' It did bring back the old plot again, but this time when they want to put on a show, they mean in New York. Mickey did a Franklin Delano Roosevelt takeoff and he and Judy triumphed in the 'Hoe Down' number. Also, the two kids did everything from imitations of Carmen Miranda and Sarah Bernhardt to minstrel numbers. A standout was Judy's singing of 'Franklin D Roosevelt Jones.'

The true-blue teens sang their hearts out again in *Girl Crazy* (1943, taken from Ziegfeld's 1930 Broadway show). It had a delightful George and Ira Gershwin score, with such songs as 'Embraceable You,' 'But Not for Me' and 'Bidin' My Time,' and its dizzying Busby Berkeley finale of 'I Got Rhythm' was the show-stopper. This time Mickey wasn't a complete goody-goody. He chased girls. So he was banished to the West by a disapproving father, where he attended Cody College, which was on the verge of financial collapse. There, he fell in love with the dean's granddaughter—Judy, of course. Mickey saved the college by coming up with his usual cure for the economic blues. The kids put on a show, but this time it was a musical rodeo. Money was raised. Everything was super. And that was that. No more Mickey-and-Judy musicals. Still, no matter how repetitious the plot, how inane the story line, those movies had style and are fun to watch even now. And they did feature two legendary talents in an important phase of their careers.

There were other all-American musicals at the time, and perhaps the best was *State Fair* (1945), which contained the first score that Richard Rodgers and Oscar Hammerstein II wrote strictly for the movies. It was an agreeable piece of rural Americana, and starred Charles Winninger, Dick Haymes, Jeanne Crain, Vivian Blaine and Dana Andrews. The story of an

A publicity still of Judy and Mickey.

Babes in Arms (193

Babes on Broadway (1941).

A publicity shot of Judy and Mickey.

Babes on Broadway (1941).

Strike Up the Band (1940).

Girl Crazy (1943).

Iowa farm family who encounter love and adventure at the state fair, it featured such songs as 'It's a Grand Night for Singing' and 'It Might As Well Be Spring.' Actually, the movie was based on a non-musical film of the same name that was made in 1933 and starred Will Rogers, Lew Ayres, Janet Gaynor and Sally Eilers. It was remade in 1961, with a different score. The picture starred Tom Ewell, Pat Boone, Pamela Tiffin and Ann-Margret, and was a disaster.

Fred Astaire, of course, continued making musicals during the war years. First there was *Broadway Melody of 1940* (1940), the last and the best of the films bearing that title. Fred had been at RKO since his debut in MGM's *Dancing Lady* (1933), and this was his return to MGM. He was to stay there for the next 20 years. The film was a standard backstage story of a dance team trying to make good, but it was memorable for its Cole Porter songs. In addition to 'I Concentrate on You,' Fred and Eleanor Powell danced to 'Begin the Beguine.'

He then made *Second Chorus* (1940) with Paulette Goddard and Burgess Meredith, a story about two hot trumpeters who try to keep their band together while vying for the affections of the same girl. Then came *You'll Never Get Rich* (1941), in which Astaire played a theatrical producer who is drafted at an inconvenient time but still manages to put on his big show. The Cole Porter score included 'So Near and Yet So Far,' and his dancing partner was Rita Hayworth.

Rita had been around for some time

Above: Dick Haymes, Jeanne Crain, Dana Andrews in *State Fair* (1945).

Opposite: *Broadway Melody of 1940* (1940).

Charles Butterworth, Paulette Goddard, Artie Shaw, Burgess Meredith, Fred Astaire in *Second Chorus* (1940).

before she got this big break. Born Margarita Carmen Cansino, she started in show business when she was six years old. Her father was a successful Spanish dancer in vaudeville and her mother had appeared in *The Ziegfeld Follies* on Broadway. Lured to California by the burgeoning movie industry of the 1920s, the Cansinos quit New York and Margarita's father opened a dance studio. The Depression forced him to rejuvenate his dance act with his daughter as his partner. She was, at the time, scarcely in her teens, an incipient beauty who looked older.

Given a contract by Fox in the mid-1930s, Margarita then appeared in a succession of 'B' pictures like *Charlie Chan in Egypt* (1935), *Trouble in Texas* (1937) and *Renegade Ranger* (1939). She was learning her craft. Margarita was in 24 films before she changed her name to Rita Hayworth, decided to lose weight, had her hairline raised through electrolysis, changed her hair color from black to red, took acting and voice lessons and developed more style. By the time *You'll Never Get Rich* (her 35th picture) came along, she was ready.

Opposite: Rita Hayworth.

Above: Frances Langford, Bing Crosby, Marjorie Reynolds, Fred Astaire in *Holiday Inn* (1942).

Ethel Waters with a representative from Heaven in *Cabin in the Sky* (1943).

Next, Astaire co-starred with Bing Crosby in *Holiday Inn* (1942), which featured what was probably Irving Berlin's finest score, including 'White Christmas,' 'Easter Parade' and 'Be Careful, It's My Heart.' Astaire was always a perfectionist. He went through one number in *Holiday Inn* 38 times before he was satisfied with it. When he started on the picture he weighed 140 pounds. At the end of the filming, he was down to 126.

Fred's next picture was *You Were Never Lovelier* (1942), and he was teamed again with Rita Hayworth. It was a film about Fred's pursuit of Rita via a matchmaking father, Adolphe Menjou, and it had such great Jerome Kern songs as 'Dearly Beloved' and 'I'm Old-Fashioned.'

He appeared with Joan Leslie in *The Sky's the Limit* (1943), as a flyer on leave who meets the photographer Leslie. The two big hits were 'One for My Baby' and 'My Shining Hour.'

A war-years musical hard to classify was *Cabin in the Sky* (1942). It was an all-black musical drama which was a variation on the Faust theme, and starred Eddie 'Rochester' Anderson (from the Jack Benny radio show) as the victim, Ethel Waters as his faithful wife and Lena Horne as the temptress.

Directed by Vincente Minnelli, the film was a step toward humanizing blacks in the popular mind, although they seemed to be living in an all-black ghetto. But the music was glorious. There was 'Cabin in the Sky,' 'Happiness Is Just a Thing Called Joe,' 'Taking a Chance on Love' and 'Honey in the Honeycomb.' And the supporting cast was excellent —Rex Ingram, Louis Armstrong, Butterfly McQueen and Duke Ellington and his Orchestra.

Lena Horne, in her second film, was superb. She was born in Brooklyn and served an apprenticeship in the chorus of the Cotton Club in Harlem, beginning when she was 16 years old. She was the first black woman ever to be signed to a long-term contract in Hollywood and the first black woman to sing with a big-league all-white dance band—Charlie Barnet's. Unfortunately, Hollywood was not ready to use her great singing voice and her warm and elegant presence until she was in her late 40s. Except for *Cabin in the Sky* and *Stormy Weather* (1943) —both all-black films—she was used only in specialty numbers in big-budget musicals. This was at a time when, in many parts of the South, record stores would not stock her albums.

Like Astaire, Bing Crosby was not idle during the war years. In addition to *Holiday Inn*, he teamed up with Joan Blondell in *The East Side of Heaven* (1939), playing a singing taxi driver who finds himself the custodian of a baby left by a young mother. The big hits were 'The East Side of Heaven' and 'Sing a Song of Sunbeams.'

He also co-starred with Bob Hope and Dorothy Lamour in that long series of 'Road' pictures, beginning with *The Road to Singapore* (1940). These films cannot perhaps technically be called musicals, but they did have some good songs. *The Road to Zanzibar* (1940) was followed by *The Road to Morocco* (1942) and its 'Moonlight Becomes You.' Then came *The Road to Utopia* (1945) with 'Personality'; *The Road to Rio* (1947) with 'But Beautiful' and 'You Don't Have

Bill Robinson in *Stormy Weather* (1943), a film starring all the black stars of the period.

Above: Bing Crosby and Mary Martin in *Rhythm on the River* (1940).

to Know the Language'; *The Road to Bali* (1952 and the only 'Road' picture to be filmed in color); and *The Road to Hong Kong* (1961).

The Birth of the Blues (1941) was a slight little film about Crosby organizing a New Orleans jazz band, but it had great songs, including the title song, 'St Louis Blues,' 'St James Infirmary' and 'Melancholy Baby.' But best of all was 'The Waiter, the Porter and the Upstairs Maid' sung by Crosby, jazz trombonist Jack Teagarden and Mary Martin.

Crosby also sang in *Going My Way* (1944) and its sequel, *The Bells of St Mary's* (1945). *Going My Way* won Academy Awards for itself as best picture of the year and for its star as best actor. The plot concerned the rivalry between an old priest (Barry Fitzgerald) and his new young assistant (Crosby), and it was one of the most beautiful, sentimental and de-

Bing Crosby and Bob Hope on *The Road to Morocco* (1942) with Dona Drake.

The Road to Zanzibar (1941).

The Road to Singapore (1940).

The Road to Rio (1947).

The Road to Morocco (1942).

Bing and the Andrews Sisters—*The Road to Rio* (1947).

The Road to Zanzibar (1941).

The Road to Utopia (1945).

The Road to Bali (1952).

lightful films ever made. In addition, the songs were special: 'Going My Way,' 'Swinging on a Star' and 'Toora-Loo-ra-Loo-ra.' *The Bells of St Mary's* teamed Crosby as the priest who schemes with Ingrid Bergman as a nun to entice a wealthy skinflint to give money to the church; its featured song was 'The Bells of St Mary's.'

With the war came jobs. The breadlines of the Depression vanished, so it was no longer necessary to provide audiences an escape into the world of the rich. Also, Europe, overrun by Hitler's troops, didn't seem a very good place to set anything as frothy as a musical. Americans, needing a way to forget the war for an hour or two, turned inward and clamored for musicals set in a prosperous and happy American past. Of course, Hollywood was happy to provide them.

Another reason for the popularity of the period musicals was that more and more pictures were being shot in color. Technicolor was strong and potent and about as realistic as a

Above: Crosby, Fitzgerald, Stevens, McHugh in *Going My Way* (1944).

Bing Crosby and Barry Fitzgerald—*Going My Way* (1944).

Above: Ingrid Bergman (left) played a nun in *The Bells of St Mary's* (1945).

picture post card. What it did for cosmetics. Crimson lipstick made the girls' mouths more kissable; their fingernails were like jewels; their costumes were sensational. So the period musicals were popular partly because the audience got a chance to see yards and yards of vivid glowing fabric.

The queen of these period pieces was Betty Grable—Twentieth Century-Fox's gift to the war effort. She personified the peaches-and-cream appeal that was required in the 1940s but which later seemed excessively bland. She was the most famous pin-up girl of World War II. The best-known photograph of Grable, in a white bathing suit at least one size too small, peeking cutely over her shoulder, with those million-dollar legs tensed up just right, found a home in at least a million barracks wall lockers.

Robert Cummings romances Betty Grable as Don Ameche looks on—*Moon Over Miami* (1941).

Three million photographs of her were scattered around the world at assorted war fronts.

'My legs made me,' she once said, admitting also that she had a small voice and below-average dancing skills. All the same, she was one of Hollywood's most popular musical-comedy actresses during the 1940s. Her 40-plus films grossed millions of dollars, her characters were fun and she took war-weary minds off their troubles. Grable was born in St Louis and honed for Hollywood by her mother, who provided both dancing and saxophone lessons. 'It's good she pushed me,' Grable said, 'because I'm basically a lazy person.'

There was a lot more to Betty Grable than a pair of legs. As a 14-year-old, she was singing with jazz bands. By the time she was 16 she had her first Hollywood contract with RKO. Betty served her time in lightweight films for more than a decade before she became a star. She was in a chorus line in *Let's Go Places* (1930); became a Goldwyn Girl in *Whoopee* (1930); sang 'Let's Knock Knees' with Edward Everett Horton in *The Gay Divorcee* (1934). After 29 films, Darryl F Zanuck, the production chief at Fox, gave her a break in *Tin Pan Alley* (1940). When Betty appeared in a sequined bra and panties, with transparent pantaloons, doing one of the hottest dance numbers ever seen up to that time ('The Sheik of Araby' with Billy Gilbert), audiences (particularly the servicemen) went wild. Grable became a star.

For about ten years she was a superstar like few before or since. When she married the band leader-trumpeter, Harry James, it made news. She had a beaming toothpaste-ad smile that came across in color. She wasn't so beautiful or so exotic that men worshipped her from afar. Rather she had a bland amiability. She was a good-looking but basically ordinary girl whom one might meet in a small-town diner or find working in a war plant in a big city. She was nice. Grable got ten thousand fan letters per week at the height of her career.

Tin Pan Alley (1940) co-starred the other Fox musical star, Alice Faye, plus Jack Oakie and John Payne. It was an entertaining musical that followed the adventures of song pluggers and composers in the period from 1915 to 1918.

Opposite: Betty Grable stands in front of the most famous pin-up of World War II.

Betty Grable and June Haver—*The Dolly Sisters* (1945).

Betty Grable, John Payne and June Haver in *The Dolly Sisters* (1945).

Grable, Adolphe Menjou and Robert Young in *Sweet Rosie O'Grady* (1943).

Betty made other backward-glancing musicals. *Coney Island* (1943) was a breezy, enjoyable, turn-of-the-century musical about saloon-entertainer Grable turned into a famous Broadway star by the hustling George Montgomery. Along the way, Montgomery and Cesar Romero fought for Betty's affections. If one can believe this picture, there was no litter in Coney Island early in this century and saloon keepers had the morals of clergymen.

Sweet Rosie O'Grady (1943) was a pleasant musical about a former burlesque star (Grable) who had made it big on the London stage, and an exposé reporter (Robert Young). Adolphe Menjou stole the show as the editor of *The Police Gazette*. The hits from the film were 'Sweet Rosie O'Grady' and 'Get Your Police Gazette' ('It's the leading periodical of the day.').

The Dolly Sisters (1945) was about the popular vaudeville sister team, played by Betty Grable and June Haver, a rising young star who in 1953 was to leave Hollywood and become a nun, then to be dispensed from her vows to marry Fred MacMurray. The film had a slew of old song favourites from vaudeville's Golden Age.

MGM took the historical musical seriously, too. *For Me and My Gal* (1942) was a film about pre-World War I Broadway life; it paired Judy Garland and Gene Kelly in his first film and established him as a versatile actor and song-and-dance man. Directed by Busby Berkeley, it featured wonderful duets for the two stars.

Then came *Meet Me in St Louis* (1944), an enjoyable period musical that had charm at a time when it was most needed. It told of the ups and downs of a middle-class family in St Louis at the turn of the century during the 1904 St Louis World's Fair. Many think that this was Judy Garland's best film, and it showcased some of the finest acting talents of the 1940s. Directed by Vincente Minnelli, the picture had wonderful songs by Hugh Martin and Ralph Blane—'The Trolley Song,' 'Have Yourself a Merry Little Christmas,' 'The Boy Next Door,' 'Meet Me in St Louis.' The movie was so popular that Fox tried to copy it with *Centennial Summer* (1946), with Jeanne Crain, Cornel Wilde, Linda Darnell and a Jerome Kern

For Me and My Gal (1942). *Right:* George Murphy, Judy Garland and Gene Kelly. *Top inset:* 'When You Wore a Tulip.' *Bottom inset:* Garland entertains the troops.

score. This film was set in Philadelphia in 1876, the year that the World's Fair was held there.

Judy also starred with Ray Bolger, Angela Lansbury and John Hodiak in *The Harvey Girls* (1946), a tale of a group of young ladies who go to the Wild West to become waitresses in a Fred Harvey restaurant and succeed in taming the town. It was a big bustling musical and featured such Johnny Mercer-Harry Warren songs as 'On the Atchison, Topeka and the Santa Fe.'

June Allyson and Kathryn Grayson starred in *Two Sisters from Boston* (1945), a musical set at the turn of the century about two well-bred Boston girls who go to work in a joint on New York's Bowery. Jimmy Durante, who once copyrighted his nose, stole the show as the owner of the tavern. Allyson, a musical mainstay at MGM, had spent five years as a Broadway chorus dancer before making her Hollywood feature debut in *Best Foot Forward* in 1943. She had also been an understudy to Betty Hutton. Grayson, born Zelma Hedrick, had begun her career in 1940 as one of Andy Hardy's dates.

Hollywood had another problem to face during the war years. Most of the export traffic to Europe had been cut off and a new market had to be invented. So the studios began to have a love affair with another part of the Western Hemisphere—Latin America.

Garland and Margaret O'Brien dance 'Under the Bamboo Tree—*Meet Me in St Louis* (1944).

Angela Lansbury and Judy Garland in *The Harvey Girls* (1946).

Down Argentine Way (1940) should have starred Alice Faye, but she couldn't make it. The girl who got the lead was Betty Grable, who played a wealthy American woman in love with a South American rancher, Don Ameche. But the person who almost ran away with the show was Carmen Miranda, who was specially imported to Hollywood to help open the Latin-American film market.

She was so small she wore six-inch heels, and she had been a well-known singer in her native Brazil before she ever reached Hollywood. Just as America demanded that its black performers behave in stereotyped ways—dumb, sexy, lazy—so all South Americans were supposed to be passionate, violent and spoiled by living in a warm climate. Carmen Miranda (born Carmen de Carmo Miranda de Cunha) had a campy accent and a style that made her a natural for the part of a hot, jealous señorita. She was always fantastically made up and emitted a force of personality that was hard to resist.

This doesn't mean that she wasn't talented. Whatever her image, Carmen Miranda sang with gusto and had a comic flair. She was enormously assisted by Technicolor, which showed off her wild costumes and headdresses to the fullest.

After *Down Argentine Way*, Miranda made *That Night in Rio* (1941) with Alice Faye and Don Ameche, and then *Weekend in Havana* (also 1941) with Faye and John Payne.

Busby Berkeley, who had an eye for the exotic, used her to perfection in *The Gang's All Here* (1943) where, in the number 'The Lady in the Tutti-Frutti Hat,' she wore a banana hat 30 feet high surrounded by strawberries that made her headdress seem to extend to infinity. It got knocked off during the filming and caused a panic so a painting of the hat was used.

This was also the era of two Latin musicians—Jose Iturbi and Xavier

Above: Betty Grable and Don Ameche recoil from J Carrol Naish—*Down Argentine Way* (1940).

Seated: June Allyson, Peter Lawford, Kathryn Grayson. Standing: Lauritz Melchior, Jimmy Durante. *Two Sisters from Boston.*

Cugat. Iturbi, a Spanish pianist and conductor, appeared in seven films as a classical musician. Cugat, a Spanish-American band leader, was a feature of many movies of the time.

Even Esther Williams got into the Latin act. *Bathing Beauty* (1944), one of her swimming extravaganzas, featured her as a swimming instructor and Red Skelton as a male student in a girls' school; it had a John Murray Anderson water ballet that rivaled Busby Berkeley. In addition, there was a lot of Latin rhythm. Ethel Smith, the pop organist, played 'Tico Tico.' 'Echo of a Serenade' was sung by Carlos Ramirez. There were several songs played by Xavier Cugat and his Orchestra and sung by Lina Romay. Finally, putting in a plug for North American music, there was Harry James and his Band.

Holiday in Mexico (1946) was a 'let's find a wife for Dad' story about the widowed American Ambassador to Mexico (Walter Pidgeon) and his daughter (Jane Powell). It also featured the 17-year-old Roddy McDowall and Ilona Massey, who had been away from the screen for seven years. Semi-classical music provided by Jose Iturbi was spiced with some Latin American melodies by Xavier Cugat in this musical treat that was stolen by Jane Powell, the 16-year-old, with her singing and acting.

Above: Miranda, Ameche, Faye and Leonid Kinsky in *That Night in Rio* (1941).

Red Skelton moons over Esther Williams in *Bathing Beauty* (1944).

The most important person in the story of the musical with a Latin beat was none other than Walt Disney. Walt (people who worked for him were instructed to call him by his first name) had already completed a number of cartoon masterpieces, but what with war raging across Europe, South America looked good to him. That, coupled with a natural attraction to what lay just across the border from Southern California, got Disney going.

He made a travelogue-cum-cartoon called *Saludos Amigos*. We meet the Disney staff, see Donald Duck play a tourist and are introduced to a new and important character, a bird named José Carioca, whose voice belonged to José Oliveira in real life. Later Walt brought us *The Three Caballeros* (1944), a combination of animation and live actors. The color was beautiful, the songs were fun and the image of a cheerful sun-drenched South America permeated the public's consciousness. That became the image of Latin lands for some years. Today, we know more about the countries of Latin America, but in the 1940s it was Disney, Carmen Miranda and the samba.

Another direction in which Hollywood went during the war years was toward the extravaganza—the type of film that featured a cast of thousands, was enormously expensive in costumes and setting, and was prepared, purely and simply, to boost morale. The first one of the period was *Ziegfeld Girl* (1941).

It was a big picture and was definitely a hybrid, part 1930s and part 1940s. Produced by Arthur Freed, it seemed to star the entire MGM studio, plus 100 beautiful girls. It was vulgar and supercolossal and had a certain galumphing zest. Among the many stars were James Stewart, Lana Turner, Judy Garland, Hedy Lamarr, Tony Martin, Jackie Cooper, Ian Hunter, Philip Dorn and Charles Winninger. Directed by Vincente Minnelli, it was the story of three Ziegfeld Girls going in different directions, Garland to stardom, Lamarr to a wealthy marriage, Turner to alcoholism.

But forget the plot. The musical numbers were directed by Busby Berkeley. 'You Stepped out of a Dream,' sung by Tony Martin to sex goddesses Hedy Lamarr and Lana

Opposite: Carmen Miranda and hat.

Turner, is probably the most famous number, but it was overshadowed by Judy Garland in her 'I'm Always Chasing Rainbows' and 'Minnie from Trinidad' renditions.

Lady Be Good (1941) came out the same year, starring Eleanor Powell, Ann Sothern, Robert Young, Lionel Barrymore and Red Skelton. It was a spunky musical about married song-writers Sothern and Young, with dancer Powell and comic Skelton thrown in for good measure. It kept only a few songs from the original Gershwin Broadway musical of 1924, in which Fred and Adele Astaire had starred. A new plot was devised and the hit song was by Jerome Kern and Oscar Hammerstein II—'The Last Time I saw Paris.' This caused a minor dust-up, since it had not been written for the movie. 'You'll Never Know' was another popular song from the film.

The rest of the score was also top-notch, and the musical numbers were directed by Busby Berkeley. The highlight was, undoubtedly, 'Fascin-atin' Rhythm' with Eleanor Powell and what seemed to be hundreds of chorus boys. Powell had been crowned 'The World's Greatest Tap Dancer' by the Dancing Masters of America in 1937. At 13 she had been discovered in Atlantic City. She appeared on Broadway for several years and then was signed by MGM. The studio used voice teachers, orthodontists and other beautifiers to prepare her for her film debut in *George White's Scandals* (1935). At her peak, she earned $125,000 per film and cut some phono-graph records tapping out dance rou-tines to musical accompaniment. When she married Glenn Ford in 1943 and retired on becoming pregnant, she said, 'I'm an old-fashioned mother. I didn't consider that I had a choice.' In 1961 she put together a successful night club act, encouraged by her son, Peter.

Paramount released *Star Spangled Rhythm* in 1942, an all-star film featuring Bing Crosby, Ray Milland, Bob Hope, Veronica Lake, Dorothy Lamour, Susan Hayward, Dick Powell, Alan Ladd, Paulette Goddard, Cecil B De Mille, Arthur Treacher, Eddie 'Rochester' Anderson and Wil-liam Bendix. It was a film with sketches and no plot. Goddard, Lamour and Lake sang 'A Sweater, a Sarong and a Peek-a-boo Bang.' Other hits were 'That Old Black Magic' and 'Time to Hit the Road to Dreamland.'

Thank Your Lucky Stars (1943) was Warner Brothers' contribution to the all-star revue. It starred Eddie Cantor, Humphrey Bogart, Olivia De Havil-land, Errol Flynn, John Garfield, Joan Leslie, Ida Lupino, Dennis Mor-gan and Ann Sheridan, but Bette Davis stole the show with her rendi-tion of 'They're Either Too Young or Too Old,' in which she lamented the

Opposite: Hedy Lamarr in *Ziegfeld Girl* (1941), 'You Stepped Out of a Dream.'

Tony Martin and Judy Garland in a production number from *Ziegfeld Girl* (1941).

lack of 'available males' who were all away in the war.

MGM gave audiences *Thousands Cheer* (1943), which starred Mickey Rooney, Judy Garland, Eleanor Powell, Ann Sothern, Lucille Ball, Virginia O'Brien, Frank Morgan, Kathryn Grayson and Lena Horne. Grayson played the part of an army brat who lived with her officer-father John Boles, and who decided to put on all-star shows for the soldiers. The film ended with the 'United Nations on the March' number, which MGM had commissioned Dmitri Shostakovitch to compose, and it seemed to have half the people in Los Angeles on the screen.

Broadway Rhythm (1943) was loosely based on the Jerome Kern-Oscar Hammerstein II Broadway musical of 1939, *Very Warm for May*. The only musical holdover, however, was 'All the Things You Are.' It was a typical 'putting on a show' musical and starred George Murphy and Ginny Simms, who was at the height of her popularity as the female vocalist with the Kay Kyser Orchestra, but it was stolen by the kids—Gloria De-Haven, Nancy Walker and Kenny Bowers.

Betty Hutton and Fred MacMurray were in *And the Angels Sing* (1944), a story of some singing sisters and the band leader who discovers them. The hit song was Hutton's 'My Rocking Horse Ran Away.'

Out of this World (1945) starred Eddie Bracken, Diana Lynn, who was an accomplished pianist, and Veronica Lake. Also in the cast were Bing Crosby's boys—Gary, Philip and Lindsay. The film had a weak plot in which Bracken appeared as a crooner (with Bing's voice dubbed in).

One musical of the war years was impossible to categorize. It was *Where Do We Go from Here?* (1945) and starred Fred MacMurray and June Haver. One critic said it deserved an 'A' for effort but a 'B' for performance. Fred, who was 4-F in the draft, had his wish granted by a genie—to get him into the Army—but the genie put him in various places at the wrong time. The result was a musical cavalcade of American history, with songs by Kurt Weill and Ira Gershwin. The highlight was probably the miniature operetta on the deck of the *Santa Maria*, with Fred and Christopher Columbus singing:

Opposite: Judy Garland in *Thousands Cheer* (1943). *Inset:* Also in the film: Kelly, Grayson, Jose Iturbi, Mary Astor, John Boles.

Astaire and Lucille Bremer in 'Limehouse Blues'—*Ziegfeld Follies* (1946).

Who'd have thought that sailing
 west meant
A terrifically expensive investment?
And who do you suppose supplied
 the means
But Isabella, Queen of Queens?

Ziegfeld Follies (1945) was MGM's first no-story musical since *The Hollywood Revue of 1929* and the third Metro-Goldwyn-Mayer film to use the showman's name. The studio had to get permission from Billie Burke, Ziegfeld's widow, and they cast William Powell again as the impresario—in heaven. The movie starred Judy Garland, Fred Astaire, Gene Kelly, Lucille Ball, Lena Horne, Esther Williams, Kathryn Grayson, Red Skelton, Cyd Charisse and Victor Moore. Several of the performers were seen at their best. Fred Astaire danced two numbers with Lucille Bremer (he was later to appear with her in *Yolanda and the Thief* in 1945) and one with Gene Kelly. (The ever-diplomatic Astaire listed Kelly as his favorite dancing partner.) Kelly and Astaire

Gene Kelly and Fred Astaire in 'The Babbit and the Bromide'—*Ziegfeld Follies* (1946).

Gene Kelly, Rita Hayworth, Phil Silvers and Edward S Brophy in *Cover Girl* (1944).

were in 'The Babbitt and the Bromide' number, which Fred and his sister Adele had introduced on stage in *Funny Face* in 1927. Judy Garland burlesqued a star's press interview. Other numbers were 'Limehouse Blues,' 'This Heart of Mine,' 'Love' and 'There's Beauty Everywhere.'

Not much was being done in the musical field in Great Britain, a condition that was to last until the 1960s. Vera Lynn, the British singing star who became 'The Forces' Sweetheart' of World War II, made a fine appearance in *We'll Meet Again* (1944), singing the title song. And there was J Arthur Rank's ambitious *London Town* (1946), which one British critic called 'An attempt by the Rank Organization to make a British musical, often quoted as proof that success in this genre is impossible outside Hollywood (a maxim not disproved until the sixties).'

In Germany there was *Die Grosse Liebe (The Grand Life)* in 1941. Starring Zarah Leander, it was an exotic musical that featured Busby Berkeley-like numbers, and it became the biggest musical hit of the period in the Axis-held countries of Europe.

For some reason, another type of musical caught the fancy of audiences during the war years—biographical films about the lives of composers and musicians. Musical biopics were not new, of course, going back at least to Richard Tauber's portrayal of Franz Schubert in *Blossom Time* (1934). But a new era had been ushered in by *Alexander's Ragtime Band* (1938), which played a different and irresistible tune—or rather a ton of tunes, all culled from the 600 compositions of Irving Berlin (Tyrone Power). The lyrics were as familiar to audiences as the stilted story, but together they constituted a cavalcade of the preceding quarter of a century, brimming over with sentiment, nostalgia and patriotism.

A slightly more classical approach was taken in *The Great Waltz* (1938), the life of Johann Strauss Jr, the Waltz King.

The Great Victor Herbert (1939), with Allan Jones, Mary Martin and Susanna Foster, starred Walter Connolly as the operetta composer. It was a fanciful biography set in turn-of-the-century New York City, and there was not much of a plot. Its compensation for that flaw was music—28 of Herbert's best songs—including 'The March of the Toys' and 'Ah, Sweet Mystery of Life.'

Don Ameche played Stephen Foster in *Swanee River* (1939). He wasn't too convincing, but Al Jolson and the wonderful Foster music kept it afloat.

The blockbuster musical biopic of those years, however, was *Yankee Doodle Dandy* (1942), starring James Cagney as George M Cohan. The United States had just entered World War II and the time was right for this flag-waving (literally) story of Cohan, perhaps the greatest composer and song-and-dance man in American history. Cagney played the part to the hilt, and danced up a storm to boot. It was probably the highest point in his career, and it won him the Academy Award as best actor that year.

Cagney had been type-cast as a gangster in such gems as *The Public Enemy* (1931), but he was, in fact, a dancer to begin with. He started in show business as a song-and-dance man, and his first film, *Sinner's Holiday* (1930), featured him in that role. He was naturally graceful—even as a gangster, he had a lithe grace that was as distinctive as his fast, clipped speech. Cagney went on from *The Public Enemy* to play a series of tough-guy roles in which he was rough on women, but the dancer side of him was always there. It surfaced when he was in *Footlight Parade* (1933) as a producer of musicals, in which he got to do some dancing.

Yankee Doodle Dandy was the best musical of the year and one of 1942's highest-grossing pictures. It was not only an affectionate, melodious biography of George M Cohan, but a nostalgic evocation of a colorful era in the American theater. But it was truly held together by the immense zest of James Cagney.

Bing Crosby played Dan Emmett, the pioneer minstrel man, in *Dixie* (1943). The atmosphere overshadowed the plot, but Bing did get to sing the title song (it had been written by Emmett) and 'Sunday, Monday or Always.'

Cole Porter was portrayed by Cary Grant in *Night and Day* (1945). The music was the only worthy aspect of this fabricated biography. It is doubtful that the composer grew up on a magnificent horse farm. Magnificent horse farms are not usually found in Peru, Indiana. It is doubtful that he composed the title song while at the front, wearing a full-dress uniform, during World War I. But the songs, of course, were great—even Cary Grant singing 'You're the Top'—especially Mary Martin's re-creation of 'My Heart Belongs to Daddy.'

Rhapsody in Blue (1945) starred Robert Alda (who later became known as Alan Alda's father) as George Gershwin. It was a sort of pulp-fiction story of the composer, but it came off

Above: Cary Grant was Cole Porter in *Night and Day* (1946)—with Alexis Smith.

James Cagney, as George M Cohan, doing the title song from *Yankee Doodle Dandy* (1942).

Above: Rhapsody in Blue (1945) starred Robert Alda as Gershwin with Joan Leslie.

more credibly than most other composer biopics, since it captured Gershwin's enthusiasm for his work and some of the inner conflicts he faced. It was loaded with his fine songs and featured an almost complete performance of the title work, 'Rhapsody in Blue.' Audiences left the theater grieving at his untimely death at the age of 48.

The Jolson Story (1946) starred Larry Parks in the title role—a film biography of the popular singer from his boyhood to his success on the stage and in talkies. The great musical numbers, like 'Swanee,' 'April Showers' and 'Mammy,' were dubbed by Jolson himself and mimed by Parks. Parks had been a light leading man whose career in 'B' pictures was interrupted by his highly successful impersonation of Al Jolson. Later he became difficult to cast, and was forced out of Hollywood after running afoul of the House Un-American Activities Committee. Jolson, on the other hand, became an international celebrity again. Unfortunately for Warner Brothers, who gave Jolson his start

Larry Parks played Al Jolson in *The Jolson Story* (1946). 'Swanee' was one of the hits.

in films, the picture made money for Columbia Pictures, who made the movie. The film was so successful that a less popular sequel, *Jolson Sings Again* (1949), which took up Jolson's life where the other film had left off, was made. The strangest scene was probably the one in which Parks (playing Jolson) meets Parks (playing Parks).

Till the Clouds Roll By (1946) was a glossy biopic on Jerome Kern with a terrible plot, offset by the old familiar musical masterpieces of the genius-composer. The story slumped but the music was worth the price of admission. Unfortunately, Kern died while the film was in production. Robert Walker played the lead role and was assisted by a *Who's Who* of Hollywood stars. June Allyson sang 'Till the Clouds Roll By.' Lucille Bremer sang 'I Won't Dance' and 'The Land Where the Good Songs Go.' Kathryn Grayson sang 'Make Believe' and 'Long Ago and Far Away.' Lena Horne sang 'Can't Help Lovin' That Man' and 'Why Was I Born?' Van Johnson sang 'I Won't Dance.' Tony Martin sang 'Make Believe' and 'All the Things You Are.' Dinah Shore sang 'The Last Yime I Saw Paris.' Frank Sinatra sang 'Ol' Man River' in a white tailcoat. Judy Garland sang 'Who,' 'Look for the Silver Lining' and 'Sunny.' (Her sequences were directed by Vincente Minnelli, who was her husband at the time; Richard Whorf directed the rest of the film.)

What would wartime film musicals be without musicals about people in service? *Ship Ahoy* (1941) starred Eleanor Powell, Red Skelton and Bert Lahr, plus Tommy Dorsey and his Orchestra, featuring an uncredited male vocalist—Frank Sinatra. It was an entertaining but trite little musical about a girl who was—it was thought—unwittingly helping enemy agents. One of the best numbers had Powell tapping out Morse code messages with her feet.

Bracken and Hutton—*The Fleet's In* (1942).

Paramount released *The Fleet's In* in 1943. It starred William Holden, the Navy's 'Champion Lover,' who tried to melt the heart of the iceberg, Dorothy Lamour. But the picture was stolen by two youngsters, Eddie Bracken and, in her first role, blonde, bouncy Betty Hutton. The music was provided by the Jimmy Dorsey Orchestra and their two vocalists, Helen O'Connell and Ray Eberle. Who can forget 'Tangerine,' 'I Remember You' and the title song, 'The Fleet's In'?

One of the most successful of the musicals in uniform was *This Is the Army* (1943), a super-duper musical that was a melange of flag-waving, star-singing, fast-stepping hokum showmanship tied up in an unbeatable bundle of box-office allure with 17 smash-hit Irving Berlin songs. It made

The rousing finale to *This Is the Army* (1943)—'This Time Is the Last Time,' with its chorus of some 350 soldiers.

Bing Crosby (right) looks on as Betty Hutton is in trouble in *Here Come the Waves* (1944).

eight and one-half million dollars, which, in terms of 1980s dollars was over 48 million, placing it right behind *South Pacific* (1958).

Two Girls and a Sailor (1944) teamed up June Allyson and Gloria DeHaven as the girls and Van Johnson as the sailor. The cast also included Jose Iturbi (who seemed to be around in every Metro-Goldwyn-Mayer musical of the time), his sister Amparo (to supply the other half in the duo-piano numbers), Jimmy Durante, Lena Horne and the Harry James and Xavier Cugat Orchestras. The highlight was Gracie Allen playing her 'Concerto for Index Finger' with a symphony orchestra. (For the uninitiated, that was really 'Chopsticks.')

Two young entertainers, both of whom were to become show-business legends, appeared in *Up in Arms* (1944). This was Danny Kaye's first picture and Dinah Shore's second, if you count a brief appearance in *Thank Your Lucky Stars* (1943) as her first. Kaye played a green Army recruit, and the film featured some of his great patter songs.

Betty Hutton, the musical firecracker, was back in *Here Come the Waves* (1944). This time she played a dual role opposite Bing Crosby and Sonny (He's a Honey) Tufts. According to the studio flackmen, 'Crosby and Tufts hit the High C's with the double-trouble Hutton.' Who could resist? It was a fairly cute nautical musical about a successful crooner (Crosby) who joins the Navy. The Johnny Mercer-Harold Arlen score included 'Let's Take the Long Way Home' and 'Ac-Cent-Tchu-Ate the Positive.'

Many would argue that the best of all was *Anchors Aweigh* (1945). It was a tuneful, lively musical about two sailors on leave in Hollywood. Gene Kelly had his first true lead role as one of the sailors and Frank Sinatra was the other. The love interest was supplied by Kathryn Grayson and Pamela Britton. Once again Jose Iturbi showed up as the kindly pianist. Some of the songs were 'All of a Sudden My Heart Sings' (the melody was merely a chromatic scale), 'What Makes the Sunset?' and 'I Fall in Love Too Easily.' Sinatra and Kelly did a dance number in a USO dormitory in which they used the cots as trampolines. But the highlight was a dream-like number featuring Kelly, as a Pomeranian sailor, teaching a mouse king (Jerry, from the *Tom and Jerry* cartoons) to dance. The combination of animation with Kelly's dancing was irresistible, and Jerry became Kelly's most memorable dancing partner.

The war years were a great and fertile period in the history of musical films. By 1943, 40 percent of the year's films were musicals, and this percentage held until the end of the war. Musicals provided escape from war worries and permitted the expression of unabashed patriotic emotion.

Opposite: Sinatra and Kelly in their USO dormitory dance in *Anchors Aweigh* (1945).

Vera-Ellen and Gene Kelly in 'Slaughter on Tenth Avenue' from *Words and Music* (1948)

AFTER THE WAR

After World War II the musical biopics kept rolling along. One of the first was *Song of Love* (1947), the story of relationships among a lot of nineteenth-century composers. It was a classy, slow-moving production about Robert Schumann, played by Paul Henried, and Johannes Brahms, played by Robert Walker, who was terribly miscast. Henry Daniell played Franz Liszt and Katharine Hepburn played Schumann's wife, Clara. One critic suggested that the best way to enjoy the film was with one's eyes shut. The music was splendid—conducted by William Steinberg, with the piano playing dubbed by Arthur Rubenstein.

Words and Music (1948) was a musical biography of the great composing team Richard Rodgers and Lorenz Hart, and almost fell under the heading of an all-star romp. Tom Drake was Rodgers and Mickey Rooney was Hart. Also in the cast were June Allyson, Perry Como, Judy Garland, Lena Horne, Gene Kelly, Ann Sothern, Cyd Charisse, Betty Garrett and Janet Leigh. It had the usual factual distortions common to biopics of composers, but the music was the thing—19 songs and 17 dancing numbers. The hits were 'Blue Room' with Como and Charisse, 'Manhattan' with Rooney and Garrett, 'Thou Swell' with Allyson, 'I Wish I Were in Love Again' with Rooney and Garland, 'The Lady Is a Tramp' with Horne and 'Blue Moon' sung by Mel Torme. The best routine in the picture was the 'Slaughter on Tenth Avenue' number—the eight-minute ballet with Gene Kelly and Vera-Ellen, a number that had been seen previously in *On Your Toes* (1939).

Above: Perry Como and Cyd Charisse at the piano in *Words and Music* (1948).

Above: Vera-Ellen and Fred Astaire in *Three Little Words* (1950).

Another song-writing team, Bert Kalmar (played by Fred Astaire) and Harry Ruby (played by Red Skelton), was the subject of yet another biopic, *Three Little Words* (1950). Arlene Dahl played Ellen Percy, the silent-movie star who married Ruby, and Vera-Ellen was Kalmar's wife. Gloria DeHaven played her real-life mother, the stage star Mrs Carter DeHaven. Debby Reynolds was Helen Kane, the 'Boop-Boop-a-Doop' star of the 1920s. The film contained 14 of the team's hits, including the title tune.

The Great Caruso (1951) starred the ill-fated Mario Lanza as the Italian opera tenor Enrico Caruso. It surprised everyone by being a hit. The music was overwhelming. Lanza dominated the picture, which had been based on an outline supplied by Caruso's widow, Dorothy. It had 27 vocal items, most of them sung by Lanza, who was occasionally joined by operatic divas Dorothy Kirsten, Blanche Thebom and Jarmila Novotna. The movie also included a pop hit, 'The Loveliest Night of the Year.'

A unique biopic of a composer was *Stars and Stripes Forever* (1952), the story of the 'March King,' John Philip Sousa, who was played a little stiffly by Clifton Webb. The many standard march tunes were worked into the plot nicely.

Then came the pictorial biography of the female vocalist Jane Froman—*With a Song in My Heart* (1952). It

Opposite: Mario Lanza.

Above: Mario Lanza had the title role in *The Great Caruso* (1951).

June Allyson played the wife to James Stewart's Glenn Miller in *The Glenn Miller Story* (1954).

was schmaltzy, but Susan Hayward was fine as the singer in this story of her early success and her comeback after a near-fatal air crash that left her almost completely crippled. Many of the songs were sung by Froman with Hayward doing an admirable miming job.

The Glenn Miller Story (1954) was a sentimental biography of the trombone-playing band leader that gave a strong nostalgic twist to the aimless pop music of the 1950s. Starring James Stewart in the title role, with June Allyson as his wife, most of the film contained marvelous music, and the rest was sentimentality. There was plenty of music—most of Miller's hits—and the big-band sound was the thing.

Sigmund Romberg came in for a biopic, *Deep in My Heart* (1954), in which he was played by Jose Ferrer. The story served as a peg for the appearance of a host of guest stars—Fred Astaire, Gene Kelly, Tony Martin, Rosemary Clooney, Ann Miller, for example. And the film had songs from some of Romberg's biggest hits—*Maytime*, *The Student Prince*, *The Desert Song* and *The New Moon*.

With the success of *The Jolson Story*, could *The Eddie Cantor Story* (1954) be avoided? Cantor was played by Keefe Brasselle. It was a disappointing biography of the famed 'Banjo Eyes' and his rise to fame and fortune as a comedian. Of course it had songs that were identified with the star, such as 'If You Knew Susie.'

Then came another 'Eddie Story'—*The Eddy Duchin Story* (1955). It was another glossy Hollywood biopic of the pianist-band leader (father of Peter Duchin) of the 1930s–40s. Tyrone Power in the lead role tried hard, especially when playing the piano to the dubbing of another band leader of the period—Carmen Cavallero.

Love Me or Leave Me (1955) was another kind of thing altogether. The biography of Ruth Etting, the star vocalist who became involved with a gangster, it was a better-than-average film biography. Doris Day had seldom been shown to more advantage, both vocally and dramatically. James Cagney, as Marty the Gimp, the racketeer who loved Etting, stole every scene he was in. Doris Day had 13 solos—most of them great songs of the 1920s, such as 'Ten Cents a Dance,' 'Never Look Back' and 'Love Me or Leave Me.' Oddly enough, many of those old Ruth Etting hits became Doris Day hits.

Another biopic of a band leader was *The Benny Goodman Story* (1956), with Steve Allen playing the clarinetist. Allen, too, was a musician of sorts, so his fingering of the clarinet was a lot more convincing than most actors' bouts with faking the piano, the drums, the trumpet, the trombone, etc. Guest performances spiced up the film. There was Gene Krupa, Harry James, 'The Liltin' Martha Tilton, Sammy Davis Jr and the sound of Benny Goodman himself on the clarinet.

St Louis Blues (1957) was the life story of composer W C Handy, and the music was everything. The great songs, including the title song, were sung by a long list of wonderful performers, like Nat 'King' Cole (in his second film, as the title character), Eartha Kitt, Pearl Bailey, Ella Fitzgerald and Cab Calloway.

This is not to say that the musical biographies were the only rage in Hollywood in the postwar years. Far from it. Some of the most memorable movies made during that time had virtually no relationship to real life.

Betty Grable was still going strong. *Pin-Up Girl* (1944) had her playing a secretary who sent pin-up photos to GIs. Hermes Pan did the choreography, but the production numbers couldn't save the picture.

Then she did *Diamond Horseshoe* (1945), which was originally titled

Opposite: James Stewart as the great band leader in *The Glenn Miller Story* (1954).

Billy Rose's Diamond Horseshoe. This one had an abundance of the Grable legs, good clowning by Phil Silvers, tongue-in-cheek writing and a good production that almost compensated for a mediocre score and a backstage plot built around Rose's once-popular night club. The one big song was 'The More I See You.'

By 1946 Betty Grable was the highest-paid American woman. She and Harry James owned a racing stable, ranches and two estates. She liked to gamble and so did he. Never burdened with excessive drive or a voracious ego, she often talked about retiring from movies and just enjoying life. But gambling losses and problems with the Internal Revenue Service made this choice impossible.

One of her best movies came out after the war—*Mother Wore Tights* (1947), in which she was cast opposite Dan Dailey. They were terrific together and became one of Hollywood's best-known star teams. The picture was an entertaining show-business cavalcade about a girl who marries and becomes part of a song-and-dance act. She and Dailey were back again in *When My Baby Smiles at Me* (1948), a musical based on the old play *Burlesque*. Even with the help of Jack Oakie, June Havoc and James Gleason, it was a strictly routine musical about a burlesque team that breaks up when one member gets a job on Broadway. Eventually, of course, they were reunited.

In *Wabash Avenue* (1950), Betty had a field day. It was a remake of *Coney Island* (1943), set in Chicago, but this time she had more fun. She sang, danced, threw vases at Victor Mature, sang some more, danced some more and ended up in Mature's arms. The musical numbers were a lot of fun, too.

Betty and Dan then appeared in *My Blue Heaven* (1950), a fast-moving musical with Grable and Dailey tapping and singing their way through a silly plot about a show-business team and their efforts to adopt a family.

Grable had never considered herself an actress, just a dancer, and the day of the big musical was coming to an end. A new crop of postwar stars was pressing for attention, most notably Marilyn Monroe, who appeared with Betty in *How to Marry a Millionaire* (1953). This wide-screen Cinemascope spectacular told the story of the maneuvering of three dumb blondes (Monroe, Grable and Lauren Bacall) to hook themselves wealthy husbands. Betty, who played a breezy huntress who cuts out a skittish gentleman (Fred Clark) and shamelessly pursues him right up to his snowbound lodge in Maine, was the funniest of the trio. And she had a delicious in-joke in the film when she failed to recognize a recording by Harry James, to whom she was married at the time.

It was typical of Betty Grable that she was gracious and helpful to Marilyn Monroe, encouraging her rather than trying to thwart her, even though Twentieth Century-Fox courted Marilyn and snubbed Betty at this time. In 1965 Betty Grable and Harry James were divorced. Grable gained custody of their daughters. Unlike her own mother, she didn't force them into show business but let them choose their own careers. Betty tore up her film contract and turned to the theater once it was obvious to her that

Betty Grable and Dan Dailey in *Mother Wore Tights* (1947).

her movie career was over. She toured in *Hello Dolly!*, did *Born Yesterday* in dinner theaters and appeared as Adelaide in *Guys and Dolls*, the part originated by Vivian Blaine. She performed on television and did Geritol commercials. She was about to tour Australia in *No, No, Nanette* when she became too ill to work. On 2 July 1973 she died of cancer.

Fred Astaire stayed busy during the postwar years. *Blue Skies* (1946) had him teamed with Bing Crosby and 20 Irving Berlin tunes. The plot was corny, but it didn't get in the way of music that included 'Blue Skies,' 'Puttin' on the Ritz' and 'A Couple of Song and Dance Men.'

Then came *Easter Parade* (1948) in which he starred with Judy Garland, Peter Lawford and Ann Miller, that great dancer who had had rickets as a child and took ballet and acrobatic dancing lessons to overcome the effects of the disease. It was a delightful Irving Berlin musical with Astaire trying to forget ex-dance partner Miller as he rises to stardom with Judy. Fred came out of a two-year retirement to make this film, and the

Judy and Fred do 'A Couple of Swells' in *Easter Parade* (1948).

Fred Astaire, Joan Caulfield and Bing Crosby starred in *Blue Skies* (1946).

Above: Judy and Fred in *Easter Parade* (1948).

Sarah, in her only Hollywood movie. The film was set in London and concerned Astaire and Powell's attempts as a brother-and-sister dance team to perform in London at the time of the wedding. Fred and Jane did well, both singing and dancing. Alan Jay Lerner wrote the book and lyrics and Burton Lane wrote the tunes. Among the songs was a ballad for Powell, 'Too Late Now,' and Fred sang the song that has probably the longest title in musical history—'How Could You Believe Me When I Said I Love You When You Know I've Been a Liar All My Life?'—which took over that distinction from 'I've Got Tears in My Ears From Lying on My Back in My Bed As I Cry over You.' There was also the dance sequence in which Fred danced up the wall, across the ceiling and down the other side.

The Belle of New York (1952) was another film in which Astaire was to have starred with Judy Garland, but she was replaced by Vera-Ellen. It was an uninspired musical set in New York City in the Gay Nineties, with Astaire as a rich playboy chasing mission-worker Vera-Ellen. It was not a success, especially since the great song-writing team of Harry Warren and Johnny Mercer created a group of songs without one hit, unless we count 'Let a Little Love Come In.'

A better vehicle for Fred Astaire was *The Band Wagon* (1953), in

critics went wild. It had 17 Irving Berlin songs including the classic 'We're a Couple of Swells.' Astaire took the role because Gene Kelly broke his ankle before production started.

After appearing with Ginger Rogers one more time in *The Barkleys of Broadway* (1949) and with Red Skelton in *Three Little Words* (1950), he made *Let's Dance* (1950) with Betty Hutton, a story about Hutton's attempts to win her son away from her Back Bay in-laws. Astaire's dancing was the only good part of the picture.

But then came *Royal Wedding* (1950). Judy Garland was supposed to have had the lead in this film, but she missed or delayed so many rehearsals that it was decided to replace her with Jane Powell. Metro-Goldwyn-Mayer was trying to cash in on the Princess Elizabeth-Prince Philip wedding season, and went so far as to hire Sir Winston Churchill's daughter,

Opposite: Astaire and Jane Powell—*Royal Wedding* (1951).

Betty Hutton and Fred Astaire interrupt some diners in *Let's Dance* (1959).

Above: Fred Astaire, Nanette Fabray and Jack Buchanan do the 'Triplets' number from *The Band Wagon* (1953).

which he danced with Cyd Charisse (born Tula Ellice Finklea), whom he later admitted was his best female dancing partner of all time. She had started dancing to counter the effects of a childhood bout with polio, and had later danced with the Ballet Russe; at the outbreak of World War II she began her Hollywood film career. It was a delightful musical, with its Howard Dietz and Arthur Schwartz songs, and concerned putting on a show. Also starring were Oscar Levant, Nanette Fabray and Jack Buchanan, and the show featured such classics as 'That's Entertainment,' 'By Myself,' 'Triplets' and Astaire's 'Shine on Your Shoes' number.

His next starring vehicle was *Daddy Long Legs* (1955), which even today can start arguments. One either loved it or hated it. At any rate, Astaire had seldom had a better dancing partner than charming and graceful Leslie Caron—their numbers were the film's highlights. The plot bordered on a modern fairy tale—a French orphan (Caron) is subsidized by a wealthy bachelor on the condition that his identity be kept secret.

Fred Astaire and Leslie Caron in *Daddy Long Legs* (1955).

Funny Face (1957) starred Astaire with Audrey Hepburn in her first musical. Astaire was at his best, and the top Gershwin tunes and colorful Parisian scenes combined to make a sprightly musical about a fashion photographer who turns a bookstore clerk into a high-fashion model.

Bing Crosby was rolling along during the postwar years, too. After he made *Blue Skies* with Fred Astaire, he appeared in a few non-musicals before he starred in *The Emperor Waltz* (1948), a schmaltzy musical set in the Austria of Franz Joseph (or a Hollywood facsimile), with Crosby trying to sell phonographs to royalty and wooing a countess (Joan Fontaine) on the side.

He made a few forgettables, such as

Opposite: Astaire and Cyd Charisse—*The Band Wagon* (1953).

Above: Al fresco Austrian music, from *The Emperor Waltz* (1948).

Top O' The Morning (1949), with Barry Fitzgerald, in which he was in Ireland crooning while he searched for the thief of the Blarney Stone. Then there was *Riding High* (1950), a sappy story about Crosby as a race-horse owner whose horse had never won, but it had a few decent songs. In *Mr Music* (1950) he was a composer who would rather play golf than work. The tunes were below par, but Groucho Marx, Peggy Lee and Marge and Gower Champion were in the cast. *Here Comes the Groom* (1951) had him as a reporter wooing Jane Wyman, but the songs were better, such as 'In the Cool, Cool, Cool of the Evening.' *Just for You* (1952) was a story-and-song affair about a man who can't be bothered with his children until Jane Wyman sets him straight. About the only highlight was the appearance of 14-year-old Natalie Wood as his daughter.

Photographer Fred Astaire shows book clerk Audrey Hepburn her picture in *Funny Face* (1957).

Rosemary Clooney, Danny Kaye, Bing Crosby and Vera-Ellen sing in *White Christmas* (1954).

But no one minded these potboilers: they remained loyal to 'Der Bingle.' After all, he had introduced more Academy Award-winning songs in films than anyone else—'Sweet Leilani' (*Waikiki Wedding* in 1937), 'White Christmas' (*Holiday Inn* in 1942), 'Swingin' on a Star' (*Going My Way* in 1944) and 'In the Cool, Cool, Cool of the Evening' (*Here Comes the Groom* in 1951).

The public had waited a long time, but finally *White Christmas* (1954) came along, in which he starred with Danny Kaye, Rosemary Clooney and Vera-Ellen. It was a colorful package of holiday entertainment and had 15 Irving Berlin musical numbers, including 'White Christmas' itself. Unfortunately, it also contained one of Berlin's most forgettable songs, 'What Can You Do with a General.' But it did have 'Count Your Blessings,' sung by Crosby and Clooney, and 'The Best Things Happen When You're Dancing,' which Kaye sang and then danced to with Vera-Ellen. The critics seemed to pay more attention to the new process of VistaVision, however.

After a fine straight acting role in *The Country Girl* with Grace Kelly (who won the Academy Award for best actress), he and she teamed up again in what might be called his best musical—*High Society* (1956), not to be confused with the *High Society* of 1955, which was a 'Bowery Boys' film. Frank Sinatra, Celeste Holm and Louis Armstrong joined them in the venture. The story was taken from Philip Barry's non-musical play *The Philadelphia Story* and concerned Samantha, a society woman (Kelly) who is about to marry a fop (John Lund) when her ex-husband (Crosby)

Bing Crosby, John Lund, Grace Kelly and Frank Sinatra in *High Society* (1956).

Bing Crosby sings 'True Love' to Grace Kelly in *High Society* (1956).

arrives on the scene, along with newspaper reporters Holm and Sinatra. Actually, Kelly filled Katharine Hepburn's shoes nicely (Hepburn had been the heroine in the play and the subsequent film version of it); however, Crosby and Sinatra were a bit miscast. But it had nine superb Cole Porter songs—'True Love' (in which Grace Kelly revealed a rather pleasant voice in a duet with Crosby), 'I Love You, Samantha,' 'Little One,' 'Now You Has Jazz,' 'High Society' (a Calypso number), 'Mind If I Make Love to You?,' 'You're Sensational,' 'Who Wants to Be a Millionaire?' and 'Well, Did You Evah!' The last was the only song not written especially for the film. It had been sung in 1939 on Broadway by Betty Grable and Charles Walters in *Du Barry Was a Lady*. Except for *The Road to Hong Kong* (1961), this was Bing's last musical.

The biggest star of the era's musicals was undoubtedly Gene Kelly. He was to receive a special Academy Award 'in appreciation of his versatility as an actor, singer, director and dancer, and especially for his brilliant achievements in the art of choreography on film.'

He starred with Judy Garland in his first postwar musical, *The Pirate* (1948), based on the S N Behrman play that had starred Alfred Lunt and Lynn Fontanne on the stage. Music by Cole Porter was added, but the songs were pretty much forgettable, except for the fans of 'Mack the Black.' There was one gem, however—Gene and Judy singing 'Be a Clown.' The thin plot involved Judy believing that circus clown Gene is a pirate and Gene pretending to be that pirate (although Walter Slezak was the real pirate who had retired and didn't want his identity to be revealed). This was Judy's first picture after her maternity leave in 1946 to have Liza Minnelli.

His next musical was *Take Me Out to the Ball Game* (1949), in which he teamed up with Frank Sinatra and Jules Munshin as baseball players who played for Esther Williams' team at the turn of the century. Somehow director Busby Berkeley was able to squeeze in a water ballet for Esther. The film had to be retitled for British audiences, since it was about baseball, which was box-office poison there. It was called *Everybody's Cheering*.

Kelly co-directed and starred in *On the Town* (1950). The film was not merely clever: it had the look and feel of a new era. Kelly had learned his trade well. From the time he first worked with Busby Berkeley, he became fascinated with what the camera could do. The shots of the real New York City in *On the Town* gave audiences a vista of freedom no cardboard backdrop could convey. Kelly starred with Frank Sinatra, Betty Garrett, Vera-Ellen, Ann Miller, Jules Munshin and Alice Pearce in this adaptation of the Broadway musical by Leonard Bernstein, with lyrics by Betty Comden and Adolph Green (the team that had played the Miller and Munshin roles on Broadway). The Broadway musical had, in turn, been based on a ballet, *Fancy Free*, with music by Bernstein and choreography by Jerome Robbins. The movie, about three sailors on a one-day liberty in New York City, doesn't really qualify as a remake of a Broadway show, since all but two of the original songs were dropped, leaving only the Bernstein

Above: Judy Garland is terrified of Gene Kelly in *The Pirate* (1948).

Betty Garrett, Ann Miller, Gene Kelly, Jules Munshin, Frank Sinatra, Alice Pearce—*On the Town* (1949).

music and some great ballet sequences.

Kelly was often working in non-musicals, and in 1950 he did *Black Hand*, a forgettable film. Then came *Summer Stock* (1950), a tuneful musical co-starring Judy Garland in her final MGM film. The plot centered on a farm, run by Judy, which is invaded by a group of show people who want to turn the barn into a summer theater. Sound familiar? After many holdups because of the unpredictable Garland, the film was finished. Then it was decided that the picture needed a flashy finale, and Garland was called back to make the famous 'Get Happy' number. But in the meantime, she had lost a great deal of weight from a diet. Thus, although she was at her best in the number, she appeared to be considerably smaller than she was in the rest of the picture.

Kelly's first complete triumph was *An American in Paris* (1951), co-starring with Leslie Caron, the French dancer whom Kelly himself had discovered in the *Ballets des Champs Elysées*. The film was a joyous, original musical built around a Gershwin score, and won the Academy Award

Judy Garland sings 'Get Happy' in *Summer Stock* (1950).

Below: Jules Munshin, Betty Garrett, Frank Sinatra, Esther Williams, Gene Kelly in *Take Me Out to the Ball Game* (1949).

Sinatra and Kelly dance in *Take Me Out to the Ball Game* (1949).

for best picture of the year. Directed by Vincente Minnelli, it told the story of an American ex-GI (Kelly) who stays in Paris after World War II to see if he can make it as an artist. The film took such risks as an 18-minute ballet featuring Kelly and Caron, but it won a total of five Academy Awards.

The score was magnificent, with 20 George and Ira Gershwin songs used, plus George's 'Concerto in F,' although only the third movement was played. These songs included one of their first, 'I'll Build a Stairway to Paradise,' as well as one of their last, 'Our Love Is Here to Stay.' The Gershwin classical music suite of the title was also included—it had first been staged on Broadway in Florenz Zeigfeld's *Show Girl* in 1929.

The final ballet was, beyond question, a truly cinematic ballet, with dancers describing vivid patterns against changing colors, designs, costumes and scenes. The whole story of a poignant romance within a fanciful panorama of Paris was conceived and performed with taste and talent. It was the uncontested high point of the film.

The final musical sequence is unmatched as a film ballet, but it might never have been in the picture had it not been for Nina Foch's chicken pox. At that point the plot had been resolved, and there was some doubt as to whether to stick a ballet on the end at all. Some people thought it would be pointless and dull. But while they waited for Foch to recuperate, Kelly and Minnelli finished their preparations and filmed the ballet. Studio bigwigs were not happy when Minnelli presented them with a bill for half a million dollars for the sequence. That would be small potatoes today, but things were done so much on the cheap then that the only studio people who went to Paris for the picture were members of a second unit that shot some street scenes to be used as backgrounds. Everything else was done right on the Metro-Goldwyn-Mayer lot.

The studio built three full-sized Parisian streets, as realistic as anyone could ask for, including a café where a lot of the action took place. The streets were filled with Parisian pedestrians and vehicles; by changing the lighting, the scene could go from day to night in a few minutes. When the Seine River was needed for a dreamy scene with Kelly and Caron, set designers came up with a lifelike Seine that was just three inches deep, with a bridge and Notre Dame Cathedral in the background painted on a backdrop

Above: Leslie Caron and Gene Kelly in *An American in Paris* (1951).

Kelly and Caron dance beside a fake Seine in *An American in Paris* (1951).

Above: Kelly in an exuberant dance routine from *Singin' in the Rain* (1952).

More Kelly dancing from *An American in Paris* (1951).

Above: Donald O'Connor and Gene Kelly clown in *Singin' in the Rain* (1952).

160 feet long and 35 feet high. The whole thing was convincing, however.

Then came what some believe to be Kelly's topper—*Singin' in the Rain* (1952), which he co-directed with Stanley Donen, and in which he starred with Debbie Reynolds, Donald O'Connor, Cyd Charisse and Jean Hagen. In this film, everything went right. Reynolds, a young girl still in her teens, had caught the public fancy singing 'Abba Dabba Honeymoon' with Carleton Carpenter in the movie *Two Weeks with Love* (1950). She got the lead in *Singin' in the Rain*. Donald O'Connor was around to do some of the best comic dancing ever. Betty Comden and Adolph Green were at their wittiest. Kelly was there. The result? A gentle spoof with the best singing and dancing in a long time, including the most famous scene from any musical picture—Gene Kelly wetly singing and dancing the title song. The picture went way over budget and it was worth every penny.

The story was about the Hollywood panic when studios were forced to go

Opposite: Singin' in the Rain (1952).

Boy (Kelly) gets girl (Reynolds) in *Singin' in the Rain* (1952). O'Connor approves.

Above: Kelly and Charisse in *Singin' in the Rain* (1952).

from silents to talkies in the late 1920s, and it brought back some grand old songs by Arthur Freed and Nacio Herb Brown, including 'Singin' in the Rain,' 'You Were Meant for Me,' 'All I Do Is Dream of You,' plus some new numbers.

O'Connor was at his peak doing 'Make 'Em Laugh,' and 'The Broadway Ballet' with Charisse and Kelly was magnificent. There was also 'My Lucky Star' and 'Good Morning.' Jean Hagen deserved an award for her portrayal of a sex goddess who cannot sing, cannot dance, cannot talk, cannot enunciate a single word without creating mounting hysteria in an audience.

Singin' in the Rain was rich in references to the old days of Hollywood, and the satire on studio moguls, stars and show business was sharp and sometimes devastating. More than that, the choreography was inspired. Each of the three great production numbers was staged differently, and their juxtaposition gave the picture its notable qualities of variety and lightness.

The first—the title number—was a simple and emotional solo by Gene Kelly. 'You Were Meant for Me,' in which Kelly and Reynolds sang and danced their love duet on an empty sound stage, was more in the Astaire-Rogers tradition. And the big production number, 'Broadway Ballet,' was a surrealistic Busby Berkeley-type extravaganza filled with magic, unexpected transitions, a huge cast and spectacular uses of light, color, costumes and sets, plus marvelous dancing by Kelly and Charisse. Add in O'Connor's acrobatic and amusing 'Make 'Em Laugh,' and a couple of other numbers that enriched the mixture and heightened the fun, and the result was an anthology of musical styles and techniques.

It's Always Fair Weather (1955) was another co-operative directing job between Kelly and Donen. Kelly starred with Dan Dailey, Cyd Charisse, Michael Kidd and Dolores Gray in this tuneful romp about three ex-soldiers who meet in New York City ten years after V-J Day. There were plenty of songs and some expert group dancing by Kelly, Dailey and choreographer Kidd.

Kelly rounded out the period with *Les Girls* (1957), in which he played a dancer with a troupe of three girls—

Opposite: Kelly and Reynolds in *Singin' in the Rain* (1952).

Gene Kelly, Cyd Charisse, Dan Dailey, Betty Garrett, Michael Kidd in *It's Always Fair Weather* (1955).

RLS

S Z 'Cuddles' Sakall, Van Johnson, Judy Garland in the shop—*In the Good Old Summertime* (1949).

Taina Elg, Kay Kendall and Mitzi Gaynor—on a European tour. The score was Cole Porter's last.

In addition to the musicals she made with Gene Kelly, Judy Garland was busy during this era, too. *Easter Parade* (1948) was followed by *In the Good Old Summertime* (1949). It was an oddity. Originally there had been a play, *The Shop Around the Corner*, by Nikolaus Laszlo, which was made into a film of the same name in 1940 by Ernst Lubitsch, starring James Stewart and Margaret Sullavan. It told the story of two pen pals who worked in a turn-of-the-century notions shop without knowing that they were carrying on a post-office romance with each other. At the shop, they can't stand each other. For the musical, starring a chubby Judy Garland and Van Johnson, the setting was switched to a music store in Chicago, with S Z Sakall as the owner. Judy sang 'I Don't Care' and other delightful songs. Later, the same theme was switched to a Budapest perfume store in the Broadway musical *She Loves Me*.

The picture that many Judy Garland fans think of as her best was *A Star Is Born* (1954). It was also her last musical. Janet Gaynor and

Opposite: Kelly with Mitzi Gaynor, Kay Kendall, Taina Elg—*Les Girls* (1957).

Judy Garland in *A Star Is Born* (1954).

Fredric March had made the original, non-musical *A Star Is Born* in 1937. It was the story of a girl's overnight success in Hollywood and the decline of her alcoholic star-husband. By the time Judy made the film as a musical, the story had often been told, but it didn't matter because of Garland's musical genius and a fine supporting cast, especially James Mason as her failing alcoholic husband. Judy was at her pinnacle singing 'The Man That Got Away' and 'Born in a Trunk.' And she was at her most winning in 'Here's What I'm Here For,' where she sang, danced and pantomimed the woman in pursuit of the man. The music by Harold Arlen, Ira Gershwin and Leonard Gershe took audiences' breath away. The advertising read '$6,000,000 and 2½ years to make it!' But it was worth the money and the wait.

After a four-year hiatus from film-making, a nervous breakdown, a divorce and an attempted suicide, Judy Garland had staged a spectacular comeback. The premier on 19 September 1954 outglittered anything Hollywood could have invented about itself. The film met with rave reviews. But when theater owners found audiences balking at its three-hour length, Warner Brothers trimmed 30 minutes from its running time. The film leaped into the headlines again in 1983 when Ronald Haver, a movie historian, searched old archives for months and recovered the missing footage. The restored version again drew out the glamorous and the great and garnered new raves from film critics.

Esther Williams was another wartime star who continued for years. *Neptune's Daughter* (1949) starred the swimming beauty with Ricardo Montalban and Red Skelton and won an Academy Award for its hit song 'Baby, It's Cold Outside,' written by Frank Loesser and sung by Williams and Montalban and later reprised by Skelton and Betty Garrett. Xavier Cugat was also in this light and tuneful romantic comedy. It was a South American romance with Williams as a bathing-suit designer and Skelton as a no-account mistaken for a famous polo player.

Pagan Love Song (1950) presented Williams as a native of Tahiti whom Howard Keel romances tunefully. In *Dangerous When Wet* (1953) she swam the English Channel and romanced with Fernando Lamas, who later became her husband. One highlight was a Tom-and-Jerry underwater car-

Esther Williams hangs suspended in *Million Dollar Mermaid* (1952).

Inset: Esther Williams in the finale of *Easy to Love* (1953).

toon sequence. In the film, Williams played a Midwestern girl who wanted to win fame with her swimming.

Easy to Love (1953) presented Williams as a swimming show star who wanted to quit and settle down, but her boss wouldn't let her because he loved her. The film was set in Cypress Gardens, Florida, and co-starred Tony Martin and Van Johnson. Busby Berkeley directed the water-skiing and swimming ballets.

Mario Lanza had a very brief but meteoric career in musicals. The American-born tenor first appeared in *That Midnight Kiss* (1949), which was a semi-autobiographical story about a singing truck driver—which Lanza had been. Also in the cast were Kathryn Grayson, Jose Iturbi and Ethel Barrymore. Lanza and Grayson sang their hearts out.

The Toast of New Orleans (1950) was next, also with Grayson. This was the one in which he sang his all-time hit 'Be My Love.' Lanza played a New Orleans fisherman who is converted into an opera star. Following *The Great Caruso* (1951) he made *Because You're Mine* (1952), this time with Doretta Morrow. He played a drafted opera singer who fell in love with his tough Army sergeant's daughter. The title song was the big hit.

Serenade (1956) cast him as a street singer who was discovered by a society playgirl (Joan Fontaine) and a concert manager (Vincent Price). The segments from operas saved the show. *Seven Hills of Rome* (1957) was a real nothing, but at least it had one great song, 'Arrivederci Roma.' The last picture that Lanza made before he died was *For the First Time* (1959). He was an opera star who found romance with a deaf girl (Johanna von Koszian). No one could know how she appreciated his singing.

An enormous number of musicals was made after the war starring singers whose names are not exactly household words today. One of them was *Two Sisters from Boston* (1945) with Kathryn Grayson, June Allyson and Peter Lawford. It was an odd musical with practically no plot, set in the 1890s and stuffed with a strange collection of types of music, from a scene from *Die Meistersinger* with Lauritz Melchior, the Danish opera star, to a

Opposite: Lanza and Grayson in *The Toast of New Orleans* (1950).

Lanza in *Because You're Mine* (1952).

Joan Fontaine, Mario Lanza, Serita Montiel in *Serenade* (1956).

Above: Larry Parks, Rita Hayworth, James Gleason in *Down to Earth* (1947).

Above: Frank Sinatra, Kathryn Grayson, Peter Lawford in *It Happened in Brooklyn* (1947).

Selena Royle, Wallace Beery, Carmen Miranda in *A Date with Judy* (1948).

song sung by Jimmy Durante, 'G'wan Home, Your Mudder's Calling.'

Wallace Beery made a rare musical appearance in *A Date With Judy* (1948), the story of two teenagers, Elizabeth Taylor and Jane Powell, and the competition between them for Robert Stack. Beery was taught to dance by Carmen Miranda as she sang '*Cuanto le Gusta*' to the accompaniment of Xavier Cugat and his Orchestra. Powell, playing Judy, sang 'It's a Most Unusual Day.' But for many the highlight was to feast their eyes on 15-year-old Elizabeth Taylor, who was obviously approaching womanhood.

It Happened in Brooklyn (1947) starred Frank Sinatra, Kathryn Grayson, Peter Lawford and Jimmy Durante. It was a pleasant, inconsequential musical about an ex-sailor (Sinatra) who moved in with a janitor in Brooklyn (Durante) and tried to make the grade in the music business. The meat of the film was the music. Grayson sang Mozart and Delibes, while Sinatra and Durante sang 'The Song's Got to Have Heart.' The best song was probably Sinatra's rendition of 'Time After Time.' The pianist on the sound track was a 17-year-old kid who worked in the Metro-Goldwyn-Mayer music department—André Previn.

Probably Frank Sinatra's biggest flop was *The Kissing Bandit* (1948), in which he (at his frailest) played the son of a Western kissing bandit who took over where his father had left off. One critic said 'The song "Siesta" sums it up.' The only good moments were Kathryn Grayson singing 'Love Is Where You Find It,' and a dance routine—added at the last minute—with Ricardo Montalban, Cyd Charisse and Ann Miller.

Lullaby of Broadway (1951) had Doris Day playing a singer who returned to New York City to find that her mother, Gladys George, was a down-and-out chanteuse. The score included standards by George Gershwin and Cole Porter, but Broadway was never like this.

Show Boat kept rolling along in 1951, this time starring Kathryn Grayson, Howard Keel, Joe E Brown, Agnes Moorehead and Marge and Gower Champion. Ava Gardner was hired for the Julie character when it was felt that Judy Garland couldn't handle it. The wonderful old songs were still there—'Make Believe,' 'Why Do I Love You?,' 'You Are Love,' 'Ol' Man River,' 'Bill' and 'Can't Help Lovin' That Man.'

Doris Day dances with Gene Nelson in *The Lullaby of Broadway* (1951).

One of the most charming films of 1952 was *Hans Christian Andersen*, with Danny Kaye, Farley Granger, Zizi Jeanmaire and Roland Petit. It was, of course, the story of the Danish writer of children's stories, and featured such Frank Loesser songs as 'Thumbelina,' 'Inchworm,' 'Ugly Duckling' and 'Wonderful, Wonderful Copenhagen.'

Kathryn Grayson came back with *Lovely to Look At* (1952), with Howard Keel and Red Skelton. It was an entertaining remake of the musical *Roberta*, with many of the lovely Jerome Kern tunes. The songs took precedence over the thin plot, set in the fashion world of Paris. Grayson and Keel sang well, and Marge and Gower Champion provided some excellent dancing. With such songs as 'Smoke Gets in Your Eyes,' 'I Won't Dance,' 'Yesterdays,' 'The Touch of Your Hand,' 'You're Devastating' and 'Lovely to Look At,' how could it have missed?

Leslie Caron and Mel Ferrer starred in *Lili* (1953), the tale of French carnival folk. Caron was captivating as Lili, an orphan who joined the carnival and fell for the charms of a

Jimmy Durante sings to Donald O'Connor in *The Milkman* (1950).

sophisticated magician (Jean-Pierre Aumont)—he is very much a ladies' man, although he is married. Ferrer played a self-pitying puppeteer. The unforgettable highlight was a charming dream sequence in which Caron danced with the life-sized replicas of the puppets who magically materialize in the road. 'Hi Lili, Hi Lo' won the Academy Award as the best song of the year.

Small Town Girl (1953) was a musical remake of *Small Town Girl* (1936), which had starred Janet Gaynor and Robert Taylor. This time around the actors were Jane Powell, Farley Granger, Ann Miller and Bobby Van. There were plenty of songs and dances in the film about a small town (Duck Creek, Connecticut) and the change it goes through after a young and handsome millionaire playboy (Granger) happens to get arrested for speeding through the village.

Rose Marie came back in another incarnation in 1954. This time it starred Ann Blyth and Howard Keel, with Busby Berkeley doing the dance numbers. Bert Lahr stole the show singing 'I'm the Mountie Who Never Got His Man.'

Above: Leslie Caron, Mel Ferrer and his puppets in *Lili* (1953).

'I've Got to Hear That Beat' danced by Ann Miller in *Small Town Girl* (1953). The dance was directed by Busby Berkeley.

Johnny Ray, Mitzi Gaynor, Dan Dailey, Ethel Merman, Donald O'Connor, Marilyn Monroe in . . . *Show Business* (1954).

There's No Business Like Show Business (1954) was just what the title might indicate—an overproduced show-biz musical. It was the story of a trouping family and their plights on and off stage—Dan Dailey and Ethel Merman were the parents. Also in the cast were Marilyn Monroe, Donald O'Connor, Mitzi Gaynor and Johnny Ray. The terrible plot was worth suffering through for the Irving Berlin songs like 'Remember,' 'Heat Wave,' 'Play a Simple Melody' and 'There's No Business Like Show Business' belted out by Ethel Merman.

The big hit for its year was *Seven Brides for Seven Brothers* (1954), based on the Stephen Vincent Benét *Sobbin' Women*, which, in turn, was based on the story of the rape of the Sabine women. It was the saga of six fur-trapping brothers who came to town to find wives after their eldest brother (Howard Keel) married Jane Powell. It included a kidnapping and many musical numbers before the happy conclusion. The sprightly dancing was choreographed by Michael Kidd. Gene de Paul and Johnny Mercer contributed 'When You're in Love,' 'Wonderful Day,' 'Bless Yore Beautiful Hide,' 'Spring' and 'Lonesome Polecat.' It worked in every department and actually created a new style of film musicals.

Meet Me in Las Vegas (1956) had a tiny little plot about a gambling rancher (Dan Dailey) and a dancer (Cyd Charisse) who brings him luck. The important thing was the dancing, especially a 'Frankie and Johnny' ballet with Cyd, Liliane Montevecchi and John Brasccia, with off-screen singing by Sammy Davis Jr. Also making appearances were Lena Horne, Frankie Lane and Jerry Colonna.

This era of musical films ended with *Gigi* (1958), and there are those who feel this was the most delightful movie ever made. Certainly Lerner and Loewe's sumptuous original music for the screen was a complete delight. Louis Jourdan was the epitome of the French man-about-town who suddenly realizes that that little girl Gigi

Powell and the six unmarried brothers in *Seven Brides for Seven Brothers* (1954).

Howard Keel and Jane Powell in *Seven Brides for Seven Brothers* (1954).

(Leslie Caron) has grown up to be a lovely young lady. Maurice Chevalier and Hermione Gingold were perfect as the older man and woman, especially when they sang 'I Remember It Well.' Other show-stoppers were 'I'm Glad I'm Not Young Any More,' 'Thank Heaven for Little Girls,' 'The Night They Invented Champagne' and 'Gigi.' The film won nine Academy Awards, including best direction to Vincente Minnelli, best score to Alan Jay Lerner and Frederick Loewe and best costumes to Cecil Beaton.

But hold on a moment. Arthur Freed, the producer, may have handed a blank check to the team of Lerner-Loewe-Beaton. Lerner and Loewe had written the book, lyrics and music for *My Fair Lady*, which was, at the time, in its third year on Broadway. Cecil Beaton happened to be the person who designed the *My Fair Lady* costumes, a task that he also performed for this movie. Instead of a flower-selling Eliza Doolittle, in this film we had a bright little teenage tomboy living in Paris at the century's turn. Sound familiar? She is also resistant to the notion that she should learn all the graces and qualities of a lady so as to become a lady. Eventually a butterfly bursts from the cocoon. Finally the hero sings a song called 'Gigi,' which lets it be known that he's grown accustomed to her face. It was suggested that Lerner and Loewe might have wanted to sue themselves.

But *Gigi* was a charming entertainment that could stand on its own two legs. Leslie Caron was a vision of youthful rapture and Louis Jourdan was suave as the hero who holds out against her blossoming charms. Chevalier was wonderful as the mellowed boulevardier.

There will never again be a period of musical abundance like the late 1940s and 1950s. Hollywood has never been quite so totally Hollywood since.

Louis Jourdan, Leslie Caron, Maurice Chevalier in *Gigi* (1959).

Bob Fosse, Janet Leigh, Betty Garrett, Tommy Rall in a fast and furious dance routine in *My Sister Eileen* (1955).

The New Moon (1930), based on the Sigmund Romberg operetta of 1928, long preceded the MacDonald-Eddy version of 1940. Cole Porter's Broadway hit of 1929, *Fifty Million Frenchmen*, was filmed in 1931, but without the music.

Maurice Chevalier's sixth film, *The Smiling Lieutenant* (1931), was actually based on a 1907 operetta, *Waltz Dream*.

Girl Crazy, George Gershwin's 1930 Broadway musical, was first filmed in 1932, then remade in 1943 with Mickey Rooney and Judy Garland. The next incarnation for the show was called *When the Boys Meet the Girls* (1965), with Connie Francis, Harve Presnell, Herman's Hermits, Louis Armstrong and Sue Ane Langdon. It had been turned into a dull guest-star showcase.

Cole Porter's 1932 musical *The Gay Divorce* became *The Gay Divorcee* (1934). Gloria Swanson and John Boles starred in *Music in the Air* (1934), which was based on the 1932 stage musical by Jerome Kern and Oscar Hammerstein II. Jerome Kern's *Roberta* of 1933 was first filmed in 1934 and then in 1952 under a new title, *Lovely to Look At*. Al Jolson, Dolores Del Rio and Dick Powell made *Wonder Bar* (1934), which had been a 1930 stage hit.

Naughty Marietta, Victor Herbert's operetta of 1910, was filmed in 1935 with Jeanette MacDonald and Nelson Eddy. The team came back in Herbert's *Rose Marie*, which had opened on Broadway in 1924. It was remade in 1954 with Ann Blyth and Howard Keel. *The Firefly* (1937) was a remake of Rudolf Friml's 1912 operetta and starred Jeanette MacDonald and Allan Jones. MacDonald also appeared in *Maytime* (1937) with Nelson Eddy—an operetta which had first been seen on stage in 1917.

Sally, Irene and Mary (1938) had first appeared on Broadway in 1922 and was a story of three stage-struck girls trying to break into show business. The film starred Alice Faye, Tony Martin, Fred Allen, Jimmy Durante and Louise Hovick (the former strip-tease star Gypsy Rose Lee). It had a couple of good songs—'I Could Use a Dream' and 'This Is Where I Came In.'

MacRae and Grayson in *The Desert Song* (1953).

The MacDonald-Eddy collaboration in *Sweethearts* (1938) was a revival of the 1913 Victor Herbert operetta. The Rooney-Garland team-up in *Babes in Arms* (1939) had a few of the Rodgers and Hart songs from their 1937 stage hit.

So taking stage musicals and making them into musical films was nothing new. What was new was the fact that the adaptations became at some point the principal staple offered in Hollywood musicals, and this trend has continued to the present.

Perhaps it started with *The Boys from Syracuse* (1940), which had been so popular on Broadway in 1938. It was a Richard Rodgers-Lorenz Hart musical, loosely based on Shakespeare's *A Comedy of Errors*, but it had a story line that Will might not have recognized. Set in Ancient Greece, it featured such songs as 'This Can't Be Love' and 'Falling in Love with Love.' It starred Allan Jones, Joe Penner, Martha Raye and Rosemary Lane.

Irene (1940) was a bit of an oddity. It was based on a 1919 stage musical,

Ava Gardner as the mulatto, Julie, in *Show Boat* (1951). Her vocals were dubbed by Eileen Wilson.

and had been filmed as a silent with Colleen Moore. This time around, it starred Anna Neagle, Ray Milland, Roland Young, Billie Burke and Arthur Treacher—none of them renowned for their musical abilities. So they took out most of the songs in this tale of a wealthy playboy (Milland) romancing a working girl (Neagle). Finally, although most of the picture was in black and white, the producers turned on the Technicolor for the 'Alice Blue Gown' number.

George M Cohan's music was featured in *Little Nellie Kelly* (1940), based on his Broadway hit of 1922. It was a lightweight musical starring Judy Garland, George Murphy (before he became a United States

Lamas and Turner in *The Merry Widow* (1952).

George Murphy, Judy Garland, Douglas McPhail in *Little Nellie Kelly* (1940).

John Carroll, Eleanor Powell, Ann Sothern, Robert Young, Virginia O'Brien, Red Skelton in *Lady Be Good* (1941).

Senator) and Charles Winninger, about how Nellie (Garland) patches up a long-standing feud between her tough New York cop father (Murphy) and her grandfather (Winninger). Judy was at her best singing 'It's a Great Day for the Irish' and a non-Cohan song that has appeared so many times in film musicals—'Singin' in the Rain.'

No, No, Nanette first appeared on Broadway in 1925 and was revived in the 1970s. It was first made into a film in 1930, then in 1940 and again in 1950 as *Tea for Two.* The last version starred Doris Day, Gordon MacRae and Eve Arden. Of course the hit song was 'Tea for Two.'

Judy Garland and Mickey Rooney's *Strike Up the Band* (1940) was a remake of Gershwin's stage musical of 1930.

The Rodgers and Hart success of 1939, *Too Many Girls,* was turned into a film in 1940 with Lucille Ball, Richard Carlson, Eddie Bracken, Ann Miller, Desi Arnaz and Francis Langford. It was a tale of a small college—Pottawatomie College at Stopgap, New Mexico—with ten girls to every man, and how everybody wanted a good football team. One sidelight—a very young Van Johnson was one of the chorus boys.

George Gershwin's *Lady Be Good* premiered on Broadway in 1924 and was remade by Hollywood in 1941. With Eleanor Powell, Robert Young, Ann Sothern, Lionel Barrymore and Red Skelton, it was the story of mar-

Above: Red Skelton and Lucille Ball frolic as Louis XV and Madame Du Barry in *Du Barry Was a Lady* (1943).

Ben Blue, Red Skelton, Ann Sothern and 'Rags' Ragland in *Panama Hattie* (1942).

ried songwriters (Young and Sothern). In addition to the title song, it featured 'Fascinatin' Rhythm,' 'You'll Never Know' and 'The Last Time I Saw Paris.'

Louisiana Purchase was a 1940 stage hit with music by Irving Berlin. When the film came out in 1941 it starred Bob Hope, Vera Zorina, Victor Moore and Irene Bordoni. It was a story about hanky-panky in Congress, and Hope had a filibuster scene that was a riot. Unfortunately, all but three songs were pared from the original, and one of them was an opening scene in which a group of chorus girls sang the lines about the characters in the film being fictitious. One critic pointed out that this was probably a movie first—and last.

Along came *Panama Hattie* (1942), the film version of the stage musical of 1940, with most of Cole Porter's music removed. The story of a night-club owner, Hattie, in Panama, and a plot to blow up the canal, it starred Ann Sothern, Red Skelton, 'Rags' Ragland, Lena Horne and Dan Dailey. Although it was a hit on the stage, it was a miss in films. The problem was that the play had been written for Ethel Merman, who had starred in it. Ann Sothern just couldn't handle the job, and was also overwhelmed by the talents of Skelton, Dailey and Horne (in her film debut). About the only memorable song left in the picture was 'Let's Be Buddies.'

One of the best stage musicals of 1941 was *Best Foot Forward*, and it was turned into one of the most entertaining film musicals of 1943. Lucille Ball starred as a fading movie queen who, as a publicity stunt, accepts an invitation to a small-town school's prom. No one was more surprised when she showed up than the boy who asked her. Who could forget a character who had won the title of 'Miss Delaware Watergap,' or the rousing song 'Buckle Down, Winsocki?'

Du Barry Was a Lady (1943) was adapted from the Cole Porter Broadway musical and featured Lucille Ball in the title role opposite Red Skelton's delightfully ridiculous Louis XV of France. The 1939 Broadway show had starred Ethel Merman and Bert Lahr. Unfortunately, most of the Porter score was missing, but the highlight was 'Friendship.' Skelton played the part of a bartender who had been slipped a Mickey Finn and imagined himself cavorting with the famous Madame Du Barry. Other featured songs were 'Do I Love You, Do I?' and 'Katie Went to Haiti.' One of the inside jokes in the film was an uncredited appearance by Lana Turner. The movie was all Lucille Ball's—that woman who had once been dismissed from a drama school for being 'too shy and reticent.'

One of the strangest plots in musical history was to be found in *Higher and Higher* (1943), the remake of the stage musical of 1940. Leon Errol played the part of a once-wealthy man, unable to pay his bills, who forms a corporation with his servants. Also in the cast were Frank Sinatra, Mel Torme, Michele Morgan, Jack Haley and Victor Borge. Sinatra's songs stood out—'The Music Stopped' and 'I Couldn't Sleep a Wink Last Night.'

Knickerbocker Holiday (1944) was a disappointing film version of the Kurt Weill-Maxwell Anderson Broadway musical of 1938 about Peter Stuyvesant, the governor of New Amsterdam, and of how love makes a fool of him. The problem was that Nelson Eddy still couldn't act very well, and Charles Coburn as Stuyvesant was no competition for Walter Huston, who had played the role on the stage. Still, the music, including the famous 'September Song,' was great.

Kurt Weill fared better with another of his musicals, *Lady in the Dark* (1944), based on his musical play of 1941. With its book by Moss Hart, it made a wonderful musical. It was about a successful magazine editor (Ginger Rogers) who was psychologically going to pieces because she was torn between her work and three different men. The dream sequences were quite good, but many of the best songs were cut. The film also marked the beginning of Hollywood's interest in psychiatry.

Allyson and Lawford in *Good News* (1947).

Something for the Boys had been a minor hit on Broadway in 1943, and reached the screen in 1944, starring Vivian Blaine, Phil Silvers and Carmen Miranda. It had a slick Cole Porter score and concerned a Southern plantation that had been recruited as a home for soldiers' wives. One of the highlights was the singing of a young newcomer, Perry Como, especially in 'I Wish I Didn't Have to Say Goodnight.'

A Golden Oldie came from Hollywood in 1947. It was *Good News*, the Broadway show of 1927 that had previously been filmed in 1930. The plot was flimsy—an average 1920s college campus musical with last-minute touchdowns and complicated subplots. But June Allyson, Peter Lawford, Joan McCracken and Mel Torme did justice to all the singing and dancing. The score contained

Ginger Rogers in the circus dream sequence from *Lady in the Dark* (1944).

Donald O'Connor, Vera-Ellen, Ethel Merman, George Sanders, Billy DeWolfe in *Call Me Madam* (1943).

such songs as 'Good News,' 'The Varsity Drag,' 'The French Lesson' and 'Just Imagine' from the original DeSylva-Brown-Henderson production.

Are You With It? (1948) was a rather pleasant musical based on the 1945 stage show, but somehow most people have forgotten it. The plot was about a mathematics whiz (Donald O'Connor) who left his job and joined a carnival. Also starring was Olga San Juan.

Another Kurt Weill musical of 1943 was made into a film—*One Touch of Venus* (1948). It starred Ava Gardner, Robert Walker and Dick Haymes, and was about a Roman statue of Venus that came to life in a department store, causing romance and misunderstandings. Some of the original songs were removed, but there was still the lovely ballad 'Speak Low.'

Up in Central Park (1948) was an old-fashioned musical even when it was on stage in 1945. It was the story of an Irish colleen and a reporter in turn-of-the-century New York City and their efforts to expose 'Boss' Tweed—the head of Tammany Hall. Deanna Durbin and Dick Haymes were helped by the songs, such as 'Carousel in the Park' and 'When You Walk in the Room.'

Red Hot and Blue (1949) was a remake of the stage success of 1936, and starred Betty Hutton, Victor Mature and June Havoc. Hutton played a girl anxious to make it big on the stage who is helped by a director and a publicist but runs afoul of gangsters. It was mainly a showcase for Hutton's brassy talents.

The dam burst in 1950. Scores of Broadway shows have been translated into films from that year to the present. They engendered new dance concepts, entwined story line with music with increased effectiveness, and have provided splendid screen vehicles for both new and long-established performers—Doris Day, Liza Minnelli, Joel Gray, Julie Andrews, Yul Brynner, Zero Mostel, Fred Astaire, Robert Preston, Barbra Streisand, Howard Keel, Cyd Charisse, Robert Morse, Ben Vereen and Gwen Verdon, to name but a few.

The first of the new invasion was *Annie Get Your Gun* (1950), based on the 1946 Irving Berlin musical about the nineteenth-century sharpshooter Annie Oakley, and her romance with a male sharpshooter, Frank Butler. Betty Hutton was Annie, Howard Keel was Frank and Louis Calhern was Buffalo Bill. On the stage, Annie had been played by Ethel Merman, that brassy, vibrant and much-loved musical star. On the screen, the role was first scheduled for Judy Garland with Busby Berkeley directing. Garland, however, had a complete breakdown, mentally and physically, and Hutton was picked for the role. But the studio had to wait for her to finish another picture, and Berkeley didn't have the time in his schedule, so he was replaced by Charles Walters. Buffalo Bill was to have been played by Frank Morgan, but he died and was replaced by Calhern. Needless to say, many scenes had to be reshot and the

Opposite: Howard Keel and Betty Hutton in *Annie Get Your Gun* (1950).

production schedule was a mess. Out of all this came a picture that some critics claimed was better than the Broadway show. It had 11 Irving Berlin songs, including 'You Can't Get a Man with a Gun,' 'Anything You Can Do,' 'Doin' What Comes Naturally' and 'There's No Business Like Show Business.'

In *Where's Charley?* (1952) Ray Bolger re-created his 1948 stage role in the musical based on Brandon Thomas' 1896 farce *Charley's Aunt.* The words and music were by Frank Loesser, and Bolger was great, especially in 'Once In Love With Amy.'

Merman got to bring one of her Broadway roles to the screen in 1953. She had starred on stage in 1950 in *Call Me Madam*, in which she played a free-wheeling Washington 'hostess with the mostest,' a role obviously patterned after Perle Mesta. With her were Donald O'Connor, George Sanders and Vera-Ellen, whose singing voice was dubbed by Carole Richards. The Irving Berlin songs included 'You're Just in Love' and 'The Hostess with the Mostest.'

Cole Porter's delightful 1948 musical with its play-within-a-play plot, *Kiss Me Kate*, came to the screen in 1953 and starred Kathryn Grayson, Howard Keel, Ann Miller, Bobby Van and Keenan Wynn. Since the story revolved around the lives of actors who were rehearsing a production of Shakespeare's *The Taming of the Shrew*, Porter had to write a score with both modern and Elizabethan rhythms. He was brilliant, and some of the 14 songs have become classics—'Too Darn Hot,' 'Why Can't You Behave?' 'So in Love,' 'Wunderbar' and 'Always True to You in My Fashion.' But purists might quibble about some of the changes that were made from the original play. For some reason, a previous Porter hit, 'From This Moment On,' was stuck in as a ballet and tap dance specialty number. The wonderful song 'I Am Ashamed that Women Are So Simple' was spoken by Grayson, rather than sung. The camera concentrated on a backstage discussion while Grayson was on stage singing the clever 'I Hate Men,' and most of the lyrics were lost. The film, oddly enough, was produced in both 3-D and flat versions, but by the time of its release, the 3-D fad was over, so only the flat version was seen in theaters.

Gentlemen Prefer Blondes (1953) was an adaptation of the Broadway musical that had been based on the Anita Loos book of the same name and that had premiered on Broadway in 1949. Marilyn Monroe played the part originated by Carol Channing on the stage—that of Lorelei Lee. Jane Russell was the other girl, and both of them were on the prowl for husbands while enroute to Paris in the 1920s. The best remembered song was 'Diamonds Are a Girl's Best Friend.'

The Band Wagon (1953), previously mentioned, was taken from the 1931 stage show. It had a wealth of great songs from the 1930s; among them were 'Triplets,' 'Louisiana Hayride,' 'I Guess I'll Have to Change My Plans,' 'Dancing in the Dark' (performed by Fred Astaire and Cyd Charisse), 'A Shine on Your Shoes,' 'By Myself,' 'Something to Remember You By,' 'I Love Louisa,' 'You and the Night and the Music' and 'That's Entertainment.' The highlight of the film was a 12-minute 'private eye' ballet danced by Fred and Cyd—'The Girl Hunt.'

Brigadoon (1954) was the screen adaptation of the Lerner and Loewe Broadway musical of 1947. It starred Gene Kelly, Cyd Charisse (whose voice was dubbed by Carole Richards, who had done the same thing for Vera-Ellen in *Call Me Madam*) and Van Johnson, and was about two American men stumbling on the Scottish village of Brigadoon—a village that comes to life for one day every hundred years. The dancing and the singing were splendid. Some of the

Marilyn Monroe and Jane Russell in *Gentlemen Prefer Blondes* (1953).

Kathryn Grayson (second from left) meets Ann Miller as Howard Keel (center) looks on—*Kiss Me Kate* (1953).

Donald O'Connor, Vera-Ellen, Ethel Merman, George Sanders, Billy DeWolfe in *Call Me Madam* (1943).

such songs as 'Good News,' 'The Varsity Drag,' 'The French Lesson' and 'Just Imagine' from the original DeSylva-Brown-Henderson production.

Are You With It? (1948) was a rather pleasant musical based on the 1945 stage show, but somehow most people have forgotten it. The plot was about a mathematics whiz (Donald O'Connor) who left his job and joined a carnival. Also starring was Olga San Juan.

Another Kurt Weill musical of 1943 was made into a film—*One Touch of Venus* (1948). It starred Ava Gardner, Robert Walker and Dick Haymes, and was about a Roman statue of Venus that came to life in a department store, causing romance and misunderstandings. Some of the original songs were removed, but there was still the lovely ballad 'Speak Low.'

Up in Central Park (1948) was an old-fashioned musical even when it was on stage in 1945. It was the story of an Irish colleen and a reporter in turn-of-the-century New York City and their efforts to expose 'Boss' Tweed—the head of Tammany Hall. Deanna Durbin and Dick Haymes were helped by the songs, such as 'Carousel in the Park' and 'When You Walk in the Room.'

Red Hot and Blue (1949) was a remake of the stage success of 1936, and starred Betty Hutton, Victor Mature and June Havoc. Hutton played a girl anxious to make it big on the stage who is helped by a director and a publicist but runs afoul of gangsters. It was mainly a showcase for Hutton's brassy talents.

The dam burst in 1950. Scores of Broadway shows have been translated into films from that year to the present. They engendered new dance concepts, entwined story line with music with increased effectiveness, and have provided splendid screen vehicles for both new and long-established performers—Doris Day, Liza Minnelli, Joel Gray, Julie Andrews, Yul Brynner, Zero Mostel, Fred Astaire, Robert Preston, Barbra Streisand, Howard Keel, Cyd Charisse, Robert Morse, Ben Vereen and Gwen Verdon, to name but a few.

The first of the new invasion was *Annie Get Your Gun* (1950), based on the 1946 Irving Berlin musical about the nineteenth-century sharpshooter Annie Oakley, and her romance with a male sharpshooter, Frank Butler. Betty Hutton was Annie, Howard Keel was Frank and Louis Calhern was Buffalo Bill. On the stage, Annie had been played by Ethel Merman, that brassy, vibrant and much-loved musical star. On the screen, the role was first scheduled for Judy Garland with Busby Berkeley directing. Garland, however, had a complete breakdown, mentally and physically, and Hutton was picked for the role. But the studio had to wait for her to finish another picture, and Berkeley didn't have the time in his schedule, so he was replaced by Charles Walters. Buffalo Bill was to have been played by Frank Morgan, but he died and was replaced by Calhern. Needless to say, many scenes had to be reshot and the

Opposite: Howard Keel and Betty Hutton in *Annie Get Your Gun* (1950).

production schedule was a mess. Out of all this came a picture that some critics claimed was better than the Broadway show. It had 11 Irving Berlin songs, including 'You Can't Get a Man with a Gun,' 'Anything You Can Do,' 'Doin' What Comes Naturally' and 'There's No Business Like Show Business.'

In *Where's Charley?* (1952) Ray Bolger re-created his 1948 stage role in the musical based on Brandon Thomas' 1896 farce *Charley's Aunt*. The words and music were by Frank Loesser, and Bolger was great, especially in 'Once In Love With Amy.'

Merman got to bring one of her Broadway roles to the screen in 1953. She had starred on stage in 1950 in *Call Me Madam*, in which she played a free-wheeling Washington 'hostess with the mostest,' a role obviously patterned after Perle Mesta. With her were Donald O'Connor, George Sanders and Vera-Ellen, whose singing voice was dubbed by Carole Richards. The Irving Berlin songs included 'You're Just in Love' and 'The Hostess with the Mostest.'

Cole Porter's delightful 1948 musical with its play-within-a-play plot, *Kiss Me Kate*, came to the screen in 1953 and starred Kathryn Grayson, Howard Keel, Ann Miller, Bobby Van and Keenan Wynn. Since the story revolved around the lives of actors who were rehearsing a production of Shakespeare's *The Taming of the Shrew*, Porter had to write a score with both modern and Elizabethan rhythms. He was brilliant, and some of the 14 songs have become classics—'Too Darn Hot,' 'Why Can't You Behave?' 'So in Love,' 'Wunderbar' and 'Always True to You in My Fashion.' But purists might quibble about some of the changes that were made from the original play. For some reason, a previous Porter hit, 'From This Moment On,' was stuck in as a ballet and tap dance specialty number. The wonderful song 'I Am Ashamed that Women Are So Simple' was spoken by Grayson, rather than sung. The camera concentrated on a backstage discussion while Grayson was on stage singing the clever 'I Hate Men,' and most of the lyrics were lost. The film, oddly enough, was produced in both 3-D and flat versions, but by the time of its release, the 3-D fad was over, so only the flat version was seen in theaters.

Gentlemen Prefer Blondes (1953) was an adaptation of the Broadway musical that had been based on the Anita Loos book of the same name and that had premiered on Broadway in 1949. Marilyn Monroe played the part originated by Carol Channing on the stage—that of Lorelei Lee. Jane Russell was the other girl, and both of them were on the prowl for husbands while enroute to Paris in the 1920s. The best remembered song was 'Diamonds Are a Girl's Best Friend.'

The Band Wagon (1953), previously mentioned, was taken from the 1931 stage show. It had a wealth of great songs from the 1930s; among them were 'Triplets,' 'Louisiana Hayride,' 'I Guess I'll Have to Change My Plans,' 'Dancing in the Dark' (performed by Fred Astaire and Cyd Charisse), 'A Shine on Your Shoes,' 'By Myself,' 'Something to Remember You By,' 'I Love Louisa,' 'You and the Night and the Music' and 'That's Entertainment.' The highlight of the film was a 12-minute 'private eye' ballet danced by Fred and Cyd—'The Girl Hunt.'

Brigadoon (1954) was the screen adaptation of the Lerner and Loewe Broadway musical of 1947. It starred Gene Kelly, Cyd Charisse (whose voice was dubbed by Carole Richards, who had done the same thing for Vera-Ellen in *Call Me Madam*) and Van Johnson, and was about two American men stumbling on the Scottish village of Brigadoon—a village that comes to life for one day every hundred years. The dancing and the singing were splendid. Some of the

Marilyn Monroe and Jane Russell in *Gentlemen Prefer Blondes* (1953).

Kathryn Grayson (second from left) meets Ann Miller as Howard Keel (center) looks on—*Kiss Me Kate* (1953).

Joe has just killed Carmen Jones (Harry Belafonte and Dorothy Dandridge) in *Carmen Jones* (1954).

songs were 'Brigadoon' and 'The Heather on the Hill.'

Carmen Jones (1954) was a screen version of a quite unusual stage musical of 1943. To begin with, *Carmen*, the highly romantic tale by the French novelist Prosper Mérimée, was turned into an opera by Georges Bizet. The opera probably holds the record for the number of films it has spawned—14. Then Oscar Hammerstein II wrote new lyrics to the arias, switched the locale from Spain to the American South during World War II and used a black cast. The result was *Carmen Jones*, which starred Harry Belafonte, Dorothy Dandridge (whose voices were dubbed by Marilyn Horne and La Verne Hutcherson) and Pearl Bailey. An example of the clever job done by Hammerstein was the changing of the toreador, Escamillo, to the prize fighter, Husky Miller; the 'Toreador Song' becomes 'Stand Up and Fight.' Unfortunately, the film contains one of the classic boo-boos.

Opposite: Gene Kelly declares his love for Cyd Charisse in *Brigadoon* (1954).

Gene Kelly and Van Johnson in their soft-shoe dance routine from *Brigadoon* (1954).

The camera tracks with Dorothy Dandridge down a shopping street and the entire crew is seen reflected in the windows that she passes.

Sigmund Romberg's old war horse *The Student Prince*, which first appeared in theaters in 1924, was made into a film in 1954, starring Ann Blyth, Edmund Purdom and Louis Calhern. It was a story of the heir to a European throne who is sent to the University of Heidelberg for one last fling, where he falls in love with barmaid Blyth. Mario Lanza had been scheduled to play the role of the prince: his temper tantrums caused him to be fired, but not until after he had recorded the songs. The result was that Edmund Purdom stepped in and mouthed the lyrics that Lanza had taped. The songs were still thrilling—'Deep in My Heart,' 'Golden Days,' 'The Drinking Song' and 'Serenade.'

Above: Joe loves Carmen. Harry Belafonte and Dorothy Dandridge in *Carmen Jones* (1954).

Guys and Dolls (1955) had first

The 'Luck Be a Lady' crap game from *Guys and Dolls* (1955). Brando in the foreground; Sinatra to his left in background.

appeared on Broadway in 1950. This Frank Loesser musical was based on the characters created by Damon Runyon and was set in the Broadway milieu of gamblers and their girl friends. It starred Marlon Brando as Sky Masterson, Jean Simmons as a Salvation Army lassie, Frank Sinatra as Nathan Detroit, Vivian Blaine as Adelaide, plus Stubby Kaye and Sheldon Leonard. MGM had wanted Gene Kelly for the lead, but despite widespread criticism of Brando, and especially of his voice, this musical comedy was most enjoyable because of its all-star list of songs, such as 'If I Were a Bell,' 'Luck, Be a Lady,' 'Take Back Your Mink,' 'Guys and

Dolls' and 'Sit Down, You're Rocking the Boat.' Loesser even added a beautiful number that had not been in the stage version—'A Woman in Love.'

The granddaddy of all the sailors-on-leave stage musicals—*Hit the Deck*—was remade in 1955. It had been a hit on Broadway in 1927 and was filmed by RKO in 1930. In 1936 it was redone as *Follow the Fleet* with Astaire and Rogers and Irving Berlin songs. This time, Metro-Goldwyn-Mayer gave it an all-star cast, including Jane Powell, Tony Martin, Debbie Reynolds, Walter Pidgeon, Vic Damone and Ann Miller. The songs by Vincent Youmans included 'Hallelujah,' 'Sometimes I'm Happy' and 'Why, Oh Why?,' which had been in the original show, and 'Keeping Myself for You,' which had been in the original film, plus others.

Kismet (1955) had been on the stage in 1953, and was an oddity of a kind. It was based on a rather stolid Arabian Nights play by Edward Knoblock, which nevertheless had been a long-running non-musical play starring Otis Skinner. Lyrics by Robert Wright and George Forrest were set to the music of the Russian classical composer Alexander Borodin. The story concerned a wise beggar (Howard Keel) and his beautiful daughter (Ann Blyth) in old Baghdad. Dolores Gray and Vic Damone also appeared in the film. It was an opulent picture, and some of the songs were 'And This Is My Beloved,' 'Baubles, Bangles and Beads' and 'Not Since Nineveh.'

One of the most important stage musicals of all time, *Oklahoma!*, which premiered on Broadway in 1943, became a film in 1955. It had the audacity to begin with a song ('Oh, What a Beautiful Morning') rather then dialogue, to have someone (Judd Frye) die in a musical comedy, and to use ballet (choreographed by Agnes DeMille) instead of a chorus line. The film starred Gordon MacRae as Curly, the cowboy; Shirley Jones as Laurey, the farm girl; Gloria Grahame as Ado Annie. The splendid Rodgers and Hammerstein score was preserved intact, and included 'People Will Say We're in Love,' 'Everything's Up to Date in Kansas City,' 'I Cain't Say No' and the title song, which was adopted by the state of Oklahoma as its state song.

Another Rodgers and Hammerstein smash stage hit appeared on screen in 1956—*Carousel*, which had premiered on stage in 1945. Based on Ferenc Molnar's play *Liliom*, it told the story

Howard Keel, Dolores Gray, Ann Blyth, Vic Damone in *Kismet* (1955).

Gordon MacRae as Curley in *Oklahoma!* (1955). 'The corn is as high as an elephant's eye.'

Shirley Jones and Gordon MacRae in 'The Surrey with the Fringe on Top' in *Oklahoma!* (1955).

The shy lovers in *Oklahoma!* (1955).

of a rowdy carousel barker, Billy Bigelow (Gordon MacRae), who tries to change for the better when he falls in love with Julie, a mill girl (Shirley Jones). In stealing money to try to provide for their child, he is killed, but is permitted to return from heaven to earth for a time to do one good deed. There wasn't a dry eye in the house. The memorable songs included 'You'll Never Walk Alone,' 'June Is Bustin' Out All Over,' 'Soliloquy,' and 'If I Loved You.'

Rodgers and Hammerstein were all over the place in those days. *The King and I* (1956) was an adaptation of their 1951 Broadway smash. It had been taken from a film, *Anna and the King of Siam* (1946), a non-musical with Rex Harrison and Irene Dunne, which had been based on a book of the same title by Margaret Landon. In the film, Yul Brynner played the king who had imported the English widow, Anna Leonowens, played by Deborah Kerr using Marni Nixon's voice, to teach his many children. It was the pictorial magnificence of the appropriately regal production that distinguished the film. Also, many of the songs have become classics—'I Whistle a Happy Tune,' 'Hello, Young Lovers,' 'We Kiss in a Shadow,' 'Getting to Know You,' 'Shall We Dance' and 'Something Wonderful.' The children's ballet, 'The Little Hut of Uncle Thomas,'

The male dancers in the 'June Is Bustin' Out All Over' ballet in *Carousel* (1956).

Julie (Shirley Jones) rides Billy Bigelow's (Gordon MacRae) merry-go-round in *Carousel* (1956).

Anna Leonowens (Deborah Kerr) is not too pleased with the King (Yul Brynner) in *The King and I* (1956).

was unforgettable. One thing to notice —when Brynner sings 'It's a Puzzlement,' he is wearing an earring in some shots and not in others.

The Vagabond King (1956) was a stale remake of the picture of the same name, released in 1930, which was a remake of the Rudolf Friml 1925 operetta about the fifteenth-century French poet François Villon. It starred Kathryn Grayson, Oreste and Rita Moreno.

Above: John Raitt and Doris Day starred in *The Pajama Game* (1957).

The Pajama Game (1957) was a wholly cinematic and successful version of the stage musical of 1954, with the unlikely subject of labor unrest in a pajama factory in Iowa. All the fun, songs, dances and laughs of the hit Broadway musical were brought to the screen with the added attraction of Bob Fosse's choreography. The key to its success, however, was in the choice of the stars—two pros who had come up the hard way—John Raitt as the foreman of the factory and Doris Day as the head of the union's grievance committee.

Cyd Charisse, Fred Astaire, Joseph Buloff, Jules Munshin, Peter Lorre in *Silk Stockings* (1957).

Raitt had been around since the late 1930s, even appearing in blackface as a minstrel in a cheap Hollywood film. He graduated to playing Curly in the Chicago production of *Oklahoma!*, later moving to Broadway to play the role. He so impressed Rodgers and Hammerstein that when they cast *Carousel*, he was given the leading role as Billy Bigelow. Doris Day, born Doris Kappelhoff, wanted to be a dancer, but at age 15 she broke her leg and turned to singing instead. She started singing on Cincinnati radio stations in the early 1940s and became the lead singer for several big bands like Bob Crosby's and Les Brown's (what World War II GI could forget her 'Sentimental Journey' with Brown?). After testing for Warner Brothers, she finally got a dramatic role in *Young Man With a Horn* (1950). After *The Pajama Game*, her star rose, and she was one of the top ten box-office draws from 1959 to 1966.

There was an interesting sidelight to *The Pajama Game*. The show, with its fine music—including 'Seven and a Half Cents,' 'Once-a-Year Day' and 'Hey, There,' was based on a not-too-popular book, *Seven and a Half Cents*, by Richard Bissell of the Bissell carpet-sweeper family. He made a bit of money on the book, then on the play, then on the film. Later he and

Kim Novak (left) and Rita Hayworth try to entice Sinatra in *Pal Joey* (1957).

'Shall We Dance?'—*The King and I.*

Gwen Verdon doing 'Whatever Lola Wants' in *Damn Yankees* (1958). Tab Hunter at left.

John Kerr, Mitzi Gaynor and Rossano Brazzi in *South Pacific* (1958).

Abe Burrows came back with another Broadway musical, *Say Darling*, in 1958 that documented in musical-comedy form how they came to write and produce *The Pajama Game*. It wasn't half bad, with the title song and 'Something's Always Happening on the River,' but it never made it to Hollywood.

Pal Joey (1957) was a most unusual musical. It was based on what could best be described as Rodgers and Hart's flop Broadway musical of 1940, which had starred Gene Kelly. The problem was that audiences couldn't relate to a musical comedy about a heel. So Hollywood made him a little more pleasant, a sort of nice guy who wanted to build a night club in San Francisco. Frank Sinatra played the part, and was fought over by Rita Hayworth and Kim Novak. The songs were the thing, however—'Bewitched, Bothered and Bewildered,' 'Small Hotel,' 'My Funny Valentine' and 'The Lady Is a Tramp' among them.

Cole Porter had taken the plot of the old Greta Garbo film *Ninotchka* (1939), in which she played a Russian agent who came to Paris and fell in love, and had written a score for it. The result was *Silk Stockings*, which opened on Broadway in 1955. It was made into a film in 1957 with Cyd Charisse as the agent and Fred Astaire as an American producer.

Damn Yankees, the baseball musical, had opened on the stage in 1955, and the film premiered in 1958. Once again, a baseball movie had to be retitled in Great Britain—it was called *What Lola Wants*. Gwen Verdon, as the sexy Lola, re-created her Broadway role as the temptress sent by the Devil (named Mr Applegate), played by Ray Walston, who was also in the role he had created. One mistake was in casting Tab Hunter as the middle-aged Washington-Senator fan who was turned into a star baseball player in a Faustian agreement. Some of the songs were 'You've Got to Have Heart,' 'Whatever Lola Wants,' 'Two Lost Souls,' 'Those Were the Good Old Days,' 'The Game' and 'Shoeless Joe from Hannibal, Mo.'

South Pacific, another Rodgers and Hammerstein musical, opened on Broadway in 1949 and promptly won the Pulitzer Prize for Drama—the first musical to achieve that honor. This love story about a United States Navy nurse and a suave French planter in the South Pacific during World War II originally starred Ezio

Sinatra and Hayworth in *Pal Joey* (1957).

M28A2
USA
BEER

Mitzi Gaynor, as Nurse Nellie Forbush, admires the handiwork of Ray Walston, as Luther Billis, in *South Pacific* (1958). *Inset:* Nellie entertains the sailors.

Above: Sidney Poitier and Dorothy Dandridge. 'Bess, You Is My Woman Now' from *Porgy and Bess* (1959).

Sammy Davis Jr as Sportin' Life in *Porgy and Bess* (1959), singing 'It Ain't Necessarily So.'

Pinza and Mary Martin on the stage. When the film was released in 1958, the stars were Rossano Brazzi (with Giorgio Tozzi's voice dubbed in) and Mitzi Gaynor. Unfortunately, these two were not good choices for the leads. The story line needed dynamic personalities to make it catch fire, and they weren't there. But the songs were —such songs as 'Bali H'ai,' 'There Is Nothing Like a Dame,' 'Happy Talk,' 'You've Got to Be Taught' and 'Some Enchanted Evening.'

The Broadway musical based on the doings of the famous cartoon characters of Dogpatch, *Li'l Abner*, opened in 1956. When the film came out in 1959, it starred Peter Palmer, who not only filled the bill by his physical resemblance to Li'l Abner, but could also sing; Stubby Kaye was Marryin' Sam. Unfortunately, the delightful Edie Adams had been replaced by Leslie Parrish as Daisy Mae. It was loud and brassy, with corny comedy, and some good songs—'Jubilation T Cornpone,' 'You Can Tell if There's Love in a Home' and 'Namely Me.'

George Gershwin's folk opera *Porgy and Bess*, about the inhabitants of Catfish Row, a black ghetto in the South, and a crippled beggar who falls in love with a beautiful but reckless girl, opened in 1935, but it wasn't until 1959 that the movie came out. It starred Sidney Poitier, Dorothy Dandridge, Sammy Davis Jr and Pearl Bailey. It was a stiff version, staged unimaginatively, but the score was the thing—'Summertime,' 'I Got Plenty o' Nuthin,' 'It Ain't Necessarily So,' 'Bess, You Is My Woman Now' and many more.

Judy Holliday, the talented comedienne whose early death ended a notable career, appeared in *Bells Are Ringing* (1960), taken from the 1956 Broadway show. She had starred in the stage production, and on the screen appeared with Dean Martin in the Jule Styne-Betty Comden-Adolph Green film about an answering-service operator who falls in love with the voice of a young show writer. Some of the songs were 'The Party's Over,' 'Long Before I Knew You,' 'Drop That Name,' 'Just in Time' and 'I'm Going Back to the Bonjour Tristesse Brassiere Factory.'

Can-Can (1960) had political overtones—not in the script, but in real life. While they were filming the musical based on the stage show of 1953, Nikita Khrushchev, then the premier of the USSR, was touring the studio and was shocked at the capitalist decadence of the can-can dance.

Judy Holliday in a moment of jealousy in *Bells Are Ringing* (1960). Dean Martin is the hugger.

Frank Sinatra removing Shirley MacLaine's garter as Maurice Chevalier looks on—*Can-Can* (1960).

So much for history. The picture starred Frank Sinatra, Shirley MacLaine, Maurice Chevalier, Louis Jourdan and Juliet Prowse, and was set in Paris in the 1890s, involving lawyer Sinatra's defense of showgirl MacLaine's right to perform her daring dance in her night club. It was a pretty lackluster film, but it did have a few good Cole Porter songs, including 'C'est Magnifique,' 'I Love Paris,' 'Let's Do It' and 'Just One of Those Things.'

Flower Drum Song (1961) was a remake of the very unusual Rodgers and Hammerstein Broadway show of 1958. It had an almost all-Oriental cast, including Nancy Kwan, James Shigeta, Miyoshi Umeki, Benson Fong and Juanita Hall. The story was about a Chinese picture-bride in San Francisco who falls for another man. It was lavish and colorful, but it just went on too long: the running time was two hours and 13 minutes. Besides that, the score was not all that memorable—the biggest hit was 'I Enjoy Being a Girl.'

Nancy Kwan leads a street dance in *Flower Drum Song* (1961).

The long-awaited *West Side Story* (1961) was a gem based on the 1957 musical about rival white and Puerto Rican gangs in a New York City ghetto. Jerome Robbins' brilliant choreography in this modern *Romeo and Juliet* story was enhanced by the magnificent New York City location photography. The book by Arthur Laurents, the music by Leonard Bernstein and the lyrics by Stephen Sondheim were magnificent. It starred Richard Beymer (whose voice was dubbed by Jim Bryant), George Chakiris (who was a former dancer himself), Rita Moreno (voice courtesy of Betty Wand, who had been Leslie Caron's voice in *Gigi* in 1958) and Natalie Wood (voice dubbed by Marni Nixon). The film hauled in the Academy Awards. It was selected best picture of the year. Robert Wise, the director, and Robbins got Oscars, as did Boris Leven (art direction), Chakiris (best supporting actor) and Moreno (best supporting actress).

The critics went wild. *The New York Times* reported, 'What they have done with *West Side Story* in knocking it down and moving it from stage to screen is to reconstruct its fine material into nothing short of a cinema masterpiece.' They raved about the songs, among them 'Tonight,' 'Maria,' 'Something's Coming,' 'There's a Place for Us' and 'America.' But what seemed to surprise critics most was Natalie Wood. They had known her as a child star, as in her sickly-sweet role in *Miracle on 34th Street* (1947). They knew her as a teenager in such films as *Rebel Without a Cause* (1955). But here she was in a musical, doing a wonderful job with real dancing and artificial singing, full of luster and charm.

Needless to say, Hollywood immediately brought her back in another musical. It was *Gypsy* (1962), from the 1959 Broadway musical play. She starred as Gypsy Rose Lee, the intellectual stripper, in this adaptation from Lee's autobiography. It was the story of the stage mother of all time, Rose Hovick, the mother of Gypsy (Louise) and June Havoc, who also went on to acting fame. Unfortunately, Rosalind Russell (voice dubbed by Lisa Kirk) did not have the same kind of pizzazz as did the Broadway Rose, Ethel Merman. And Karl Malden, as her patient suitor, was no Jack Klugman, who had the part on stage. But Natalie turned in a fine performance, as did the Jule Styne-Stephen Sondheim songs such as 'Everything's Coming Up Roses,' 'Small World,' 'Let Me Entertain

The rumble between the Jets and the Sharks in *West Side Story* (1961).

Wood, Russell and Malden in *Gypsy* (1962).

Doris Day and Stephen Boyd in *Billy Rose's Jumbo* (1962).

Natalie Wood was spectacular in the title role in *Gypsy* (1962).

Richard Beymer reacts to a knifing in *West Side Story* (1961).

You,' 'Rose's Turn' and 'You'll Never Get Away From Me.'

Billy Rose's Jumbo (1962) was a remake of the Broadway musical *Jumbo* of 1935. It was an elaborate film about a circus and the efforts of its owners to save it, and starred Doris Day, Stephen Boyd, Jimmy Durante and Martha Raye. It was not top quality, but the Busby Berkeley choreography and the Rodgers and Hart songs made it pleasant. Among the songs were 'The Most Beautiful Girl in the World,' 'My Romance' and 'This Can't Be Love.'

The blockbuster of 1962 was *The Music Man*, from the Meredith Willson stage musical of 1957. It was a happy summer-day type of picture about Professor Harold Hill (Robert Preston), who arrives in River City, Iowa, to organize a boy's band, and, incidentally, to sell instruments to all the kids. There he meets and falls in love with Marian, the librarian (Shir-

ley Jones), who reforms him. Preston was superb (he had made a triumphal comeback in the stage version) and the tunes were made for whistling. Some of them were 'Till There Was You,' 'Seventy-six Trombones,' 'Trouble,' 'My White Knight,' 'Marian the Librarian,' 'Lida Rose,' 'The Wells Fargo Wagon' and 'Gary, Indiana.'

Bye Bye Birdie (1963), taken from the 1960 Broadway production, gave audiences a more up-to-date story line. The character of Conrad Birdie was obviously patterned after Elvis Presley, and the story line was about a rock and roll singing idol, about to be drafted, and about to make his final television appearance on the Ed Sullivan show, resulting in many confrontations with his adoring fans and their frustrated parents. Among the more popular songs from the production were 'What's the Matter With Kids?,' 'Bye Bye Birdie' and 'Put on a Happy Face.' It starred Dick Van Dyke, Janet Leigh and Paul Lynde, but the movie was stolen by Ann-Margret, a young performer, born Ann Margaret Olson in Sweden. She had been discovered singing and dancing in Las Vegas by none other than George Burns. She was not the best dancer in the world. She was not the best singer in the world. But she was a presence—a naive, sultry entertainer who was seldom ignored.

The Threepenny Opera (1963) was a film with a rather complicated life story. It was a musical play by Berthold Brecht with music by Kurt Weill that was inspired by John Gay's *Beggar's Opera*, an English burlesque of 1727. Brecht and Weill kept the setting in London's Soho, but upped the time to Queen Victoria's coronation year. The story concerned a thief and murderer, Macheath (Mack the Knife) and his various love affairs with Polly Peachum, Lucy Lockit and Jenny, the prostitute. Originally performed in Germany in 1928 as *Die Dreigro-*

Opposite: Preston and Jones in *The Music Man* (1962).

Jessie Pearson as Conrad Birdie in *Bye Bye Birdie* (1963).

Robert Preston leads his '76 Trombones' in *The Music Man* (1962).

Harrison and Hepburn in 'The Rain in Spain'—*My Fair Lady* (1964).

'Move your bloomin' arse!' The 'Ascot Gavotte' number from *My Fair Lady* (1964).

Eliza gets no credit from Higgins after the triumphal ball—*My Fair Lady* (1964).

schenoper, it was an immediate success, and was made into a film in Germany in 1931, starring Lotte Lenya, Weill's wife, playing the part of Jenny. (The director, G W Pabst, simultaneously shot a French version with a different cast.) It wasn't until 1954 that Americans became aware of the musical play. It opened off-Broadway with a new libretto translation by Marc Blitzstein, and played for years. This new version was made into the film *The Threepenny Opera* (1963) starring Curt Jurgens as Mack and Hildegard Neff. Some of the songs were 'Mack the Knife,' 'Pirate Jenny' and 'The Moon Over Dock Street.'

The public had waited eight years for *My Fair Lady* to appear on the screen. The stage version had premiered in 1956 and the film was released in 1964. It had been in the news even when it was in production. Professor Henry Higgins had to be played by Rex Harrison, who had starred in the original Broadway production. But Hollywood was suspicious of the charming newcomer, Julie Andrews, who had been the stage Eliza Doolittle, and cast Audrey Hepburn in the role instead, with her singing voice dubbed by the redoubtable Marni Nixon. Of course Julie showed them two years later when she won the Academy Award for best actress for her work in *Mary Poppins* (1964), another musical.

By now the whole world must know that *My Fair Lady* was a musical version of George Bernard Shaw's *Pygmalion*, in which Professor Henry Higgins turns a guttersnipe, Eliza Doolittle, into a regal lady to win a bet. Harrison won the Academy Award as best actor. The sets and costumes were resplendent. The movie was sumptuously filmed. But the credit should go to the Alan Jay Lerner-Frederick Loewe score, with such memorable tunes as 'The Rain in Spain,' 'Just You Wait,' 'I Could Have Danced All Night,' 'On the Street Where You Live,' 'I'm Getting Married in the Morning' and Harrison's splendid soliloquies.

Probably the best surprise, however, was Audrey Hepburn. Audiences had been prepared to resent her, but she gave one of the best performances of her life. She justified the decision of the producer, Jack L Warner, to get her to play the title role that Julie Andrews had so charmingly and popularly originated on the stage. It was her brilliance that gave the extra touch

Audrey Hepburn in her Ascot gown.

of subtle magic and individuality to the film. One critic said, 'It is true that Marni Nixon provides the lyric voice that seems to emerge from Miss Hepburn, but it is an excellent voice, expertly synchronized. And everything Miss Hepburn mimes to it is in sensitive tune with the melodies and words.'

There was an interesting censorship problem while the film was in production. In the stage version, at the end of the Ascot race sequence, the ladylike Eliza loses her sense of decorum in the excitement of the race, and, in her loudest and best Cockney, shouts at the horse, 'Move your bloomin' arse!' This was almost deleted from the film, but calmer heads prevailed and the shout remained. Had it been deleted, it would have seemed like history repeating itself. In the original non-musical film version of *Pygmalion*, another line had been deleted by the censors of the day—'Not bloody likely!'

An interesting sidelight to these movies of the early 1960s was that the superspectacular musical had replaced the superspectacular Biblical film as the bonanza picture of the times. Because so much money was being spent, studio bigwigs felt that under the current market conditions a multimillion dollar picture must command a worldwide audience to turn a profit. It could not, therefore, reflect facets of national life that would not be understood in foreign countries. But there were two exceptions to the rule—*West Side Story*, about juvenile gangs in the streets of New York, and *My Fair Lady*, a story built around English class distinctions. Both of them did very well indeed throughout the world. Perhaps it was because they shared with other popular musicals a fairy-tale approach to their subjects. The musical form, after all, has always depended strongly on fantasy and artificiality.

Another volatile and exciting Meredith Willson Broadway musical was made into a film in 1964. It was his 1960 hit *The Unsinkable Molly Brown*. The plot revolved around Molly, played by Debbie Reynolds, the Colorado mining camp hellion who becomes a social-climbing heiress and eventually the wealthiest woman in Denver in the late 1880s. Harve Presnell, as her gold-prospecting husband, had a good voice and cut a romantic figure. Debbie was fine in her best role since *Singin' in the Rain*, especially when she sang 'I Ain't Down Yet.'

There was no question that the biggest Broadway-to-Hollywood musical of 1965 was *The Sound of Music*, adapted from the 1959 Rodgers and Hammerstein stage presentation. Indeed, it was referred to in some quarters as 'The Sound of Money.' It made almost 80 million dollars, which made it the biggest money-maker in the history of movie musicals. In terms of 1984 dollars, it would come to more than $200 million. Of course it was so sweet that certain other unnamed people called it 'The Sound of Mucus.' Call it corn if you like, but the fact is that this blockbuster pleased more people than practically any other

Debbie Reynolds in a riotous moment from *The Unsinkable Molly Brown* (1964).

movie in history. A certain Myra Franklin of Cardiff, Wales, for example, claimed to have sat through the film 940 times in its first ten years.

As almost everyone knows, it was the musical story of Maria von Trapp, who was born aboard a train as her mother hurried to the hospital. She was orphaned at age six and became the ward of a left-leaning anti-Catholic. As if to make amends, she converted to Catholicism at age 18 and decided to become a nun. It was at this point that the film began.

Because of her independent, tomboyish nature and lack of formal religious training, she became the black sheep of the convent. Nine months before she was to take her vows, she was assigned to work as governess for the family of Baron Georg von Trapp, a World War I naval hero. She was torn when the widowed baron proposed marriage, but married him with her Mother Superior's blessing in 1927. The family lost its wealth in the worldwide Depression of the 1930s, and their home was turned into a hostel for traveling students and clergy. One of their guests, the Reverend Franz Wasner, heard the family singing together and appointed himself their manager. At the urging of Wasner and singer Lotte Lehmann, they entered the 1936 Salzburg Festival, where they won top honors. They fled Austria after the 1938 Nazi takeover.

Mary Martin had played Maria on the stage, but in the film it was Julie Andrews who starred—the sweet, wholesome, ebullient Julie Andrews. Maria von Trapp later admitted that she thought Martin came closer to hitting the mark, but felt that she had finally developed an affection for the movie which she once considered almost unbearably syrupy.

The baron was played by Christopher Plummer, with a singing voice supplied by Bill Lee. And Marni Nixon, the American singer who was a former MGM messenger, the woman who was the voice for Margaret O'Brien in *The Big City* (1948), for Deborah Kerr in *The King and I* (1956), for Natalie Wood in *West Side Story* (1961) and for Audrey Hepburn in *My Fair Lady* (1964), finally appeared on the screen—in a bit part as a nun.

The music was wonderful—'Climb Every Mountain,' 'The Sound of Music,' 'Edelweiss' and 'Do, Re, Mi.' The simple story, the happy ending and the sumptuous Austrian locales marked a public desire for less sophisticated fare. The movie won Academy Awards for best picture, best direction (Robert Wise), best editing (William Reynolds), best sound recording (Jane Corcoran) and best photography (Ted McCord).

Stop the World, I Want to Get Off had been quite a success on the London and Broadway stages in 1961, but when it was released as a film in 1966, it was not the smash it had been in New York or the West End. To begin with, the story line was esoteric, concerning a character called Littlechap, a sort of everyday Everyman, who goes through his life in song, dance and mime in an allegorical story

The Trapp Family from *The Sound of Music* (1965). Julie Andrews as Maria and Christopher Plummer as the Baron (center).

set in a circus. Then there was the problem of casting. In the film, Tony Tanner was nowhere near as inventive a performer as was Anthony Newley on the stage. Unfortunately, only the score by Newley and Leslie Bricusse remained, featuring the hit 'What Kind of Fool Am I?'

A Funny Thing Happened on the Way to the Forum (1966) had opened on Broadway in 1962. It was a frenzied adaptation of Stephen Sondheim's musical about a conniving slave (Zero Mostel) in ancient Rome. It also starred Phil Silvers, Buster Keaton and Jack Gilford. It was burlesque at its best, but, sad to say, many of the original songs were deleted. Probably the best of those that were kept was 'Lovely.'

Opposite: 'The hills are alive with the sound of music.'

How to Succeed in Business . . . — Lee and Morse.

The Baron summons the children for Maria in *The Sound of Music* (1965).

Franco Nero, Richard Harris and Vanessa Redgrave in *Camelot* (1967).

How to Succeed in Business Without Really Trying (1967) came from the delightful Pulitzer Prize-winning Broadway show of 1961 about a window washer (Robert Morse) with a captivating charm who uses his wiles and a handbook to rise to prominence in the Worldwide Wicket Company, whose president was Rudy Vallee. Morse offered an instructive lesson in how to climb the corporate ladder. Frank Loesser wrote the score, which featured 'The Company Way' and 'I Believe in You.'

The 1960 stage musical *Camelot*, by Lerner and Loewe, was released as a movie in 1967. One critic called it 'an appalling film version with only good orchestrations and sporadically good acting to recommend it.' Part of the problem was that the original cast was not in the film. Instead of Richard Burton there was Richard Harris; instead of Julie Andrews, Vanessa Redgrave; instead of Robert Goulet, Franco Nero. Besides that, it was too long—one minute short of three hours. It also had too little of the wit of T H White's *The Once and Future King*, the trilogy on which the original play had been based. The result was that Harris and Redgrave were probably the last non-singers to be entrusted with major singing roles. By the way, Redgrave wore one of the strangest costumes ever known in one scene in the picture—a gown completely covered with pumpkin seeds stitched into the fabric. And it contained one classic mistake. King Pellinore, played by Lionel Jeffries, first meets King Arthur about an hour into the movie, but 20 minutes before he was plainly visible at the King's wedding. The songs, however, were there—'Camelot,' '*C'est Moi*,' 'If Ever I Would Leave You' and the rest.

One of the most unusual sources for a stage musical was a novel by H G Wells—his 1905 book *Kipps: The Story of a Simple Soul*. It was made into the musical play *Half a Sixpence*, which premiered in 1963 and became a 1967 movie. It was a boisterous but cardboard film about a draper's assistant who inherited a fortune and tried to break into London society, and starred Tommy Steele, Julia Foster and Cyril Ritchard.

Nineteen sixty-eight was a banner year for filmed Broadway shows. There was *Finian's Rainbow*, which had opened on the stage in 1947. Starring Fred Astaire, Petula Clark, Tommy Steele, Keenan Wynn and Al Freeman Jr, it was a fantasy with political overtones in which an elderly Irishman steals a leprechaun's crock of gold and plants it in America. The leprechaun follows and the magic crock finally grants everyone's wishes. This Burton Lane-E Y Harburg musical combined subtle social commentary with a tuneful Irish musical setting. Its examination of racial discrimination in the South, while ahead of its time in the 1940s, was a bit old-fashioned 20 years later. Still, it had 'If This Isn't Love,' 'Look to the Rainbow' and 'How Are Things in Glocca Morra?'

Funny Girl (1968) was an adaptation

Opposite: Harris in *Camelot* (1967).

Fred Astaire (Finian McLonergan) and Petula Clark (his daughter Sharon) in *Finian's Rainbow* (1968).

Barbra Streisand in *Funny Girl* (1968).

of the 1964 stage musical, roughly based on the life of singer-comedienne Fanny Brice and her love affair with a mobster. As Fanny, Barbra Streisand made her film debut and won the Academy Award as best actress for her trouble. She was simply fabulous—brassy and vulnerable—and was able to toss off such lines as (indicating her nose) 'You think beautiful girls are going to stay in style forever?' And what she did with the Robert Merrill-Jule Styne songs like 'People' and 'Don't Rain on My Parade'—was perfection.

Oliver! (1968) had opened on the stage in 1960 and brought audiences Fagin's old gang, prettied up for the kids' crowd, but still with plenty of punch. It won Academy Awards for best film, best direction (Carol Reed), best art direction (John Box and Terence Marsh), best score (John Green), best sound (Shepperton Studios) and best choreography (Onna White). Based on Charles Dickens' *Oliver Twist*, this musical with book and additional lyrics by Lionel Bart (the lyricist and composer who can't read music), told the story of a young boy swept into a gang of youthful thieves overseen by the scurrilous Fagin, whose character had been sanitized so that virtually all the anti-Semitic implications of the original story were deleted. Mark Lester, playing Oliver, was one of the most appealing child actors to come along in a good while, and Ron Moody, as Fagin, acted the part with relish. Among the many hummable songs were 'Oliver,' 'Food, Glorious Food,' 'Pick a Pocket or Two,' 'Consider Yourself,' 'Who Will Buy?' and 'As Long As He Needs Me.'

Opposite: Streisand as Fanny Brice.

Streisand sings 'People' in *Funny Girl* (1968) while Omar Sharif looks on.

'Please, Sir, I want some more.' Mark Lester is hungry in *Oliver!* (1968).

Shirley MacLaine in a wild number from *Sweet Charity* (1969).

Sweet Charity, which had opened on Broadway in 1966 with Gwen Verdon, was an adaptation of Frederico Fellini's non-musical film *Nights of Cabiria (Notti di Cabiria)* of 1957—a story of a prostitute with a heart of gold. The plot had been switched from the ladies of the night to dance-hall hostesses. On Broadway it was a hit, but when it was transferred to the screen in 1969, some of the bloom had gone off the rose. Shirley MacLaine was wonderful in the title role, but Bob Fosse directed with too much flash, as if he distrusted the impact of the material, and some of the production numbers were really overproduced. For example, MacLaine sang the 'I'm a Brass Band' number on a rooftop dressed in a drum majorette's uniform. But the Cy Coleman-Dorothy Fields score made up for much of this, with 'Big Spender,' 'If They Could See Me Now' and 'Rhythm of Life.'

'Hey, Big Spender' from *Sweet Charity* (1969).

MacLaine deserved better treatment. She was born Shirley MacLean Beatty (she is Warren Beatty's sister) in Richmond, Virginia, and was studying ballet at the age of two years. Her first Broadway musical was *Me and Juliet* (1953), a Rodgers and Hammerstein effort that never made it to the screen, as a dancer in the chorus. Her next musical was *The Pajama Game* (1954), in which she understudied Carol Haney, the leading dancer. She replaced an injured Haney, was spotted by a Hollywood producer and began her movie career in *The Trouble With Harry* (1954). MacLaine has been nominated for an Academy Award, but, although she is a magnificent musical-comedy star, she has been in few musical pictures. Indeed, her typecasting seemed to go in another direction. She admitted that she has played a hooker in 14 films.

Barbra Streisand reappeared on the screen as Dolly Levi in *Hello, Dolly!* (1969), the screen version of the 1964 stage musical which seems to have

Streisand sings 'Before the Parade Passes By' in *Hello Dolly!* (1969).

Streisand leads the cast in song at the Yonkers railway station in *Hello Dolly!* (1969).

gone on forever—starring, among others, Carol Channing, Pearl Bailey, Ginger Rogers, Betty Grable, Mary Martin, Martha Raye and Ethel Merman. The stage musical was an adaptation of a play, *The Matchmaker*, by Thornton Wilder, who had borrowed the plot himself. Actually, the musical, either on stage or on film, was not much of an entertainment, but with a strong actress-singer in the title role (and all of them were), it was irresistible. Dolly is the matchmaker whose real aim is to snare a Yonkers, New York, merchant, Horace Vandergelder (played by Walter Matthau). Gene Kelly directed this $20-million extravaganza, whose Jerry Herman score included 'Hello, Dolly,' 'Before the Parade Passes By,' 'Put on Your Sunday Clothes,' and 'It Only Takes a Moment.' Blooper-catchers love to point out the scene in which, although the film was set at the turn of the century, a modern car was parked beside the railroad track.

There are those who say that the film version of the Broadway musical *Paint Your Wagon* was the worst adaptation in history. The stage musical premiered in 1951 and the film was released in 1969. The story about life in the California boom towns during the Gold Rush of the 1840s didn't have much going for it to begin with, but at least the stage version had singers for the only two Alan Jay Lerner songs worth remembering—'They Call the Wind Maria' and 'I Talk to the Trees.' Harve Presnell did a fine job with the former in the film, but letting Clint Eastwood sing the latter was a disaster. And Lee Marvin's singing left much to be desired, even though a film in which Marvin plays a drunk can't be completely bad. And the scenery was beautiful. The picture ran for almost three hours, and as one critic said, 'A boring, dated Broadway musical of the late 40s has been turned into an enormously expensive [$20

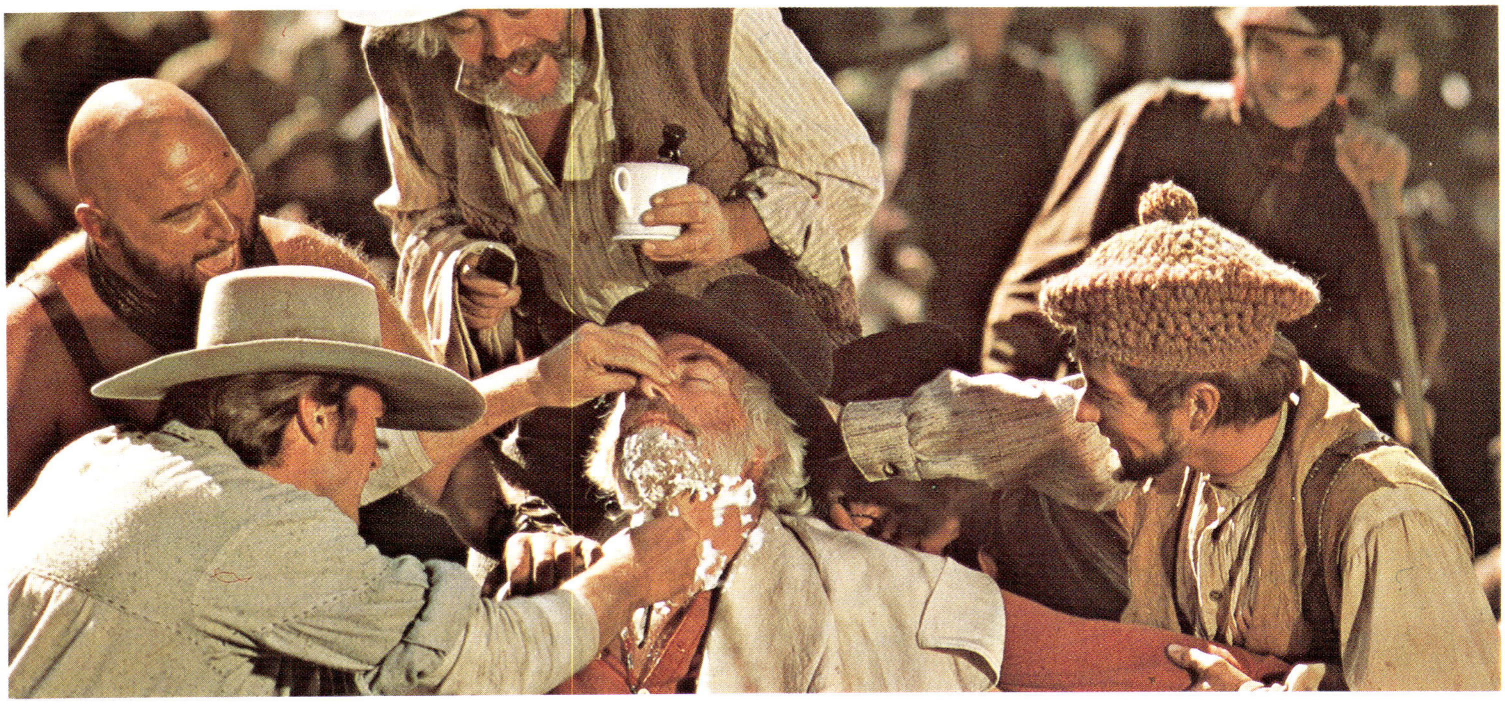

Lee Marvin gets shaved for his impending wedding in *Paint Your Wagon* (1969).

million], stupefyingly boring movie musical . . . a clinker . . . Let this wagon roll by without you.'

The 1970s rolled in with *On a Clear Day You Can See Forever* (1970), based on the Broadway show of 1965. It had an all-star cast, with Barbra Streisand playing the part of a girl whose psychiatrist, Yves Montand, discovers that she lived a former life and, under hypnosis, sends her back to relive it. It also starred Bob Newhart, Larry Blyden and Jack Nicholson. Director Vincente Minnelli was at top form, especially when mounting the sequences taking place amid the pomp and pageantry of nineteenth-century English aristocracy. Some of the Alan Jay Lerner-Burton Lane songs were 'On a Clear Day You Can See Forever,' 'He Wasn't You,' 'Come Back to Me' and 'Go to Sleep.'

Some of the more polite critics characterized *Song of Norway* (1970) as a bomb. The film, taken from the 1944 stage musical, was loosely based on the life of the Norwegian composer Edvard Grieg, and starred Florence Henderson and Toralv Maurstad. The music was stolen from Grieg himself, and when the audience heard performers sing 'Norway waits for the song of one man' to the tune of one of the themes from Grieg's *Piano Concerto*, they walked out in droves.

The Boy Friend (1971) had been a stage musical in 1954 starring Julie Andrews. It was a pleasant little satire on 1920s musicals and was made into a big production, with Ken Russell directing, adding a backstage story outside the story, and updating it into a spoof of 1930s musicals. But it worked on several levels, from the tacky matinee performances of a show to a fantasy-world conception. The Busby Berkeley-like numbers came amazingly close to the spirit and execution of The Master himself. It starred Twiggy and Tommy Tune, and had in it 'You Are My Lucky Star,' 'All I Do Is Dream of You,' 'The Boy Friend' and many, many more songs.

Fiddler on the Roof opened on Broadway in 1964, and went on and on, being presented all over the world. People wondered how it could appeal to the Japanese, for example, but the answer was probably that it was not solely a Russian-Jewish musical, it encompassed the feeling of family in all parts of the world. Even today, it is presented by amateur groups everywhere, possibly every day. Based on the stories of Sholem Aleichem, the production was set in a small Ukrainian town, Anatevka, in 1905, and told the story of Tevye, a milkman who tried to preserve his Jewish heritage against growing odds—his daughters' desires to marry the men they want rather than those picked for them by a matchmaker—the impending Russian pogrom against the Jews—the necessity to leave the village. The world awaited the film version of 1971, and it was not disappointed. Chaim Topol, the Israeli actor, could not match the exuberance of Zero Mostel, the original Tevye, but no one else could have done that, either. The supporting cast included Molly Picon, Norma Crane and Leonard Frey, with an assist on the sound track by Isaac Stern playing

Barbra Streisand in *On a Clear Day You Can See Forever* (1970).

his violin as 'The Fiddler.' The Sheldon Harnick-Jerry Bock score included 'Fiddler on the Roof,' 'Tevye's Dream,' 'If I Were a Rich Man,' 'Miracle of Miracles,' 'Anatevka' and many more.

The 1969 stage musical *1776* was unique. No chorus line. Only two female roles. Lyrical singing roles for such personages as Benjamin Franklin, Thomas Jefferson and John Adams. Unabashed patriotism. But it worked. The Pulitzer Prize-winning show about America's first Congress trying to come up with a Declaration of Independence from Britain had audiences on the edges of their seats. Will they or won't they agree? The final scene, which re-created the actual signing of the Declaration to the accompaniment of the calling of the roll and the ringing of the Liberty Bell, was memorable. Fortunately, the movie version (1972) recaptured the drama and thrills quite well, and had the added charm of occasionally moving the camera outside Independence Hall to the streets of old Philadelphia. William Daniels was Adams, Howard da Silva was Franklin and Ken Howard was Jefferson. Some of the songs were 'Sit Down, John,' 'Till Then,' 'The Lees of Virginia,' 'He Plays the Violin,' 'Mamma Look Sharp,' 'The Egg,' 'Molasses to Rum' and 'Is Anybody There?'

Left: Fiddler on the Roof (1971).
Inset: Chaim Topol as Tevye.

vestism and rock music. It concerned a straight couple (Susan Sarandon and Barry Bostwick) stranded in an old dark house full of weirdos from Transylvania. The songs by Richard O'Brien included 'Dammit Janet,' 'Over at the Frankenstein Place,' 'Sweet Transvestite' and 'Wild and Untamed Thing.' It became a cult flick for the younger set and was usually found on Saturday midnight bills, where the kids who attended all seemed to know the dialogue by heart and conducted a huge sing-along, often attired in the costumes of their favorite creep.

A Little Night Music (1978) was adapted from the stage musical of 1973, and went to all the trouble of casting Elizabeth Taylor, Diana Rigg (of *The Avengers* television series), Len Cariou (of *Sweeney Todd*) and Hermione Gingold. But it turned out to be a laughingly stilted film version of the Stephen Sondheim stage musical (called in Germany, naturally enough, *Eine Kleine Nachtmusik*) which was based on Ingmar Bergman's *Smiles of a Summer Night* (1955), a zingy, yet tasteful tale of wife-swapping on a country estate. Liz's rendition of 'Send in the Clowns' sent out the audiences.

John Travolta was a performer who proved the old adage that it isn't so much a star's age, as it is the age that the audience wants him to be. He was the Vinnie Barbarino of the unruly bunch of Brooklyn high-school students in the television series *Welcome Back, Kotter* when he was in his mid-20s. He then went on to score a triumph in *Saturday Night Fever* (1977). A teenager is what people wanted Travolta to be, and he dutifully played one in *Grease* (1978), which had opened on Broadway in 1972. The film was a stock musical that fantasized the life of the young in the 1950s. Travolta co-starred with Olivia Newton-John, Stockard Channing, Eve Arden and Sid Caesar.

It was a multi-million dollar evocation of the B-picture quickies, like the Beach Party films, of the 1950s. The gang at old Rydell High was unlike any high-school class that anyone had ever seen, except in the movies. For one thing, they were all a little long in the tooth to hang around malt shops. For another, they were loaded with the kind of exuberance and talent that is not often found too far from a musical stage. Some of the songs by Jim Jacobs and Warren Casey were great—'Beauty School Dropout,'

A dance number in *Grease* (1978). John Travolta (center) with the high school principal (Eve Arden) at front right.

John Travolta leads the chorus in *Grease* (1978).

'Look at Me, I'm Sandra Dee' and 'There Are Worse Things I Could Do.'

Several characters who were famous in the 1950s appeared in the film as sort of inside jokes. Eve Arden (the English teacher from the television series *Our Miss Brooks*) was the school principal. Sid Caesar was the football coach. Edd Byrnes was the lecherous host of a television show. Frankie Avalon was in a dream sequence counseling an unhappy student. It was a large, funny, witty and imaginative film, and Travolta was better than in *Saturday Night Fever*. Newton-John was funny and charming. Stockard Channing almost stole the show in her two numbers.

The Wiz (1978) had appeared on Broadway in 1975. It was a black version of *The Wizard of Oz*—stunning in its costumes. But the movie failed despite a lot of talent in the form of Diana Ross, Michael Jackson, Richard Pryor, Nipsey Russell and Lena Horne. It had some good musical numbers, but a dreary finale, and a drearier performance by the usually talented Ross, as Dorothy, weighed it down.

Hair, based on the 1968 stage musical, finally made it to the screen in 1979. *Grease*, that paean to the 1950s, made it at the box office. *Hair*, eulogizing the 1960s, did not. We had a *Grease 2*, but no *Hair 2*. The problem was that it turned out to be a period musical celebrating 'The Age of Aquarius,' rather than a spoof, as was *Grease*, and its impact was considerably muffled. It was the story of a strait-laced Midwesterner who falls in with New York hippies. It didn't hang together, although it did have its musical moments—'Aquarius,' 'Where Do I Go?,' 'Good Morning Starshine' and 'Let the Sunshine In.'

Annie (1982), the musical about the little orphan girl who wins the heart of multi-billionaire Oliver 'Daddy' Warbucks, was a smash hit on Broadway in 1976. But the film missed the point and was turned into an overblown production by director John

Dorothy and her friends. Diana Ross in *The Wiz* (1978).

Huston, who was filming his first musical. It cost more than 40 million dollars and had a cast of thousands. Aileen Quinn, as Annie, and Albert Finney, as Warbucks, turned in appealing performances, but the rest of the cast (including, amazingly enough, Carol Burnett, who grossly overacted her role as the evil orphanage supervisor, Miss Hannigan), was uninspired. But still, there were 'Tomorrow,' 'It's a Hard-Knock Life' and 'Easy Street' to listen to.

So Hollywood has always been fond of importing hits from the theater world—proven successes, that is. There will probably never be screen versions of the less successful ones, but everyone will be waiting for *A Chorus Line* and *Cats*.

Inset: Daddy Warbucks (Albert Finney) dances with Annie (Aileen Quinn) in *Annie* (1983).

Below: John Travolta (standing) in a relaxing moment at the athletic field in *Grease* (1978).

Right: Inside the Emerald City—*The Wiz* (1978). *Below right:* Dolly Parton and Burt Reynolds in *The Best Little Whorehouse in Texas* (1983).

Elvis Presley in *Jailhouse Rock* (1957).

THE RECENT PAST

One of the most significant types of film to come after the semi-revolution against the Arthur Freed principle that music should be integrated with action began as a whimper in 1955, and it was not born in a musical film. Oddly enough, it was a drama that spawned it—*The Blackboard Jungle*, a film about the terror a young teacher encounters while working in a New York slum high school. But the sound track was filled with the piercing, pulsating sound of Bill Hayley and his Comets, a musical combo that played the new music called rock and roll. Anyone in the audience over the age of 25 was shocked and fascinated.

Rock Around the Clock (1956), starring the same Bill Hayley and his Comets, was quickly made to capitalize on his instant popularity. It stands today as a curio, but it is a good social history of that early rock phase of musical life. The plot was almost nonexistent—something about an unknown band brought to New York where they become famous. Thrown in were The Platters, Tony Martinez and his Band, Freddie Bell and his Bellboys, disc jockey Alan Freed and pop singer Johnny Johnston, who seemed out of place.

Rock and roll was in, and 1956 marked the debut in films of a heavy-lidded pop singer and guitarist who was known as 'The Pelvis' because of his swivel-hipped style—Elvis Presley. The film was *Love Me Tender*, and it was a smash. It was a sort of Civil War Western, involving robberies, double-crosses and the usual ingredients of a typical cowboy film. Elvis sang a couple of songs, including the title song, and had a death scene.

He came back with *Loving You* (1957), in which Lizabeth Scott discovered him and he became a singing idol.

Presley leads the convict chorus line in *Jailhouse Rock* (1957).

Elvis in *Love Me Tender* (1956).

Probably Presley's most successful film was his third picture, *Jailhouse Rock* (1957), a story casting him as a young convict serving a term for manslaughter who learns to play the guitar in prison and later becomes a top pop singer. Presley shivered and shook with gusto and his fans went wild. His recording of the title song sold two million records in its first two weeks in release. As he said in the film, 'Uh got wars [wires] 'n' letters from all over the worl'.' The sound technicians must have closed in, for this time most of his singing could actually be understood. In two numbers, 'Treat Me Nice' and the title song, done as a convict jamboree, he broke loose with his St Vitus specialty. As one critic said, 'Ten to one, next time he'll make it—finally getting those kneecaps turned inside out and cracking them together like coconuts. Never say die, El.'

Even with time out to serve in the Army, Presley made 28 more films in the next 13 years, and toward the end he had toned down his act and become part of the normal public scene, tolerated, if not accepted, by people of all ages.

More rock came along with the appearance of the Beatles, that Liverpudlian pop group made up of John Lennon, George Harrison, Paul McCartney and Ringo Starr. Their first picture was *A Hard Day's Night* (1964), and it was a gem, a whale of a comedy. Directed by Richard Lester, it staked out new ground synthesizing the new music with the new cinema in an exciting way. It contained no dream sequences, no dancing, no fantasy, and was not even shot in color. The film was conceived as a star vehicle to exploit the worldwide mania for the Beatles. Executives at United Artists were convinced the group's popularity would crest in 1964 and wanted to complete the film before the bubble burst. The result was a musical about music, a pseudo-documentary about an immensely popular rock band whose members' lives center around music and who attempt both to escape from and build rapport with their many thousands of screaming fans. There were plenty of songs, some played voice-over and some rendered live from the concert stage. The final 17 minutes, which were shot in a single day with six movie cameras and three television cameras, was as much of a fantastic extravaganza as anything ever cooked up by Busby Berkeley.

The story of a day in the life of the Beatles featured a dozen or so of their hit songs combined with madcap clowning in the old Marx Brothers style and a dazzling use of the camera that tickled the intellect and electrified the nerves. With practically nothing substantial in the way of a story to tell—nothing more than a loosely strung fable of how the boys take under their wings the wacky old grandfather of one of them while preparing for a London television show—the film discovered a nifty little satire in the paradox of the old man being more of

Elvis Presley wearing racing stripes in *Speedway* (1968).

The Beatles get directions in *A Hard Day's Night* (1964).

A scene from *The Yellow Submarine* (1968).

a problem, more of a 'troublemaker and a mixer,' than the boys. One of the Beatles says of him, ''E's a nice old man, isn't 'e?' And another replies with courteous unction, parodying the standard comment about the Beatles themselves, ''E's very clean.' The picture came in fast-flowing spurts of sight gags and throw-away dialogue.

The whole film was a fantasy, an entertaining vision of how the Beatles lived and the absurd claustrophobic world they inhabited. The movie had lightness, exuberance, froth, and was great escapist entertainment. Add to this surrealism and satire and the film was a winner. The rising shot of the Beatles as they cavorted around a field in a kind of mad ballet was a perfect example of lightness of touch in musical film-making. Their final concert was the picture's great escapist production number. Their relations with each other, the 'clean old man,' their managers and the public were enriched by put-down dialogue delivered with ingenuous charm.

One critic said, 'It is good to know there are people in this world, up to and including the major parties, who don't take the Beatles seriously.'

The Beatles joined Lester again in *Help!* (1965). It was another crazy, funny film, with lots of wild gags, many songs and several really far-out sequences involving some sort of spying.

Their next film was a switch. *The Yellow Submarine* (1968) was a delightful, engaging animated fantasy in which the Beatles fight off the Blue Meanies, who have the audacity to disrupt the tranquil amiability of the mythical kingdom of Pepperland (of

A zany scene with the Beatles in *Help!* (1965).

John Lennon and Yoko Ono in *Let It Be* (1970).

Bernadette Peters and Steve Martin starred in *Pennies from Heaven* (1981).

Lucie Arnaz and Neil Diamond in the 1980 remake of *The Jazz Singer*.

Sergeant Pepper's Lonely Hearts Club Band fame). Songs, puns, non-sequitur jokes combined with surreal pop-art visions. The songs included 'All You Need Is Love,' 'A Little Help from My Friends,' 'Lucy in the Sky with Diamonds' and 'The Yellow Submarine.'

Let It Be (1970) was an uneven, draggy documentary in which the audience was allowed to peek in on a Beatles recording session. The songs were lilting and poetic, but the rest of the film was a bore.

And then it was over. The Beatles broke up and each of them went his own way—to seclusion, to making other films, to forming a new group, to death.

There were a couple of interesting semi-biographical pictures about dead rock stars. The first was *The Buddy Holly Story* (1978). It was a standard biopic about the 1950s rock performer who created an influential new sound, but Gary Busey's electrifying performance as Holly set the film apart. The movie also had a vibrant sound track, probably because Busey and two other actors, Don Stroud and Charles Martin Smith, actually played their instruments live in the film.

The Rose (1979) was a spin-off of the Janis Joplin story equating show business with Hell, but, as one critic said, 'It gives the audience too much of the latter.' Bette Midler, however, gave life to the title character with a dynamic performance.

After Al Jolson made the original *Jazz Singer* in 1927, it was remade in 1953, starring Danny Thomas and Peggy Lee. It was a fairly well-done remake and the score did receive an Academy Award nomination. But the third try at *The Jazz Singer* in 1980 was an absolute bomb. It starred Neil Diamond in the title role and a totally miscast Sir Laurence Olivier as his Orthodox Jewish father. This time the hero became a rock star, but the film contained more clichés than the original.

Pennies from Heaven (1981) was not a remake of the 1936 Bing Crosby film. Rather it was a unique and remarkable film based on Dennis Potter's British television series of the same name about a sheet-music salesman during the Depression, whose unhappy life was contrasted with the cheery songs of the day. Starring Steve Martin and Bernadette Peters, it was provocative and troub-

Opposite: Bette Midler as *The Rose* (1979) with Alan Bates.

ling. The non-musical parts were set in the bleak world of the lower middle class during that period of want, but when a song came into the picture, it was changed into a dream sequence in the 1930s musical style, with the music furnished by original recordings of the time. It was a picture that one either loved or hated.

Grease 2 had nowhere near the charm of *Grease* (1978). It opened with a good back-to-school number, then went downhill, as most sequels do. Most of the talented kids of the original were missing, leaving only the newcomer, Lorna Luft (another Judy Garland daughter from her marriage to Sid Luft) and Eve Arden to take up the slack.

Perhaps some tribute should be given in passing to four of the worst big-budget musical bombs ever to be inflicted on an unsuspecting public.

The first was *Doctor Doolittle* (1967), based on the leading character in the wonderful Hugh Lofting books for children—Doctor Doolittle of Puddelby-on-the-Marsh—the veterinarian who can talk to animals. It was a no-expenses-barred, wide-screen film for which the film-makers went to England to find Victorian atmosphere, but once there, found it necessary to virtually rebuild an entire English village to make it look picturesque enough for the screen. It starred Rex Harrison and his talking-lyrics style of singing as the doctor, with Anthony Newley and Samantha Eggar. The movie was disappointing; Harrison was more Henry Higgins than Doctor Doolittle. Several of Leslie Bricusse's

Opposite: Dick Van Dyke and Julie Andrews in *Mary Poppins* (1964).

Steve Martin in a dream dance sequence in *Pennies from Heaven* (1981).

Maxwell Caulfield and Michele Pfeiffer in *Grease 2* (1982).

Rex Harrison as *Doctor Doolittle* (1967). The Pushmi-Pullu is behind him.

A scene from *Fame* (1980).

melodies were fun, including 'I Talk to the Animals,' but all-in-all it was a colossal musical dud that almost ruined its studio financially. One critic said, 'One merit: if you have unruly children, it may put them to sleep.'

Goodbye, Mr Chips (1969) was an attempt to add music to the wonderful non-musical picture of 1938 that had starred Robert Donat and Greer Garson, based on the novel by James Hilton. It didn't work. Peter O'Toole played the shy teacher who fell in love with a young girl, played by Petula Clark. In this version, the girl is a musical-comedy actress, complete with outlandish friends and a racy past. O'Toole carried the film and not even he was up to par. The songs were laughable, and about the only decent one was Clark's rendition of 'London Is London.' Add to that the fact that it lasted two hours and a half, and it follows that the audience had both their brains and their bottoms numbed. Even if it had not been as bad as most people thought, it was doomed to failure. Older people couldn't forget Garson and Donat in the original—a brilliant, impeccably produced picture (Donat won the Academy Award for best actor)—and younger people didn't like the Leslie Bricusse songs. At any rate, both Roger Ebert, film critic of the *Chicago Sun-Times*, and Fred W McDarrah, critic of *The Village Voice*, put it on their short lists of the worst films of all time.

The third was *Lost Horizon* (1973). With a book based on another popular novel by James Hilton, whose memory was being punished enough, and the equally popular film of 1937 starring Ronald Coleman; with a score by Burt Bacharach and Hal David; with such stars as Liv Ullman, Peter Finch, Sally Kellerman, Charles Boyer and Sir John Gielgud, how could it miss? It did. Instead of discovering Shangri-La, the film was mired in an almost cartoon-like self-parody. For the first half hour the movie copied the 1937 film scene for scene, and everything was fine. Then it got to Shangri-La and the awful songs, and the film fell apart.

The fourth bomb was *At Long Last Love* (1975) with Burt Reynolds, Cybill Shepherd, Madeline Kahn, Dulio Del Prete and Eileen Brennan. To quote a critic: 'It's deplorable! It's disgraceful! It's disastrous! Cole Porter would spin in his grave if he knew how his sophisticated songs were used in this inane musical, clumsily directed, written and produced by Peter Bogdanovich. Intending to make a valentine to the 1930s, Bogdanovich has instead fashioned a poison-pen letter.' The plot was ridiculous. Oliver Pritchard III (Reynolds) is bored with his 1930s life. He falls in love with Broadway singer Kitty O'Kelley (Kahn). Johnny Spanish (Del Prete), an Italian card shark, meets Brooke Carter (Shepherd), an heiress. Kitty and Brooke were school chums, so the four people start double-dating. They go to parties and dances and usually end up singing and dancing. That's the excuse to use 16 Cole Porter songs. The picture cost 6 million dollars, but the returns were just 1.5 million. Twentieth Century took a big tax writeoff. Critics characterized it as dancing on Cole Porter's grave, and even Reynolds was quoted as saying 'I think we bombed.'

Glynis Johns (center) as Mrs Banks in *Mary Poppins* (1964).

Lavish musicals were still being made, of course, and one of the big winners was *Mary Poppins* (1964), in which Julie Andrews got her revenge for not getting the Eliza Doolittle part in *My Fair Lady* (1964) by winning the Academy Award for best actress—in her first film outing. Co-starring with Andrews, who played the title role, were Dick Van Dyke, Glynis Johns, Ed Wynn, Hermione Baddeley, Arthur Treacher and Reginald Owen. There was charm, wit, movie magic to spare in Walt Disney's adaptation of the P L Travers children's book about a 'practically perfect' nanny who brings a profound change to the Banks Family of London in 1910. In addition to Andrews' Oscar, the film earned Academy Awards for best score (Richard and Robert Sherman), best song ('Chim-Chim-Cheree') and best visual effects. Other song hits included 'A Spoonful of Sugar,' 'Jolly Holiday' and 'Supercalifragilisticexpialidocious.'

Andrews went on to diverse roles, both in drama and in musicals. Her next musical was *Thoroughly Modern Millie* (1967), with James Fox, Mary Tyler Moore and Carol Channing. It was an entertaining extravaganza with its songs, dances and comedy sequences in a 1920s setting, reminiscent of Andrews' stage success, *The Boy Friend.* Julie was a delight as the heroine who finds love, true love, but not until she dances and warbles her way through many production numbers.

Star! (1968) was a disappointing musical based on the life and career of the legendary London and Broadway theater star, English-born actress Gertrude Lawrence. Co-starring with her was Daniel Massey as Noel Coward. It had songs by Coward and Porter, but it became overly sentimental and wound up depicting Lawrence as a grown-up Girl Scout modeled on Mary Poppins. In short, it never rang true, but it did have some mammoth production numbers worth seeing. After its box-office flop it was trimmed down to 120 minutes from 175 minutes and retitled *Those Were the Happy Times.*

Her next musical was *Darling Lili* (1970) with Rock Hudson. It was a fine, though underrated and overlooked, musical spoof—a tongue-in-cheek, but never coy, story about a German spy (Andrews) posing as a London entertainer during World War II who falls in love with a squadron commander, played by Hudson.

Victor Victoria (1982) was Julie Andrews' finest musical since *Mary Poppins* (unless one counts *The Sound of Music*). It was the tale of a down-

Barbra Streisand in the remake of *A Star Is Born* (1976).

and-out singer in France (Andrews) who masquerades as Victor, a male female impersonator, much to the delight of her gay mentor (Robert Preston) and the confusion of an American mobster admirer (James Garner), his moll (Lesley Ann Warren) and his closet-gay bodyguard (Alex Karras). It was a stylish, sophisticated, hilarious comedy that was based on a 1933 German film, *Viktor und Viktoria* (with Hermann Thimig and Renate Müller), which was remade in 1936 as *First A Girl* with Jessie Matthews.

But the superstar of the period was undoubtedly Barbra Streisand. She has displayed the delicacy of a Sherman Tank since she began her career in a smokey club in Greenwich Village, when she grabbed the mike as if it were a weapon and snarled her way through a song. Her success has been stunning, and while she may not evoke warmth, no one can deny that her talent is one in a million. Her Greenwich Village appearance, an off-Broadway one-nighter and a few television appearances brought her to the attention of Broadway producer David Merrick, and he signed her up for the role of Miss Marmelstein in his stage production of *I Can Get It for*

Julie Andrews played Gertrude Lawrence in *Star!* (1968).

Barbra Streisand doing a number in *Funny Lady* (1975).

You Wholesale (1962). Now she was in show biz. After her Academy Award-winning role in *Funny Girl* (1968) and her roles in *Hello Dolly!* (1969) and *On A Clear Day You Can See Forever* (1970, the year she won a Tony for 'Star of the Decade' for her work in the theater) she came back in a few non-musical films.

Then came *Funny Lady* (1975), the sequel to *Funny Girl*, showing Fanny Brice at the height of her career, meeting and marrying ambitious showman Billy Rose (James Caan). It wasn't as good as *Funny Girl*, but when Barbra was singing it was magic all the way. Her songs included 'It's Gonna Be a Great Day' and 'Me and My Shadow.'

She made a mistake in 1976 with her remake of *A Star Is Born*, in which Judy Garland had become the definitive Vicky Lester of all time. It was self-indulgent and a little insulting, and Streisand deserved the blame since she had had complete control over every aspect of the picture. Director Jerry Schatzberg was fired after shooting a part of the film and her boy friend-producer Jon Peters directed a few scanes before being replaced by Frank Pierson. A big mistake was to switch the story line from the Hollywood movie world to the rock world of the 1970s. The audience just never cared about Esther Hoffman. Kris Kristofferson sang

Streisand with Kris Kristofferson in *A Star Is Born* (1976).

Above: Andrews in *Victor Victoria*. *Right: Viktor und Viktoria.*

Julie Andrews and James Garner are reunited after a night club brawl in *Victor Victoria* (1982).

adequately and did what he could with some dumb dialogue, but that is to be expected from a Rhodes Scholar. The only parts that worked were those in which Streisand sang. She got an Academy Award, however, not for her acting or singing, but for her music.

Yentl (1983) starred Streisand in her crowning achievement. She was the star, the producer, the director, the co-author. Based on Isaac Bashevis Singer's story of a Jewish girl in Eastern Europe who disguises herself as a boy in order to get an education, it got mixed reviews. There was no doubt that it was a labor of love for Streisand, and certainly no one complained about hearing her sing, but there was a feeling that the songs by Michel Legrand and Marilyn and Alan Bergman seemed to slow things down; that they neither advanced nor amplified the action, and sometimes stopped it cold. This may have been the first musical (although it was not advertised as a musical) in which one person sang all the songs. Sometimes she sang over other people's dialogue, sometimes the songs served as an internal monologue for Yentl. The music burst forth irregularly, sometimes from Yentl's mouth and at other times from her private thoughts, and that was confusing. In one scene, she sings on a boat—reminding everyone of *Funny Girl*—as she sails toward the New World. There must have been thousands of immigrants on the vessel, but she was able to find an entire empty deck to prance across. It was a strange film, and people, once again, either loved it or hated it.

Opposite: John Travolta in his dancing costume in *Saturday Night Fever* (1977).

A revolution seemed to be brewing in 1978. That was the year that *Saturday Night Fever* was released, and this film may have heralded a new direction for the musical film—from concentration on singing to filling the screen with dancers. This was John Travolta's first starring film, and it was a cliché movie that somehow touched the hearts of the audiences. It was a thoughtful study of a Brooklyn youth who finds the only meaning to his life when he is dancing at a local disco, and the film pulsed to the dynamic music of the Bee Gees. Travolta, as the best disco dancer in Brooklyn, was insolent, yet vulnerable. The theme music, 'Staying Alive,' hit the top of the charts.

Bob Fosse came up with another dance musical in *All That Jazz* (1979).

Ann Reinking (left) dances with Erzsebet Foldi in *All That Jazz* (1979).

Starring Roy Scheider, Jessica Lange, Ann Reinking and Ben Vereen, it was actually a sort of semi-autobiography of Fosse himself. There were great show-business moments and wonderful dancing, but it sometimes leaned toward pretentiousness and self-indulgence. The finale was interminable and what can one say about a dream-sequence dance number while Scheider was having heart-bypass surgery?

Flashdance (1983) was an oddity. It was a low-budget film about a young girl who desperately wants to be a dancer. She works as a welder during the day, and dances at Mawby's Bar, a seedy Pittsburgh tavern, at night. Actually, the photography was good, the dancing was interesting and the music was rather compelling, beginning with the title music—'What a Feeling' and going on to such numbers as 'I Love Rock and Roll,' 'Seduce Me Tonight,' 'Manhunt,' 'Lady, Lady, Lady' and 'Gloria.' It starred Jennifer Beals, Michael Nouri and Lilia Skala.

But even the producers were surprised at the reception of the picture. It zoomed to second place in moneymakers during the summer of 1983, having grossed almost $88 million, just behind *Return of the Jedi*, the third *Star Wars* film. People were seeing it more than once, partly because of a publicity gimmick. The star of the film was Jennifer Beals, as mentioned, but it was discovered by the public that most of her dancing had been done by a 25-year-old, French-born dancer, Marine Jahan, who had not been given a movie credit. Apparently people found that out and went back to look at the clever way that the film had been edited. For example, there was a scene in which Jahan bends over the bar and the camera goes directly to Beals' face. Asked how she got the part, Jahan admitted that it wasn't exclusively her talent. 'I put on a long black wig and I looked like Jennifer Beals.'

John Travolta came back to star in *Staying Alive* (1983)—a sequel to his *Saturday Night Fever* (1978). It was a disaster. The film was written and directed by Sylvester Stallone, who had been brilliant in his *Rocky* films, but made a mistake in this tale of how the Brooklyn kid went on to star as a dancer in a Broadway musical. For one thing, the camera kept zooming in on closeups of the dancers' faces so that the audience could not see the footwork. The audience wanted to see Travolta dance. Was that too much to ask? What they got was the lissome John pumped up to Rocky size by Stallone, some dance sequences that looked like championship bouts and Stallone's brother Frank thumping his music ominously in the background.

No discussion of musical films should omit that paean to the Hollywood singing and dancing film—*That's Entertainment* (1974). Fortunately for those who were too young to see the old musicals on their first time around, Metro-Goldwyn-Mayer released this film, which was a collection of bits and snippets of their best. It became one of the box-office smashes of 1974, and it turned out that the old musicals looked just as good the second time around as they had the first. In fact, they looked so much better than most of the 1970s films that older fans got weepily nostalgic about the good old days, which they hadn't appreciated at the time.

It was written, produced and directed by Jack Haley Jr (his father had played the Tin Woodman with Judy Garland, and Haley Jr had married Judy's daughter, Liza Minnelli) and included scenes from MGM musicals from 1929 to 1958. It was a rousing tribute to the first 50 Metro-Goldwyn-Mayer musical years. It had Gene Kelly dancing sublimely through puddles in *Singin' in the Rain*, Judy Garland singing 'Get Happy' over a series of clips of her face at all ages, Donald O'Connor dancing on his knees, Fred Astaire and Eleanor Powell in their breath-stopping challenge-dance duet from *Broadway Melody of 1940*, Clark Gable singing and dancing in *Idiot's Delight* (1939), Astaire in his walls-and-ceiling dance from *Royal Wedding*, Jimmy Durante coaching the young Frank Sinatra in *It Happened in Brooklyn*. Also in the cast were Bing Crosby, Peter Lawford, Liza Minnelli, Debbie Reynolds, Mickey Rooney, James Stewart and Elizabeth Taylor in scenes from nearly 100 musical films. The only complaint anyone made was that the ballet from *An American in Paris* was not complete. *Variety* magazine summed it up: 'While many may ponder the future of Metro-Goldwyn-Mayer, nobody can deny that it has one hell of a past.'

Musical films have been around since the beginning of the sound era, and it may well be true that their 'Golden Age'—the 1930s and 1940s—has long passed. But the continual quality of the films made since then undeniably indicates that the movie musical is in good health. May that health, for the joy that audiences everywhere take from singing and dancing, continue forever.

Roy Scheider in a dream sequence in *All That Jazz* (1979).

Opposite: Fred Astaire and Eleanor Powell dance 'Begin the Beguine.'

Jennifer Beals in *Flashdance* (1983).

Below: A hospital dream sequence from *All That Jazz* (1979).

Liza Minnelli and Joel Grey sing 'The Money Song' in *Cabaret* (1972).

THE BOX OFFICE WINNERS

According to a survey made in January of 1983, a list of the top 100 largest-grossing films, in terms of 1982 dollars, contained 12 musicals. Based on their total earnings the rundown went like this:

Title	Rank	Earning in $ millions
Grease (1978)	6	96,300
The Sound of Music (1965)	10	79,748
Saturday Night Fever (1977)	14	74,100
Mary Poppins (1964)	39	45,000
Fiddler on the Roof (1971)	50	40,499
A Star Is Born (1976)	56	37,100
Snow White (1937)	92	26,900
Funny Girl (1968)	95	26,325
West Side Story (1961)	166	19,450
South Pacific (1958)	193	17,500
My Fair lady (1964)	330	12,000
This Is the Army (1943)	486	8,500

But when the list was revised into 1982 dollars, the picture changed drastically.

The Sound of Music	4	208,833
Grease	10	130,829
Mary Poppins	15	110,143
Saturday Night Fever	21	101,729
Snow White	26	87,890
Fiddler on the Roof	31	76,703
West Side Story	49	62,520
Funny Girl	53	61,234
A Star Is Born	60	54,865
My Fair Lady	62	54,580
South Pacific	68	53,364
This Is the Army	84	48,739

A couple of swells — Fred and Judy in *Easter Parade* (1948).

FILMOGRAPHY

D = Director
S = Stars
R = Running time

Alexander's Ragtime Band (1938).
D: Henry King. S: Tyrone Power, Alice Faye, Don Ameche, Ethel Merman. R: 1h, 25m.

All That Jazz (1979).
D: Bob Fosse. S: Roy Scheider, Jessica Lange, Ann Reinking, Leland Palmer, Cliff Gorman, Ben Vereen, Erzsebet Foldi. R: 2h, 3m.

American in Paris, An (1951).
D: Vincente Minnelli. S: Gene Kelly, Leslie Caron, Oscar Levant, Georges Guetary, Nina Foch. R: 1h, 53m.

Anchors Aweigh (1945).
D: George Sidney. S: Frank Sinatra, Kathryn Grayson, Gene Kelly, Jose Iturbi, Dean Stockwell, Pamela Britton. R: 2h, 20m.

And the Angels Sing (1944).
D: George Marshall. S: Dorothy Lamour, Fred MacMurray, Betty Hutton, Diana Lynn, Raymond Walburn, Eddie Foy Jr. R: 1h, 36m.

Annie (1982).
D: John Huston. S: Albert Finney, Carol Burnett, Aileen Quinn, Bernadette Peters, Tim Curry, Ann Reinking, Geoffrey Holder. R: 2h, 8m.

Annie Get Your Gun (1950).
D: George Sidney. S: Betty Hutton, Howard Keel, Louis Calhern, Edward Arnold, Keenan Wynn, J Carrol Naish. R: 1h, 47m.

Applause (1929).
D: Rouben Mamoulian. S: Helen Morgan, Joan Peers, Henry Wadsworth, Dorothy Cummins. R: 1h, 18m.

Are You with It? (1948).
D: Jack Hively. S: Donald O'Connor, Olga San Juan, Martha Stewart, Lew Parker. R: 1h, 30m.

At Long Last Love (1975).
D: Peter Bogdanovich. S: Burt Reynolds, Cybill Shepherd, Madeline Kahn, Duilio Del Prete, Eileen Brennan, John Hillerman, Mildred Natwick. R: 1h, 58m.

Babes in Arms (1939).
D: Busby Berkeley. S: Mickey Rooney, Judy Garland, Charles Winninger, Guy Kibbee, June Preisser, Douglas McPhail. R: 1h, 36m.

Babes in Toyland (1934).
D: Gus Meins, Charles R Rogers. S: Stan Laurel, Oliver Hardy, Charlotte Henry, Henry Brandon, Felix Knight, Jean Darling, Johnny Downs. R: 1h, 13m.

Babes on Broadway (1941).
D: Busby Berkeley. S: Mickey Rooney, Judy Garland, Fay Bainter, Virginia Weidler, Richard Quine. R: 1h, 58m.

Balalaika (1939).
D: Reinhold Schunzel. S: Nelson Eddy, Ilona Massey, Charles Ruggles, Frank Morgan, Lionel Atwill, George Tobias. R: 1h, 42m.

Band Wagon, The (1953).
D: Vincente Minnelli. S: Fred Astaire, Cyd Charisse, Oscar Levant, Nanette Fabray, Jack Buchanan. R: 1h, 52m.

Barkleys of Broadway, The (1949).
D: Charles Waters. S: Fred Astaire, Ginger Rogers, Oscar Levant, Billie Burke, Gale Robbins. R: 1h, 49m.

Bathing Beauty (1944).
D: George Sidney. S: Red Skelton, Esther Williams, Basil Rathbone, Ethel Smith, Xavier Cugat, Bill Goodwin. R: 1h, 41m.

Because You're Mine (1952).
D: Alexander Hall, S: Mario Lanza, James Whitmore, Doretta Morrow, Dean Miller, Paula Corday, Jeff Donnell, Spring Byington, Don Porter, Eduard Franz, Bobby Van. R: 1hr, 43m.

Belle of New York, The (1952).
D: Charles Walters. S: Fred Astaire, Vera-Ellen, Marjorie Main, Keenan Wynn, Alice Pearce. R: 1h, 22m.

Bells Are Ringing (1960).
D: Vincente Minnelli. S: Judy Holliday, Dean Martin, Fred Clark, Eddie Foy Jr. R: 2h, 7m.

Bells of St Mary's, The (1945).
D: Leo McCarey. S: Bing Crosby, Ingrid Bergman, Henry Travers, William Gargan, Ruth Donnelly, John Carroll, Martha Sleeper, Rhys Williams. R: 2h, 6m.

Benny Goodman Story, The (1956).
D: Valentine Davies. S: Steve Allen, Donna Reed, Sammy Davis Sr, Gene Krupa, Harry James, Martha Tilton. R: 1h, 56m.

Best Foot Forward (1943).
D: Edward Buzzell. S: Lucille Ball, William Gaxton, Virginia Weidler, Tommy Dix, Nancy Walker, Gloria DeHaven, June Allyson. R: 1h, 35m.

Big Broadcast, The (1932).
D: Frank Tuttle. S: Bing Crosby, Kate Smith, George Burns, Gracie Allen, Stuart Erwin, Leila Hyams, Cab Calloway, The Mills Brothers, The Boswell Sisters. R: 1h, 18m.

Big Broadcast of 1936, The (1935).
D: Norman Taurog. S: Jack Oakie, George Burns, Gracie Allen, Lyda Roberti, Henry Wadsworth, Wendy Barrie, C Henry Gordon, Ethel Merman, Charlie Ruggles, Mary Boland, Bill Robinson. R: 1h, 37m.

Big Broadcast of 1937, The (1936).
D: Mitchell Liesen. S: Jack Benny, George Burns, Gracie Allen, Bob Burns, Martha Raye, Shirley Ross, Ray Milland. R: 1h, 42m.

Big Broadcast of 1938, The (1938).
D: Mitchell Liesen. S: W C Fields, Martha Raye, Dorothy Lamour, Shirley Ross, Lynne Overman, Bob Hope, Ben Blue, Leif Erickson. R: 1h, 30m.

Billy Rose's Diamond Horseshoe.
See: **Diamond Horseshoe.**

Billy Rose's Jumbo (1962).
D: Charles Walters. S: Doris Day, Stephen Boyd, Jimmy Durante, Martha Raye, Dean Jagger. R: 2h, 5m.

Birth of the Blues, The (1941)
D: Victor Schertzinger. S: Bing Crosby, Brian Donlevy, Carolyn Lee, Eddie Anderson, Mary Martin. R: 1h, 25m.

Bitter Sweet (1940).
D: W S Van Dyke II. S: Jeanette

MacDonald, Nelson Eddy, George Sanders, Felix Bressart, Lynne Carver, Ian Hunter. **R:** 1h, 32m.

Blue Skies (1946).
D: Stuart Heisler. **S:** Fred Astaire, Bing Crosby, Joan Caulfield, Billy DeWolfe, Olga San Juan. **R:** 1h, 44m.

Born To Dance (1936).
D: Roy Del Ruth. **S:** Eleanor Powell, James Stewart, Virginia Bruce, Una Merkel, Sid Silvers, Frances Langford, Raymond Walburn, Buddy Ebsen. **R:** 1h, 45m.

Boy Friend, The (1971).
D: Ken Russell. **S:** Twiggy, Christopher Gable, Moyra Fraser, Max Adrian, Georgina Hale, Tommy Tune. **R:** 1h, 50m.

Boys From Syracuse, The (1940).
D: A Edward Sutherland. **S:** Allan Jones, Joe Penner, Martha Raye, Rosemary Lane, Irene Hervey, Eric Blore. **R:** 1h, 13m.

Brigadoon (1954).
D: Vincente Minnelli. **S:** Gene Kelly, Van Johnson, Cyd Charisse. **R:** 1h, 48m.

Bright Eyes (1934).
D: David Butler, **S:** Shirley Temple, James Dunn, Judith Allen, Jane Withers, Lois Wilson, Charles Sellon. **R:** 1h, 23m.

Broadway Melody, The (1929).
D: Harry Beaumont. **S:** Bessie Love, Anita Page, Charles King, Jed Prouty, Kenneth Thompson, Edward Dillon, Mary Doran. **R:** 1h, 44m.

Broadway Melody of 1936 (1935).
D: Roy Del Ruth. **S:** Jack Benny, Eleanor Powell, Robert Taylor, Una Merkel, Sid Silvers, Buddy Ebsen. **R:** 1h, 50m.

Broadway Melody of 1938 (1937).
D: Roy Del Ruth. **S:** Robert Taylor, Eleanor Powell, Judy Garland, Sophie Tucker, Binnie Barnes, Buddy Ebsen, Billy Gilbert, Raymond Walburn. **R:** 1h, 50m.

Broadway Melody of 1940 (1940).
D: Norman Taurog. **S:** Fred Astaire, George Murphy, Eleanor Powell, Frank Morgan, Ian Hunter, Florence Rice. **R:** 1h, 42m.

Broadway Rhythm (1944).
D: Roy Del Ruth. **S:** George Murphy, Ginny Sims, Charles Winninger, Gloria De Haven, Nancy Walker, Ben Blue, Tommy Dorsey and his Orchestra. **R:** 1h, 54m.

Broadway Serenade (1939).
D: Robert Z Leonard. **S:** Jeanette MacDonald, Lew Ayres, Ian Hunter, Frank Morgan, Rita Johnson, Virginia Grey, William Gargan, Katharine Alexander. **R:** 1h, 54m.

Broadway to Hollywood (1933).
D: Willard Mack. **S:** Alice Brady, Frank Morgan, Jackie Cooper, Russell Hardie, Madge Evans, Mickey Rooney, Eddie Quillan. **R:** 1h, 25m.

Buddy Holly Story, The (1978).
D: Steve Rash. **S:** Gary Busey, Don Stroud, Charles Martin Smith, Bill Jordan, Maria Richwine, Conrad Janis, Dick O'Neill. **R:** 1h, 54m.

Bye Bye Birdie (1963).
D: George Sidney. **S:** Janet Leigh, Dick Van Dyke, Ann-Margret, Maureen Stapleton, Paul Lynde, Ed Sullivan. **R:** 1h, 52m.

Cabaret (1972).
D: Bob Fosse. **S:** Liza Minnelli, Michael York, Helmut Griem, Joel Grey, Fritz Wepper, Marisa Berenson. **R:** 2h, 8m.

Cabin in the Sky (1943).
D: Vincente Minnelli. **S:** Eddie Anderson, Lena Horne, Ethel Waters, Louis Armstrong, Rex Ingram, Duke Ellington and his Orchestra. **R:** 1h, 40m.

Cairo (1942).
D: W S Van Dyke II. **S:** Jeanette MacDonald, Robert Young, Ethel Waters, Reginald Owen, Lionel Atwill, Dooley Wilson. **R:** 1h, 41m.

Call Me Madam (1953).
D: Walter Lang. **S:** Ethel Merman, Donald O'Connor, George Sanders, Vera-Ellen, Billy DeWolfe, Walter Slezak, Lilia Skala. **R:** 1h, 57m.

Camelot (1967).
D: Joshua Logan. **S:** Richard Harris, Vanessa Redgrave, Franco Nero, David Hemmings, Lionel Jeffries. **R:** 2h, 38m.

Can-Can (1960).
D: Walter Lang. **S:** Frank Sinatra, Shirley MacLaine, Maurice Chevalier, Louis Jourdan, Juliet Prowse. **R:** 2h, 11m.

Captain January (1936).
D: David Butler. **S:** Shirley Temple, Guy Kibbee, Slim Summerville, Buddy Ebsen. **R:** 1h, 15m.

Carefree (1938).
D: Mark Sandrich. **S:** Fred Astaire, Ginger Rogers, Ralph Bellamy, Luella Gear, Jack Carson. **R:** 1h, 20m.

Carmen Jones (1954).
D: Otto Preminger. **S:** Dorothy Dandridge, Harry Belafonte, Pearl Bailey, Roy Glenn, Diahann Carroll, Brock Peters. **R:** 1h, 45m.

Carousel (1956).
D: Henry King. **S:** Gordon MacRae, Shirley Jones, Cameron Mitchell, Barbara Ruick, Claramae Turner, Robert Rounseville, Gene Lockhart. **R:** 2h, 8m.

Centennial Summer (1946).
D: Otto Preminger. **S:** Jeanne Crain, Cornel Wilde, Linda Darnell, Dorothy Gish, William Eythe, Constance Bennett, Walter Brennan. **R:** 1h, 42m.

Chocolate Soldier, The (1941).
D: Roy Del Ruth. **S:** Nelson Eddy, Rise Stevens, Nigel Bruce, Florence Bates, Dorothy Gilmore, Nydia Westman. **R:** 1h, 42m.

Coney Island (1943).
D: Walter Lang, **S:** Betty Grable, George Montgomery, Cesar Romero, Charles Winninger, Phil Silvers, Matt Briggs. **R:** 1h, 36m.

Curly Top (1935).
D: Irving Cummings. **S:** Shirley Temple, John Boles, Rochelle Hudson, Jane Darwell, Rafaela Ottiano, Arthur Treacher. **R:** 1h, 15m.

Daddy Long Legs (1955).
D: Jean Negulesco. **S:** Fred Astaire, Leslie Caron, Terry Moore, Thelma Ritter, Fred Clark. **R:** 2h, 6m.

Dames (1934).
D: Ray Enright. **S:** Joan Blondell, Dick Powell, Ruby Keeler, ZaSu Pitts, Hugh Herbert, Guy Kibbee, Phil Regan. **R:** 1h, 30m.

Damn Yankees (1958).
D: George Abbott, Stanley Donen. **S:** Tab Hunter, Gwen Verdon, Ray Walston, Russ Brown. **R:** 1h, 50m.

Damsel in Distress, A (1937).
D: George Stevens. **S:** Fred Astaire, George Burns, Gracie Allen, Joan Fontaine, Constance Collier, Reginald Gardiner, Montagu Love. **R:** 1h, 38m.

Dancing Lady (1933).
D: Robert Z Leonard. S: Joan Crawford, Clark Gable, Franchot Tone, May Robson, Nelson Eddy, Fred Astaire, Robert Benchley, Ted Healy, the Three Stooges. R: 1h, 34m.

Dangerous When Wet (1953).
D: Charles Walters. S: Esther Williams, Fernando Lamas, Jack Carson, Charlotte Greenwood, Denise Darcel. R: 1h, 35m.

Darling Lili (1970).
D: Blake Edwards. S: Julie Andrews, Rock Hudson, Jeremy Kemp, Lance Percival, Jacques Marin, Michael Witney. R: 2h, 16m.

Date With Judy, A (1948).
D: Richard Thorpe. S: Wallace Beery, Jane Powell, Elizabeth Taylor, Carmen Miranda, Xavier Cugat, Robert Stack. R: 1h, 53m.

Deep in My Heart (1954).
D: Stanley Donen. S: Jose Ferrer, Merle Oberon, Helen Traubel, Doe Avedon, Walter Pidgeon, Paul Henreid. R: 2h, 12m.

Desert Song, The (1953).
D: H Bruce Humberstone. S: Kathryn Grayson, Gordon MacRae, Steve Cochran, Raymond Massey. R: 1h, 50m.

Diamond Horseshoe (1945).
D: George Seaton. S: Betty Grable, Dick Haymes, Phil Silvers, William Gaxton, Beatrice Kay, Carmen Cavallero. R: 1h, 44m.

Dimples (1936).
D: William Seiter. S: Shirley Temple, Frank Morgan, Helen Westley, Robert Kent, Stepin Fetchit, Astrid Allwyn. R: 1h, 18m.

Dixie (1943).
D: A Edward Sutherland. S: Bing Crosby, Dorothy Lamour, Billy DeWolfe, Marjorie Reynolds, Lynne Overman, Raymond Walburn, Eddie Foy Jr, Grant Mitchell. R: 1h, 29m.

Doctor Doolittle (1967).
D: Richard Fleischer. S: Rex Harrison, Samantha Eggar, Anthony Newley, Richard Attenborough, Peter Bull. R: 2h, 32m.

Dolly Sisters, The (1945).
D: Irving Cummings. S: Betty Grable, John Payne, June Haver, S Z Sakall, Reginald Gardiner. R: 1h, 54m.

Don Juan (1926).
D: Alan Crosland. S: John Barrymore, Mary Astor, Willard Louis, Estelle Taylor, Helene Costello, Warner Oland, Montagu Love, Myrna Loy, Hedda Hopper. R: 1h, 51m.

Double or Nothing (1937).
D: Theodore Reed. S: Bing Crosby, Martha Raye, Andy Devine, Mary Carlisle, William Frawley, Fay Holden, Frances Faye. R: 1h, 35m.

Down Argentine Way (1940).
D: Irving Cummngs. S: Don Ameche, Betty Grable, Carmen Miranda, Charlotte Greenwood, J Carrol Naish, Henry Stephenson. R: 1h, 34m.

DuBarry Was a Lady (1943).
D: Roy Del Ruth. S: Red Skelton, Lucille Ball, Gene Kelly, Virginia O'Brien, Zero Mostel, Donald Meek, George Givot, Louise Beavers, Tommy Dorsey and his Orchestra. R: 1h, 41m.

East Side of Heaven, The (1939).
D: David Butler. S: Bing Crosby, Joan Blondell, Mischa Auer, Irene Hervey, C Aubrey Smith, Baby Sandy. R: 1h, 30m.

Easter Parade (1948).
D: Charles Walters. S: Judy Garland, Fred Astaire, Peter Lawford, Ann Miller, Jules Munshin. R: 1h, 43m.

Easy to Love (1953).
D: Charles Walters. S: Esther Williams, Van Johnson, Tony Martin, Carroll Baker. R: 1h, 36m.

Eddie Cantor Story, The (1953).
D: Alfred E Green. S: Keefe Brasselle, Marilyn Erskine, Aline MacMahon, Marie Windsor. R: 1h, 56m.

Eddy Duchin Story, The (1956).
D: George Sidney. S: Tyrone Power, Kim Novak, Victoria Shaw, James Whitmore. R: 2h, 3m.

Emperor Waltz, The (1948).
D: Billy Wilder. S: Bing Crosby, Joan Fontaine, Roland Culver, Lucile Watson, Richard Hayden, Sig Ruman. R: 1h, 46m.

Everybody Sing (1938).
D: Edwin L Marin. S: Allan Jones, Judy Garland, Fanny Brice, Reginald Owen, Billie Burke, Reginald Gardiner. R: 1h, 20m.

Everything Happens at Night (1939).
D: Irving Cummings. S: Sonja Henie, Ray Milland, Robert Cummings, Alan Dinehart, Fritz Feld, Jody Gilbert, Victor Varconi. R: 1h, 17m.

Expresso Bongo (1960).
D: Val Guest. S: Laurence Harvey, Sylvia Syms, Yolande Donlan, Cliff Richard. R: 1h, 48m.

Fashions of 1934 (1934).
D: William Dieterle. S: William Powell, Bette Davis, Veree Teasdale, Reginald Owen, Frank McHugh, Phillip Reed, Hugh Herbert. R: 1h, 18m.

Fiddler on the Roof (1971).
D: Norman Jewison. S: Chaim Topol, Norma Crane, Leonard Frey, Molly Picon, Paul Mann, Rosalind Harris, Michele Marsh, Neva Small, Candice Bonstein. R: 3h, 1m.

Finian's Rainbow (1968).
D: Francis Ford Coppola. S: Fred Astaire, Petula Clark, Tommy Steele, Keenan Wynn, Al Freeman Jr, Don Franks, Barbara Hancock. R: 2h, 25m.

Firefly, The (1937).
D: Robert Z Leonard. S: Jeanette MacDonald, Allan Jones, Warren William, Billy Gilbert, Henry Daniell, Douglass Dumbrille, George Zucco. R: 2h, 11m.

First Love (1939).
D: Henry Koster. S: Deanna Durbin, Robert Stack, Helen Parrish, Eugene Pallette, Leatrice Joy, Marcia Mae Jones, Frank Jenks. R: 1h, 24m.

Flashdance (1983).
D: Adrian Lyne. S: Jennifer Beals, Michael Nouri, Lilia Skala. R: 1h, 35m.

Fleet's In, The (1942).
D: Victor Schertzinger. S: Dorothy Lamour, William Holden, Betty Hutton, Eddie Bracken, Rod Cameron, Leif Erickson, Jimmy Dorsey Orchestra with Helen O'Connell, Bob Eberle. R: 1h, 33m.

Flower Drum Song (1961).
D: Henry Koster. S: Nancy Kwan, James Shigeta, Miyoshi Umeki, Juanita Hall, Benson Fong. R: 2h, 13m.

Flying Down to Rio (1933).
D: Thornton Freeland. S: Dolores Del Rio, Gene Raymond, Paul Roulien, Ginger Rogers, Fred Astaire, Blanche Frederici, Eric Blore. R: 1h, 29m.

Flying High (1931).
D: Charles F Riesner. S: Bert Lahr,

Charlotte Greenwood, Pat O'Brien, Kathryn Crawford, Charles Winninger, Hedda Hopper, Guy Kibbee. **R:** 1h, 20m.

Follow the Fleet (1936).
D: Mark Sandrich. **S:** Fred Astaire, Ginger Rogers, Randolph Scott, Harriet Hilliard, Astrid Allwyn, Betty Grable. **R:** 1h, 50m.

Footlight Parade (1933).
D: Lloyd Bacon. **S:** James Cagney, Joan Blondell, Ruby Keeler, Dick Powell, Guy Kibbee, Ruth Donnelly, Hugh Herbert, Frank McHugh. **R:** 1h, 45m.

For Me and My Gal (1942).
D: Busby Berkeley. **S:** Judy Garland, Gene Kelly, George Murphy, Horace (later Stephen) McNally, Marta Eggerth, Keenan Wynn, Richard Quine, Ben Blue. **R:** 1h, 44m.

For the First Time (1959).
D: Rudy Maté. **S:** Mario Lanza, Johanna von Koszian, Kurt Kasznar, Zsa Zsa Gabor, Hans Sohnker. **R:** 1h, 37m.

Forty-Second Street (1933).
D: Lloyd Bacon. **S:** Warner Baxter, Ruby Keeler, George Brent, Bebe Daniels, Dick Powell, Guy Kibbee, Una Merkel, Ginger Rogers, Ned Sparks, George E Stone. **R:** 1h, 30m.

Funny Face (1957).
D: Stanley Donen. **S:** Audrey Hepburn, Fred Astaire, Kay Thompson, Michel Auclair, Suzy Parker, Ruta Lee. **R:** 1h, 43m.

Funny Girl (1968).
D: William Wyler. **S:** Barbra Streisand, Omar Sharif, Kay Medford, Anne Francis, Walter Pidgeon, Lee Allen, Gerald Mohr. **R:** 2h, 35m.

Funny Lady (1975).
D: Herbert Ross. **S:** Barbra Streisand, James Caan, Omar Sharif, Roddy McDowall, Ben Vereen, Carole Wells. **R:** 2h, 17m.

Funny Thing Happened on the Way to the Forum, A (1966).
D: Richard Lester. **S:** Zero Mostel, Phil Silvers, Buster Keaton, Jack Gilford, Michael Crawford, Annette Andre, Michael Hordern. **R:** 1h, 33m.

Gang's All Here, The (1943).
D: Busby Berkeley. **S:** Alice Faye, Carmen Miranda, James Ellison, Charlotte Greenwood, Eugene Pallette, Edward Everett Horton, Benny Goodman, Sheila Ryan. **R:** 1h, 43m.

Gay Divorcee, The (1934).
D: Mark Sandrich. **S:** Fred Astaire, Ginger Rogers, Alice Brady, Edward Everett Horton, Erik Rhodes, Betty Grable. **R:** 1h, 47m.

Gentlemen Prefer Blondes (1953).
D: Howard Hawks. **S:** Jane Russell, Marilyn Monroe, Charles Coburn, Tommy Noonan, George Winslow. **R:** 1h, 31m.

George White's Scandals (1935).
D: George White. **S:** Alice Faye, James Dunn, Ned Sparks, Lyda Roberti, Cliff Edwards, Arline Judge, Eleanor Powell, George White, Benny Rubin. **R:** 1h, 23m.

Gigi (1959).
D: Vincente Minnelli. **S:** Leslie Caron, Maurice Chevalier, Louis Jourdan, Hermione Gingold, Jacques Bergerac, Eva Gabor. **R:** 1h, 56m.

Girl Crazy (1943).
D: Norman Taurog. **S:** Mickey Rooney, Judy Garland, Gil Stratton, Robert E Strickland, 'Rags' Ragland, June Allyson, Nancy Walker, Guy Kibbee. **R:** 1h, 39m.

Girl of the Golden West, The (1938).
D: Robert Z Leonard. **S:** Jeanette MacDonald, Nelson Eddy, Walter Pidgeon, Leo Carillo, Buddy Ebsen, Leonard Penn. **R:** 2h.

Glenn Miller Story, The (1954).
D: Anthony Mann. **S:** James Stewart, June Allyson, Charles Drake, George Tobias, Harry Morgan, Frances Langford, Louis Armstrong, Gene Krupa. **R:** 1h, 56m.

Godspell (1973).
D: David Greene. **S:** Victor Garber, David Haskell, Jerry Sroka, Lynne Thigpen, Katie Hanley, Robin Lamont. **R:** 1h, 43m.

Going Hollywood (1933).
D: Raoul Walsh. **S:** Marion Davies, Bing Crosby, Fifi D'Orsay, Stuart Erwin, Ned Sparks, Patsy Kelly. **R:** 1h, 20m.

Going My Way (1944).
D: Leo McCarey. **S:** Bing Crosby, Barry Fitzgerald, Rise Stevens, Gene Lockhart, Frank McHugh, James Brown, Jean Heather, Stanley Clements, Carl Switzer, Porter Hall. **R:** 2h, 10m.

Gold Diggers of 1933 (1933).
D: Mervyn LeRoy. **S:** Joan Blondell, Ruby Keeler, Aline MacMahon, Dick Powell, Guy Kibbee, Warren William, Ned Sparks, Ginger Rogers, Sterling Holloway. **R:** 1h, 36m.

Gold Diggers of 1935 (1935).
D: Busby Berkeley. **S:** Dick Powell, Adolphe Menjou, Gloria Stuart, Alice Brady, Glenda Farrell, Frank McHugh, Winifred Shaw. **R:** 1h, 35m.

Gold Diggers of 1937 (1936).
D: Lloyd Bacon. **S:** Dick Powell, Joan Blondell, Glenda Farrell, Victor Moore Lee Dixon, Osgood Perkins. **R:** 1h, 40m.

Goldwyn Follies, The (1938).
D: George Marshall. **S:** Adolphe Menjou, Andrea Leeds, Kenny Baker, the Ritz Brothers, Vera Zorina, Helen Jepson, Bobby Clark, Edgar Bergen and Charlie McCarthy. **R:** 2h.

Good News (1947).
D: Charles Walters. **S:** June Allyson, Peter Lawford, Patricia Marshall, Joan McCracken, Mel Torme. **R:** 1h, 35m.

Godbye, Mr Chips (1969).
D: Herbert Ross, **S:** Peter O'Toole, Petula Clark, Michael Redgrave, George Baker, Sian Phillips, Michael Bryant. **R:** 2h, 31m.

Grease (1978).
D: Randal Kleiser. **S:** John Travolta, Olivia Newton-John, Stockard Channing, Jeff Conaway, Didi Conn, Eve Arden, Sid Caesar. **R:** 1h, 50m.

Grease 2 (1982).
D: Patricia Birch. **S:** Maxwell Caulfield, Michele Pfeiffer, Adrian Zmed, Lorna Luft, Didi Conn, Eve Arden, Sid Caesar, Dody Goodman, Tab Hunter, Connie Stevens. **R:** 1h, 54m.

Great Caruso, The (1951).
D: Richard Thorpe. **S:** Mario Lanza, Ann Blyth, Jarmila Novotna, Dorothy Kirstin. **R:** 1h, 49m.

Great Victor Herbert, The (1939).
D: Andrew L Stone. **S:** Allan Jones, Mary Martin, Walter Connolly, Lee Bowman, Susanna Foster, Jerome Cowan. **R:** 1h, 24m.

Great Waltz, The (1938).
D: Julien Duvivier. **S:** Luise Rainer, Fernand Gravet, Miliza Korjus, Hugh Herbert, Lionel Atwill, Curt Bois. **R:** 1h, 42m.

Great Waltz, The (1972).
D: Andrew L Stone. S: Horst Buchholz, Mary Costa, Rossano Brazzi, Nigel Patrick, Yvonne Mitchell, James Faulkner. R: 2h, 15m.

Great Ziegfeld, The (1936).
D: Robert Z Leonard. S: William Powell, Myrna Loy, Luise Rainer, Frank Morgan, Fanny Brice, Virginia Bruce, Reginald Owen, Ray Bolger, Dennis Morgan. R: 2h, 56m.

Guys and Dolls (1955).
D: Joseph L Mankiewicz. S: Frank Sinatra, Marlon Brando, Jean Simmons, Vivian Blaine, Stubby Kaye, Veda Ann Borg, Sheldon Leonard. R: 2h, 30m.

Gypsy (1962).
D: Mervyn LeRoy. S: Rosalind Russell, Natalie Wood, Karl Malden, Paul Wallace, Betty Bruce, Parley Baer, Harry Shannon. R: 2h, 29m.

Hair (1979).
D: Milos Forman. S: John Savage, Treat Williams, Beverly D'Angelo, Annie Golden, Dorsey Wright, Don Dacus, Cheryl Barnes, Nicholas Ray. R: 2h, 1m.

Half a Sixpence (1969).
D: George Sidney. S: Tommy Steele, Julia Foster, Penelope Horner, Cyril Ritchard, Grover Dale. R: 2h, 28m.

Hallelujah (1929).
D: King Vidor. S: Daniel L Haynes, Nina Mae McKinney, William Fountaine, Everett McGarrity, Victoria Spivey. R: 1h, 46m.

Hans Christian Andersen (1952).
D: Charles Vidor. S: Danny Kaye, Farley Granger, Jeanmaire, Roland Petit, John Qualen. R: 1h, 25m.

Hard Day's Night, A (1964).
D: Richard Lester. S: John Lennon, Paul McCartney, George Harrison, Ringo Starr, Wilfred Bramble, Victor Spinetti, Anna Quale. R: 1h, 25m.

Harvey Girls, The 91946).
D: George Sidney. S: Judy Garland, Ray Bolger, John Hodiak, Angela Lansbury, Preston Foster, Virginia O'Brien, Marjorie Main, Kenny Baker, Cyd Charisse. R: 1h, 41m.

Hello Dolly! (1969).
D: Gene Kelly. S: Barbra Streisand, Walter Matthau, Michael Crawford, E J Peaker, Louis Armstrong. R: 1h, 58m.

Hello, Frisco, Hello (1943).
D: H Bruce Humberstone. S: Alice Faye, John Payne, Jack Oakie, Lynn Bari, Laird Cregar, June Havoc, Ward Bond. R: 1h, 38m.

Help! (1965).
D: Richard Lester. S: John Lennon, Paul McCartney, George Harrison, Ringo Starr, Leo McKern, Eleanor Bron, Victor Spinetti, Roy Kinnear, Patrick Cargill. R: 1h, 30m.

Here Come the Waves (1944).
D: Mark Sandrich. S: Bing Crosby, Betty Hutton, Sonny Tufts, Ann Doran, Catherine Craig. R: 1h, 39m.

Here Comes the Groom (1951).
D: Frank Capra. S: Bing Crosby, Jane Wyman, Franchot Tone, Alexis Smith, James Barton, Anna Maria Alberghetti. R: 1h, 53m.

High Society (1956).
D: Charles Walters. S: Bing Crosby, Grace Kelly, Frank Sinatra, Celeste Holm, Louis Calhern, Louis Armstrong. R: 1h, 47m.

Higher and Higher (1943).
D: Tim Whelan. S: Michele Morgan, Jack Haley, Frank Sinatra, Leon Errol, Marcy McGuire, Victor Borge, Mary Wickes, Mel Torme. R: 1h, 30m.

Hit the Deck (1955).
D: Roy Rowland. S: Jane Powell, Tony Martin, Debbie Reynolds, Ann Miller, Vic Damone, Russ Tamblyn, Walter Pidgeon, Kay Armen, Gene Raymond. R: 1h, 52m.

Holiday in Mexico (1946).
D: George Sidney. S: Walter Pidgeon, Ilona Massey, Roddy McDowall, Jose Iturbi, Xavier Cugat, Jane Powell. R: 2h, 7m.

Holiday Inn (1942).
D: Mark Sandrich. S: Bing Crosby, Fred Astaire, Marjorie Reynolds, Virginia Dale, Walter Abel, Louise Beavers. R: 1h, 41m.

Hollywood Cavalcade (1939).
D: Irving Cummings. S: Alice Faye, Don Ameche, Al Jolson, Mack Sennett, Stuart Erwin, Buster Keaton, Mary Forbes, Chester Conklin, Rin-Tin-Tin Jr. R: 1h, 36m.

Hollywood Revue of 1929, The (1929).
D: Charles Riesner. S: Conrad Nagel, Jack Benny, John Gilbert, Norma Shearer, Joan Crawford, Stan Laurel, Oliver Hardy, Bessie Love, Lionel Barrymore, Marion Davies, Buster Keaton, Marie Dressler, Polly Moran. R: 2h, 10m.

How to Marry a Millionaire (1953).
D: Jean Negulesco. S: Marilyn Monroe, Betty Grable, Lauren Bacall, William Powell, Rory Calhoun, David Wayne, Fred Clark. R: 1h, 35m.

How to Succeed in Business without Really Trying (1967).
D: David Swift. S: Robert Morse, Michele Lee, Rudy Vallee, Anthony Teague, Maureen Arthur, Sammy Smith. R: 2h, 1m.

I Dream Too Much (1935).
D: John Cromwell. S: Lily Pons, Henry Fonda, Eric Blore, Lucille Ball, Osgood Perkins. R: 1h, 35m.

I Married an Angel (1942).
D: W S Van Dyke II. S: Jeanette MacDonald, Nelson Eddy, Edward Everett Horton, Binnie Barnes, Reginald Owen, Douglass Dumbrille. R: 1h, 24m.

Iceland (1942).
D: H Bruce Humberstone. S: Sonja Henie, John Payne, Jack Oakie, Felix Bressart, Osa Massen, John Merrill. R: 1h, 19m.

I'll Take Romance (1937).
D: Edward H Griffith. S: Grace Moore, Melvyn Douglas, Stuart Erwin, Helen Westley, Margaret Hamilton. R: 1h, 25m.

In the Good Old Summertime (1949).
D: Robert Z Leonard. S: Judy Garland, Van Johnson, S Z Sakall, Spring Byington, Buster Keaton. R: 1h, 42m.

Irene (1940).
D: Herbert Wilcox. S: Anna Neagle, Ray Milland, Roland Young, Alan Marshall, May Robson, Billie Burke, Arthur Treacher. R: 1h, 44m.

It Happened in Brooklyn (1947).
D: Richard Whorf. S: Frank Sinatra, Kathryn Grayson, Jimmy Durante, Peter Lawford, Gloria Grahame. R: 1h, 45m.

It's a Date (1949).
D: William A Seiter. S: Deanna Durbin, Walter Pidgeon, Kay Francis, Eugene Pallette, Lewis Howard, S Z Sakall, Samuel S Hinds, Cecilia Loftus. R: 1h, 43m.

It's Always Fair Weather (1955).
D: Gene Kelly, Stanley Donen. S: Gene Kelly, Dan Dailey, Michael Kidd, Cyd Charisse, Dolores Gray, David Burns. R: 1h, 42m.

Jailhouse Rock (1957).
D: Richard Thorpe. S: Elvis Presley, Judy Tyler, Vaughn Taylor, Dean Jones, Mickey Shaughnessy. R: 1h, 36m.

Jazz Singer, The (1927).
D: Alan Crosland. S: Al Jolson, May McAvoy, Warner Oland, Eugenie Besserer, Otto Lederer. R: 1h, 29m.

Jazz Singer, The (1953).
D: Michael Curtiz. S: Danny Thomas, Peggy Lee, Mildred Dunnock, Eduard Franz. R: 1h, 47m.

Jazz Singer, The (1980).
D: Richard Fleischer. S: Neil Diamond, Laurence Olivier, Lucie Arnaz, Catlin Adams, Franklyn Ajaye, Paul Nicholas, Sully Boyar, Mike Kellin. R: 1h, 55m.

Jesus Christ, Superstar (1973).
D: Norman Jewison. S: Ted Neeley, Carl Anderson, Yvonne Elliman, Barry Dennen, Joshua Mostel, Bob Bingham. R: 1h, 43m.

Jolson Sings Again (1949).
D: Henry Levin. S: Larry Parks, Barbara Hale, William Demarest, Ludwig Donath. R: 1h, 36m.

Jolson Story, The (1946).
D: Alfred E Green. S: Larry Parks, Evelyn Keyes, William Demarest, Bill Goodman, Ludwig Donath. R: 2h, 8m.

Jumbo: See **Billy Rose's Jumbo.**

Just Around the Corner (1938).
D: Irving Cummings. S: Shirley Temple, Joan Davis, Charles Farrell, Amanda Duff, Bill Robinson, Bert Lahr. R: 1h, 10m.

Just for You (1952).
D: Elliott Nugent. S: Bing Crosby, Jane Wyman, Ethel Barrymore, Natalie Wood, Cora Witherspoon. R: 1h, 44m.

King and I, The (1956).
D: Walter Lang. S: Deborah kerr, Yul Brynner, Rita Moreno. Martin, Benson, Terry Saunders, Rex Thompson. Alan Mowbray. R: 2h, 13m.

King Steps out, The (1938).
D: Josef von Sternberg. S: Grace Moore, Franchot Tone, Walter Connolly, Raymond Walburn, Elizabeth Risdon, Nana Bryant, Victor Jory. R: 1h, 25m.

Kismet (1955).
D: Vincente Minnelli. S: Howard Keel, Ann Blyth, Dolores Gray, Monty Wooley, Sebastian Cabot, Vic Damone. R: 1h, 53m.

Kiss Me Kate (1953).
D: George Sidney. S: Kathryn Grayson, Howard Keel, Ann Miller, Bobby Van, Keenan Wynn, James Whitmore, Bob Fosse. R: 1h, 49m.

Kissing Bandit, The (1948).
D: Laslo Benedek. S: Frank Sinatra, Kathryn Grayson, Ann Miller, J Carrol Naish, Ricardo Montalban, Mildred Natwick, Cyd Charisse, Billy Gilbert. R: 1h, 42m.

Knickerbocker Holiday (1944).
D: Harry Brown. S: Nelson Eddy, Charles Coburn, Constance Dowling, Shelley Winters, Percy Kilbride, Chester Conklin. R: 1h, 25m.

Lady Be Good (1941).
D: Norman Z McLeod. S: Eleanor Powell, Ann Sothern, Robert Young, Lionel Barrymore, John Carroll, Red Skelton, Virginia O'Brien. R: 1h, 51m.

Lady in the Dark (1944).
D: Mitchell Leisen. S: Ginger Rogers, Ray Milland, Jon Hall, Warner Baxter, Barry Sullivan, Gail Russell, Mischa Auer. R: 1h, 40m.

Lady's Morals, A (1930).
D: Alexander Hall. S: Grace Moore, Reginald Denny, Wallace Beery, Jobyna Howland. R: 1h, 15m.

Les Girls (1957).
D: George Cukor. S: Gene Kelly, Kay Kendall, Mitzi Gaynor, Taina Elg, Jacques Bergerac. R: 1h, 54m.

Let It Be (1970).
D: Michael Lindsay-Hogg. S: John Lennon, Paul McCartney, Ringo Starr, George Harrison. R: 1h, 20m.

Let's Dance (1959).
D: Norman Z McLeod. S: Betty Hutton, Fred Astaire, Roland Young, Ruth Warrick, Shepperd Strudwick. R: 1h, 52m.

Li'l Abner (1959).
D: Melvin Frank. S: Leslie Parrish, Peter Palmer, Stubby Kaye, Howard St John, Julie Newmar, Stella Stevens, Billie Hayes, Robert Strauss. R: 1h, 53m.

Lili (1953).
D: Charles Walters. S: Leslie Caron, Mel Ferrer, Zsa Zsa Gabor, Jean-Pierre Aumont, Amanda Blake, Kurt Kasznar. R: 1h, 21m.

Lillian Russell (1940).
D: Irving Cummings. S: Alice Faye, Don Ameche, Henry Fonda, Edward Arnold, Warren William, Leo Carillo, Nigel Bruce. R: 2h, 7m.

Listen, Darling (1938).
D: Edwin L Marin. S: Judy Garland, Freddie Bartholomew, Mary Astor, Walter Pidgeon, Alan Hale, Scotty Beckett. R: 1h, 10m.

Little Colonel, The (1935).
D: David Butler. S: Shirley Temple, Lionel Barrymore, Evelyn Venable, John Lodge, Sidney Blackmer, Bill Robinson. R: 1h, 20m.

Little Miss Broadway (1938).
D: Irving Cummings. S: Shirley Temple, George Murphy, Jimmy Durante, Phyllis Brooks, Edna May Oliver, George Barbier. R: 1h, 10m.

Little Nellie Kelly (1940).
D: Norman Taurog. S: Judy Garland, George Murphy, Charles Winninger, Douglas McPhail. R: 1h, 40m.

Little Night Music, A (1978).
D: Harold Prince. S: Elizabeth Taylor, Diana Rigg, Len Cariou, Lesley-Anne Down, Hermione Gingold, Lawrence Guittard. R: 2h, 4m.

Little Princess, The (1939).
D: Walter Lang. S: Shirley Temple, Richard Greene, Anita Louise, Ian Hunter, Cesar Romero, Arthur Treacher, Marcia Mae Jones. R: 1h, 31m.

Littlest Rebel, The (1935).
D: David Butler. S: Shirley Temple, John Boles, Jack Holt, Karen Morley, Bill Robinson. R: 1h, 10m.

Lost Horizon (1973).
D: Charles Jarrott. S: Peter Finch, Liv Ullmann, Sally Kellerman, George Kennedy, Michael York, Olivia Hussey, Bobby Van, James Shigeta, Charles Boyer, John Gielgud. R: 2h, 23m.

Lost in the Stars (1974).
D: Daniel Mann. S: Brock Peters,

Melba Moore, Raymond St Jacques, Clifton Davis, Paula Kelly. **R:** 1h, 54m.

Louisiana Purchase (1941).
D: Irving Cummings. **S:** Bob Hope, Vera Zorina, Victor Moore, Irene Bordoni, Dona Drake. **R:** 1h, 38m.

Love Me Forever (1935).
D: Victor Schertzinger. **S:** Grace Moore, Leo Carillo, Robert Allen, Spring Byington, Douglass Dumbrille. **R:** 1h, 30m.

Love Me or Leave Me (1955).
D: Charles Vidor. **S:** Doris Day, James Cagney, Robert Keith, Tom Tully. **R:** 2h, 2m.

Love Me Tender (1956).
D: Robert D Webb. **S:** Richard Egan, Debra Paget, Elvis Presley, Robert Middleton, William Campbell, Neville Brand, Mildred Dunnock. **R:** 1h, 29m.

Love Me Tonight (1932).
D: Rouben Mamoulian. **S:** Maurice Chevalier, Jeanette MacDonald, Charlie Ruggles, Myrna Loy, C Aubrey Smith, Charles Butterworth. **R:** 1h, 36m.

Love Parade, The (1929).
D: Ernst Lubitsch. **S:** Maurice Chevalier, Jeanette MacDonald, Lillian Roth, Lionel Belmore, Lupino Lane, Ben Turpin. **R:** 1h, 30m.

Loving You (1957).
D: Hal Kanter. **S:** Elvis Presley, Lizabeth Scott, Wendell Corey, Dolores Hart, James Gleason. **R:** 1h, 41m.

Lullaby of Broadway, The (1951).
D: David Butler. **S:** Doris Day, Gene Nelson, S Z Sakall, Billy DeWolfe, Gladys George. **R:** 1h, 32m.

Mad About Music (1938).
D: Norman Taurog. **S:** Deanna Durbin, Herbert Marshall, Gail Patrick, Arthur Treacher, Helen Parrish, Marcia Mae Jones, William Frawley. **R:** 1h, 38m.

Mame (1974).
D: Gene Saks. **S:** Lucille Ball, Beatrice Arthur, Robert Preson, Jane Connell, Bruce Davison, Kirby Furlong. **R:** 2h, 11m.

Mammy (1930).
D: Michael Curtiz. **S:** Al Jolson, Lois Moran, Louise Dresser, Lowell Sherman, Hobart Bosworth. **R:** 1h, 24m.

Man of La Mancha (1972).
D: Arthur Hiller. **S:** Peter O'Toole, Sophia Loren, James Coco, Harry Andrews, John Castele. **R:** 2h, 10m.

Mary Poppins (1964).
D: Robert Stevenson. **S:** Julie Andrews, Dick Van Dyke, David Tomlinson, Glynis Johns, Ed Wynn, Hermione Baddeley, Karen Dotrice, Matthew Garber, Arthur Treacher, Reginald Owen. **R:** 2h, 20m.

Maytime (1937).
D: Robert Z Leonard. **S:** Jeanette MacDonald, Nelson Eddy, John Barrymore, Herman Bing, Rafaela Ottiano, Paul Porcasi, Sig Ruman. **R:** 2h, 12m.

Meet Me in Las Vegas (1956).
D: Roy Rowland. **S:** Dan Dailey, Cyd Charisse, Agnes Moorehead, Lili Darvas, Jim Backus. **R:** 1h, 52m.

Meet Me in St Louis (1944).
D: Vincente Minnelli. **S:** Judy Garland, Margaret O'Brien, Mary Astor, Lucille Bremer, Marjorie Main, June Lockhart, Harry Davenport, Leon Ames, Tom Drake. **R:** 1h, 53m.

Merry Widow, The (1934).
D: Ernst Lubitsch. **S:** Maurice Chevalier, Jeanette MacDonald, Una Merkel, Edward Everett Horton, George Barbier, Herman Bing. **R:** 1h, 39m.

Merry Widow, The (1952).
D: Curtis Bernhardt. **S:** Lana Turner, Fernando Lamas, Una Merkel, Richard Haydn. **R:** 1h, 45m.

Mikado, The (1939).
D: Victor Schertzinger. **S:** Kenny Baker, John Barclay, Martyn Green, Jean Colin, Constance Wills, **R:** 1h, 30m.

Million Dollar Mermaid (1952).
D: Mervyn LeRoy. **S:** Esther Williams, Victor Mature, Walter Pidgeon, David Brian, Jesse White. **R:** 1h, 55m.

Mississippi (1935).
D: A Edward Sutherland. **S:** Bing Crosby, W C Fields, Joan Bennett, Queenie Smith, Gail Patrick, Claude Gillingwater. **R:** 1h, 13m.

Mr Music (1950).
D: Richard Hadyn. **S:** Bing Crosby, Nancy Olson, Charles Coburn, Ruth Hussey, Marge and Gower Champion, Peggy Lee, Groucho Marx. **R:** 1h, 53m.

Monte Carlo (1930).
D: Ernst Lubitsch. **S:** Jeanette MacDonald, Jack Buchanan, ZaSu Pitts, Claude Allister, Tyler Brooke. **R:** 1h, 30m.

Mother Wore Tights (1947).
D: Walter Lang. **S:** Betty Grable, Dan Dailey, Mona Freeman, Connie Marshal, Vanessa Brown, Veda Ann Borg. **R:** 1h, 47m.

Music in the Air (1934).
D: Joe May. **S:** Gloria Swanson, John Boles, Douglass Montgomery, June Lang, Reginald Owen, Al Shean. **R:** 1h, 25m.

Music Man, The (1962).
D: Morton Da Costa. **S:** Robert Preston, Shirley Jones, Buddy Hackett, Hermione Gingold, Paul Ford, Pert Kelton. **R:** 2h, 31m.

My Blue Heaven (1950).
D: Henry Koster. **S:** Betty Grable, Dan Dailey, David Wayne, Jane Wyatt, Mitzi Gaynor, Una Merkel. **R:** 1h, 36m.

My Fair Lady (1964).
D: George Cukor. **S:** Rex Harrison, Audrey Hepburn, Stanley Holloway, Wilfrid Hyde-White, Gladys Cooper, Jeremy Brett, Theodor Bickel. **R:** 2h, 50m.

My Lucky Star (1938).
D: Roy Del Ruth. **S:** Sonja Henie, Richard Greene, Cesar Romero, Buddy Ebsen, Joan Davis, Arthur Treacher. **R:** 1h 24m.

Naughty Marietta (1935).
D: W S Van Dyke II. **S:** Jeanette MacDonald, Nelson Eddy, Frank Morgan, Elsa Lanchester, Douglass Dumbrille, Cecilia Parker. **R:** 1h, 46m.

Neptune's Daughter (1949).
D: Edward Buzzell. **S:** Esther Williams, Red Skelton, Keenan Wynn, Betty Garrett, Ricardo Montalban, Mel Blanc. **R:** 1h, 33m.

New Moon (1940).
D: Robert Z Leonard. **S:** Jeanette MacDonald, Nelson Eddy, Mary Boland, George Zucco, H B Warner, Grant Mitchell, Stanley Fields. **R:** 1h, 45m.

Nice Girl (1941).
D: William A Seiter. **S:** Deanna Durbin, Franchot Tone, Walter Brennan, Robert Stack, Robert Benchley. **R:** 1h, 35m.

Night and Day (1946).
D: Michael Curtiz. S: Cary Grant, Alexis Smith, Monty Wooley, Ginny Simms, Jane Wyman, Eve Arden, Mary Martin, Victor Francen, Alan Hale, Dorothy Malone. R: 2h, 8m.

Oklahoma! (1955).
D: Fred Zinnemann. S: Gordon MacRae, Shirley Jones, Charlotte Greenwood, Rod Steiger, Gloria Grahame, Eddie Albert, James Whitmore, Gene Nelson. R: 2h, 25m.

Oliver! (1968).
D: Carol Reed. S: Ron Moody, Oliver Reed, Shani Wallis, Mark Lester, Jack Wild, Harry Secombe, Hugh Griffith, Sheila White. R: 2h, 33m.

On a Clear Day You Can See Forever (1970).
D: Vincente Minnelli. S: Barbra Streisand, Yves Montand, Bob Newhart, Larry Blyden, Simon Oakland, Jack Nicholson. R: 2h, 9m.

On the Town (1949).
D: Gene Kelly, Stanley Donen. S: Gene Kelly, Frank Sinatra, Vera-Ellen, Betty Garrett, Ann Miller, Jules Munshin, Alice Pearce. R: 1h, 38m.

On Your Toes (1939).
D: Ray Enright. S: Vera Zorina, Eddie Albert, Frank McHugh, Alan Hale, James Gleason. R: 1h, 34m.

One Hour With You (1932).
D: Ernst Lubitsch, George Cukor. S: Maurice Chevalier, Jeanette MacDonald, Genevieve Tobin, Roland Young, Charlie Ruggles. R: 1h, 20m.

One Hundred Men and a Girl (1937).
D: Henry Koster. S: Deanna Durbin, Leopold Stokowski, Adolphe Menjou, Alice Brady, Eugene Pallette, Mischa Auer, Frank Jenks, Billy Gilbert. R: 1h, 24m.

One in a Million (1936).
D: Sidney Lanfield. S: Sonja Henie, Adolphe Menjou, Don Ameche, Ned Sparks, Jean Hersholt, The Ritz Brothers, Arline Judge. R: 1h, 35m.

One Night of Love (1934).
D: Victor Schertzinger. S: Grace Moore, Tullio Carminati, Lyle Talbot, Mona Barrie, Luis Alberni, Jessie Ralph. R: 1h, 20m.

One Touch of Venus (1948).
D: William A Seiter. S: Ava Gardner, Robert Walker, Dick Haymes, Eve Arden, Olga San Juan, Tom Conway. R: 1h, 21m.

Out of This World (1945).
D: Hal Walker. S: Eddie Bracken, Veronica Lake, Diana Lynn, Cass Daley, Parkyakarkus, Donald MacBride, Florence Bates, Gary, Philip, Dennis and Lindsay Crosby. R: 1h, 36m.

Pagan Love Song (1950).
D: Robert Alton. S: Esther Williams, Howard Keel, Minna Gombell, Rita Moreno. R: 1h, 16m.

Paint Your Wagon (1969).
D: Joshua Logan. S: Lee Marvin, Clint Eastwood, Jean Seberg, Harve Presnell, Ray Walston, Tom Ligon, Alan Dexter. R: 2h, 46m.

Pajama Game, The (1957).
D: George Abbott, Stanley Donen. S: Doris Day, John Raitt, Carol Haney, Eddie Foy Jr, Barbara Nichols, Reta Shaw. R: 1h, 41m.

Pal Joey (1957).
D: Don Weis. S: Rita Hayworth, Frank Sinatra, Kim Novak, Barbara Nichols, Elizabeth Patterson, Bobby Sherwood. R: 1h, 51m.

Palmy Days (1931).
D: A Edward Sutherland. S: Eddie Cantor, Charlotte Greenwood, Charles Middleton, George Raft, Walter Catlett. R: 1h, 17m.

Panama Hattie (1942).
D: Norman Z McLeod. S: Ann Sothern, Red Skelton, 'Rags' Ragland, Ben Blue, Marsha Hunt, Virginia O'Brien, Alan Mowbray, Lena Horne, Dan Dailey, Carl Esmond. R: 1h, 19m.

Paramount on Parade (1930).
D: Dorothy Arzner, Otto Brower, Edmund Goulding, Victor Heerman, Edwin Knopf, Rowland V Lee, Ernst Lubitsch, Lothar Mendes, Victor Schertzinger, A Edward Sutherland, Frank Tuttle. S: Jean Arthur, Clara Bow, Maurice Chevalier, Gary Cooper, Nancy Carroll, Leon Errol, Stuart Erwin, Kay Francis, Fredric March, Helen Kane, Jack Oakie, William Powell, Buddy Rogers. R: 1h, 42m.

Pennies from Heaven (1936).
D: Norman Z McLeod. S: Bing Crosby, Edith Fellows, Madge Evans, Donald Meek, Louis Armstrong. R: 1h, 21m.

Pennies from Heaven (1981).
D: Herbert Ross. S: Steve Martin, Bernadette Peters, Christopher Walken, Jessica Harper, Vernel Bagneris, John McMartin, Jay Garner, Tommy Rall. R: 1h, 47m.

Pigskin Parade (1936).
D: David Butler. S: Stuart Erwin, Judy Garland, Patsy Kelly, Jack Haley, Johnny Downs, Betty Grable. R: 1h, 35m.

Pin-Up Girl (1944).
D: H Bruce Humberstone. S: Betty Grable, Martha Raye, John Harvey, Joe E Brown, Eugene Pallette, Mantan Moreland, Charlie Spivak and his Orchestra. R: 1h, 23m.

Pirate, The (1948).
D: Vincente Minnelli. S: Judy Garland, Gene Kelly, Walter Slezak, Gladys Cooper, Reginald Owen, George Zucco, The Nicholas Brothers. R: 1h, 42m.

Poor Little Rich Girl (1936).
D: Irving Cummings. S: Shirley Temple, Alice Faye, Jack Haley, Gloria Stuart, Michael Whalen, Claude Gillingwater, Henry Armetta. R: 1h, 12m.

Porgy and Bess (1959).
D: Otto Preminger. S: Sidney Poitier, Dorothy Dandridge, Pearl Bailey, Sammy Davis Jr. Brock Peters, Diahann Carroll, Ivan Dixon. R: 2h, 18m.

Rebecca of Sunnybrook Farm (1938).
D: Allan Dwan. S: Shirley Temple, Randolph Scott, Jack Haley, Gloria Stuart, Phyllis Brooks, Helen Westley, Slim Summerville. R: 1h, 20m.

Red Hot and Blue (1949).
D: John Farrow. S: Betty Hutton, Victor Mature, William Demarest, June Havoc, Frank Loesser, Raymond Walburn. R: 1h, 24m.

Rhapsody in Blue (1945).
D: Irving Rapper, S: Robert Aida, Joan Leslie, Alexis Smith, Oscar Levant, Charles Coburn, Julie Bishop, Albert Bassermann, Morris Carnovsky, Rosemary DeCamp, Paul Whiteman, Hazel Scott. R: 2h, 19m.

Rhythm on the Range (1936).
D: Norman Taurog. S: Bing Crosby, Frances Farmer, Bob Burns, Martha Raye, Lucile Gleason, Samuel S Hinds. R: 1h, 25m.

Riding High (1950).
D: Frank Capra. S: Bing Crosby, Coleen Gray, Charles Bickford, Margaret Hamilton, Frances Gifford, James Gleason, Raymond Walburn. R: 1h, 52m.

Rio Rita (1942).
D: S Sylvan Simon. S: Bud Abbott, Lou Costello, Kathryn Grayson, John Carroll, Tom Conway, Barry Nelson. R: 1h, 31m.

Road to Bali, The (1952).
D: Hal Walker. S: Bob Hope, Dorothy Lamour, Bing Crosby, Murvyn Vye, Ralph Moody. R: 1h, 30m.

Road to Hong Kong, The (1962).
D: Norman Panama. S: Bob Hope, Bing Crosby, Joan Collins, Dorothy Lamour, Robert Morley, Walter Gotell, Peter Sellers. R: 1h, 31m.

Road to Morocco, The (1942).
D: David Butler. S: Bing Crosby, Dorothy Lamour, Bob Hope, Anthony Quinn, Vladimir Sokoloff, Monte Blue, Yvonne De Carlo, Dona Drake. R: 1h, 23m.

Road to Rio, The (1947).
D: Norman Z McLeod. S: Bing Crosby, Bob Hope, Dorthy Lamour, Gale Sondergaard, Frank Faylen, The Wiere Brothers. R: 1h, 40m.

Road to Singapore, The (1940).
D: Victor Schertzinger. S: Bing Crosby, Bob Hope, Dorothy Lamour, Charles Coburn, Judith Barrett, Anthony Quinn. R: 1h, 24m.

Road to Utopia, The (1945).
D: Hal Walker. S: Bing Crosby, Bob Hope, Dorothy Lamour, Hillary Brooke, Douglass Dumbrille, Jack LaRue. R: 1h, 30m.

Road to Zanzibar, The (1941).
D: Victor Schertzinger. S: Bing Crosby, Bob Hope, Dorothy Lamour, Una Merkel, Eric Blore. R: 1h, 32m.

Roberta (1935).
D: William A Seiter. S: Irene Dunne, Fred Astaire, Ginger Rogers, Randolph Scott, Helen Westley, Claire Dodd, Victor Varconi. R: 1h, 45m.

Rock Around the Clock (1956).
D: Fred F Sears. S: Bill Haley and his Comets, The Platters, Tony Martinez and his Band, Freddie Bell and his Bellboys, Alan Freed, Johnny Johnston. R: 1h, 17m.

Rocky Horror Picture Show, The (1975).
D: Jim Sharman. S: Tim Curry, Susan Sarandon, Barry Bostwick, Richard O'Brien, Jonathan Adams, Meatloaf, Little Nell (Campbell), Charles Gray, Patricia Quinn. R: 1h, 40m.

Roman Scandals (1933).
D: Frank Tuttle. S: Eddie Cantor, Ruth Etting, Gloria Stuart, David Manners, Veree Teasdale, Alan Mowbray, Edward Arnold. R: 1h, 25m.

Rosalie (1937).
D: W S Van Dyke. S: Eleanor Powell, Nelson Eddy, Frank Morgan, Edna May Oliver, Ray Bolger, Ilona Massey, Billy Gilbert. R: 2h, 2m.

Rose, The (1979).
D: Mark Rydell. S: Bette Midler, Alan Bates, Frederic Forrest, Harry Dean Stanton, Barry Primus, David Keith. R: 2h, 5m.

Rose Marie (1936).
D: W S Van Dyke II. S: Jeanette MacDonald, Nelson Eddy, Reginald Owen, Allan Jones, James Stewart, Alan Mowbray, Gilda Gray. R: 1h, 50m.

Rose Marie (1954).
D: Mervyn LeRoy. S: Ann Blyth, Howard Keel, Fernando Lamas, Bert Lahr, Marjorie Main, Joan Taylor, Ray Collins. R: 1h, 55m.

Rose of Washington Square (1939).
D: Gregory Ratoff. S: Tyrone Power, Alice Faye, Al Jolson, William Frawley, Horace McMahon, Moroni Olsen. R: 1h, 26m.

Royal Wedding (1951).
D: Stanley Donen. S: Fred Astaire, Jane Powell, Sarah Churchill, Keenan Wynn. R: 1h, 33m.

St Louis Blues (1958).
D: Allen Reisner. S: Nat 'King' Cole, Eartha Kitt, Ruby Dee, Pearl Bailey, Cab Calloway, Ella Fitzgerald, Mahalia Jackson. R: 1h, 33m.

Sally, Irene and Mary (1938).
D: William A Seiter. S: Alice Faye, Tony Martin, Fred Allen, Joan Davis, Marjorie Weaver, Gregory Ratoff, Jimmy Durante, Louise Hovick (Gypsy Rose Lee). R: 1h, 12m.

San Francisco (1936).
D: W S Van Dyke II. S: Jeanette MacDonald, Spencer Tracy, Clark Gable, Jack Holt, Jessie Ralph, Ted Healy, Shirley Ross, R: 1h, 55m.

Saturday Night Fever (1977).
D: John Badham. S: John Travolta, Karen Lynn Gorney, Barry Miller, Joseph Cali, Paul Papa, Donna Pescow. R: 1h, 59m.

Second Chorus (1940).
D: H C Potter. S: Fred Astaire, Paulette Goddard, Artie Shaw and his Orchestra, Charles Butterworth, Burgess Meredith. R: 1h, 23m.

Second Fiddle (1939).
D: Sidney Lanfield. S: Sonja Henie, Tyrone Power, Rudy Vallee, Edna May Oliver, Lyle Talbot, Brian Sisters. R: 1h, 26m.

Serenade (1956).
D: Anthony Mann. S: Mario Lanza, Joan Fontaine, Sarita Montiel, Vincent Price, Joseph Calleia, Vince Edwards. R: 2h, 1m.

Seven Brides for Seven Brothers (1954).
D: Stanley Donen. S: Howard Keel, Jane Powell, Jeff Richards, Russ Tamblyn, Tommy Rall, Virginia Gibson, Julie Newmeyer (Newmar), Ruta Kilmonis (Lee), Matt Mattox. R: 1h, 43m.

Seven Hills of Rome (1958).
D: Roy Rowland. S: Mario Lanza, Peggie Castle, Marisa Allasio, Renato Rascel, Rosella Como. R: 1h, 44m.

1776 (1972).
D: Peter H Hunt. S: William Daniels, Howard da Silva, Donald Madden, Ron Holgate, David Ford, Blythe Danner, Ken Howard, Virginia Vestoff. R: 2h, 21m.

Shall We Dance (1937).
D: Mark Sandrich. S: Fred Astaire, Ginger Rogers, Eric Blore, Edward Everett Horton, Ann Shoemaker. R: 1h, 56m.

Ship Ahoy (1942).
D: Edward Buzzell. S: Eleanor Powell, Red Skelton, Virginia O'Brien, Bert Lahr, John Emery, Tommy Dorsey Orchestra with Frank Sinatra and Joe Stafford. R: 1h, 35m.

Show Boat (1936).
D: James Whale. S: Irene Dunne, Alan Jones, Helen Morgan, Paul Robeson, Charles Winninger, Hattie McDaniel. R: 1h, 53m.

Show Boat (1951).

D: George Sidney. S: Kathryn Grayson, Ava Gardner, Howard Keel, Joe E Brown, Marge and Gower Champion, Agnes Moorehead, Robert Sterling, William Warfield. R: 1h, 47m.

Silk Stockings (1957).
D: Rouben Mamoulian. S: Fred Astaire, Cyd Charisse, Janis Paige, Peter Lorre, George Tobias. R: 1h, 47m.

Sing You Sinners (1938).
D: Wesley Ruggles. S: Bing Crosby, Fred MacMurray, Donald O'Connor, Elizabeth Patterson, Ellen Drew, John Gallaudet. R: 1h, 28m.

Singin' in the Rain (1952).
D: Gene Kelly, Stanley Donen. S: Gene Kelly, Debbie Reynolds, Donald O'Connor, Jean Hagen, Cyd Charisse, Madge Blake, Millard Mitchell, Douglas Fowley. R: 1h, 43m.

Sky's the Limit, The (1943).
D: Edward H Griffith. S: Fred Astaire, Joan Leslie, Robert Benchley, Robert Ryan, Elizabeth Patterson, Marjorie Gateson. R: 1h, 29m.

Small Town Girl (1953).
D: Leslie Kardos. S: Jane Powell, Farley Granger, Ann Miller, S Z Sakall, Billie Burke, Bobby Van, Robert Keith, Nat 'King' Cole R: 1h, 33m.

So This Is Love (1953).
D: Gordon Douglas. S: Kathryn Grayson, Merv Griffin, Walter Abel, Rosemary DeCamp, Jeff Donnell. R: 1h, 41m.

Something for the Boys (1944).
D: Lewis Seiler. S: Carmen Miranda, Michael O'Shea, Vivian Blaine, Phil Silvers, Sheila Ryan, Perry Como, Glenn Langan, Cara Williams, Thurston Hall. R: 1h, 25m.

Song of Love (1947).
D: Clarence Brown. S: Katharine Hepburn, Paul Henreid, Robert Walker, Henry Daniell, Leo G Carroll, Gigi Perreau, Tala Birel, Henry Stephenson, Else Jannssen. R: 1h, 49m.

Song of Norway (1970).
D: Andrew L Stone. S: Florence Henderson, Toralv Maurstad, Christina Schollin, Frank Poretta, Edward G Robinson, Harry Secombe, Robert Morley, Oscar Homolka. R: 2h, 22m.

Sound of Music, The (1965).
Robert Wise. S: Julie Andrews, Christopher Plummer, Eleanor Parker, Peggy Wood, Richard Haydn. R: 2h, 54m.

South Pacific (1958).
D: Joshua Logan. S: Rossano Brazzi, Mitzi Gaynor, John Kerr, Ray Walston, Juanita Hall, France Nuyen. R: 2h, 51m.

Stand Up and Cheer (1934).
D: Hamilton MacFadden. S: Warner Baxter, Madge Evans, James Dunn, John Boles, Shirley Temple. R: 1h, 20m.

Star! (1968).
D: Robert Wise. S: Julie Andrews, Richard Crenna, Michael Craig, Daniel Massey, Robert Reed, Bruce Forsyth, Beryl Reid. R: 2h, 55m.

A Star Is Born (1954).
D: George Cukor. S: Judy Garland, James Mason, Jack Carson, Charles Bickford, Tom Noonan. R: 2h, 34m.

A Star Is Born (1976).
D: Frank Pierson. S: Barbra Streisand, Kris Kristofferson, Gary Busey, Oliver Clark, Paul Mazursky. R: 2h, 20m.

Star Spangled Rhythm (1942).
D: George Marshall. S: Bing Crosby, Ray Milland, Bob Hope, Veronica Lake, Dorothy Lamour, Susan Hayward, Dick Powell, Alan Ladd, Paulette Goddard, Cecil B DeMille, Arthur Treacher, Eddie Anderson, William Bendix. R: 1h, 39m.

Stars and Stripes Forever (1952).
D: Henry Koster. S: Clifton Webb, Robert Wagner, Ruth Hussey, Debra Paget, Finlay Currie. R: 1h, 29m.

State Fair (1945).
D: Walter Lang. S: Jeanne Crain, Dana Andrews, Dick Haymes, Vivian Blaine, Charles Winninger, Fay Bainter, Donald Meek, Frank McHugh. R: 1h, 40m.

State Fair (1962).
D: Jose Ferrer. S: Pat Boone, Bobby Darin, Pamela Tiffin, Ann-Margret, Alice Faye, Tom Ewell. R: 1h, 58m.

Stop the World – I Want to Get Off (1966).
D: Philip Saville. S: Tony Tanner, Millicent Martin, Leila Croft, Valerie Croft. R: 1h, 38m.

Stormy Weather (1943).
D: Andrew L Stone. S: Lena Horne, Bill Robinson, Cab Calloway and his Band, Katherine Dunham, Fats Waller, Dooley Wilson, the Nicholas Brothers. R: 1h, 17m.

Story of Vernon and Irene Castle, The (1939).
D: H C Potter. S: Fred Astaire, Ginger Rogers, Edna May Oliver, Walter Brennan, Lew Fields. R: 1h, 33m.

Stowaway (1936).
D: William A Seiter. S: Robert Young, Alice Faye, Shirley Temple, Eugene Pallette, Helen Westley, Arthur Treacher. R: 1h, 26m.

Strike Up the Band (1940).
D: Busby Berkeley. S: Mickey Rooney, Judy Garland, Paul Whiteman, June Preisser, William Tracy, Larry Nunn. R: 2h.

Student Prince, The (1954).
D: Richard Thorpe. S: Ann Blyth, Edmund Purdom, John Ericson, Louis Calhern, Edmund Gwenn. R: 1h, 47m.

Summer Stock (1950).
D: Charles Walters. S: Judy Garland, Gene Kelly, Eddie Bracken, Marjorie Main, Gloria DeHaven, Phil Silvers, Hans Conried. R: 1h, 40m.

Sun Valley Serenade (1941).
D: H Bruce Humberstone. S: Sonja Henie, John Payne, Glenn Miller, Milton Berle, Lynn Bari, Joan Davis. R: 1h, 26m.

Swanee River (1939).
D: Sidney Lanfield, S: Don Ameche, Al Jolson, Andrea Leeds, Felix Bressart, Russell Hicks. R: 1h, 24m.

Sweet Charity (1969).
D: Bob Fosse. S: Shirley MacLaine, John McMartin, Ricardo Montalban, Sammy Davis Jr, Chita Rivera, Paula Kelly, Stubby Kaye. R: 2h, 13m.

Sweet Rosie O'Grady (1943).
D: Irving Cummings. S: Betty Grable, Robert Young, Adolphe Menjou, Reginald Gardiner, Virginia Grey, Phil Regan. R: 1h, 14m.

Sweethearts (1938).
D: W S Van Dyke II. S: Jeanette MacDonald, Nelson Eddy, Frank Morgan, Florence Rice, Ray Bolger, Mischa Auer. R: 2h.

Swing Time (1936).
D: George Stevens. S: Fred Astaire, Ginger Rogers, Victor Moore, Helen

Broderick, Eric Blore, Betty Furness. **R:** 1h, 45m.

Take Me Out to the Ball Game (1949).
D: Busby Berkeley. **S:** Frank Sinatra, Esther Williams, Gene Kelly, Betty Garrett, Edward Arnold, Jules Munshin, Richard Lane, Tom Dugan. **R:** 1h, 33m.

Tea for Two (1959).
D: David Butler. **S:** Doris Day, Gordon MacRae, Gene Nelson, Eve Arden, Billy DeWolfe. **R:** 1h, 38m.

Thank Your Lucky Stars (1943).
D: David Butler. **S:** Eddie Cantor, Humphrey Bogart, Bette Davis, Olivia de Haviland, Errol Flynn, John Garfield, Joan Leslie, Ida Lupino, Dennis Morgan, Ann Sheridan. **R:** 2h, 7m.

That Midnight Kiss (1949).
D: Norman Taurog. **S:** Kathryn Grayson, Mario Lanza, Jose Iturbi, Ethel Barrymore, Keenan Wynn, J Carrol Naish, Jules Munshin. **R:** 1h, 36m.

That Night in Rio (1941).
D: Irving Cummings. **S:** Alice Faye, Don Ameche, Carmen Miranda, S Z Sakall, J Carrol Naish, Curt Bois, Leonid Kinsky, Frank Puglia. **R:** 1h, 30m.

That's Entertainment (1974).
D: Jack Haley Jr. **S:** Fred Astaire, Gene Kelly, Bing Crosby, Peter Lawford, Liza Minnelli, Donald O'Connor, Debbie Reynolds, Mickey Rooney, Frank Sinatra, James Stewart, Elizabeth Taylor. **R:** 2h, 12m.

There's No Business Like Show Business (1954).
D: Walter Lang. **S:** Ethel Merman, Donald O'Connor, Marilyn Monroe, Dan Dailey, Johnny Ray, Mitzi Gaynor. **R:** 1h, 57m.

This Is the Army (1943).
D: Michael Curtiz. **S:** George Murphy, Joan Leslie, George Tobias, Alan Hale, Ronald Reagan, Joe Louis, Kate Smith, Irving Berlin **R:** 2h, 1m.

Thoroughly Modern Millie (1967).
D: George Roy Hill. **S:** Julie Andrews, Mary Tyler Moore, Carol Channing, James Fox, John Gavin, Beatrice Lillie. **R:** 2h, 18m.

Those Were the Happy Times. See: **Star!**

Thousands Cheer (1943).
D: George Sidney. **S:** Mickey Rooney, Judy Garland, Gene Kelly, Red Skelton, Eleanor Powell, Ann Sothern, Lucille Ball, Virginia O'Brien, Frank Morgan, Kathryn Grayson, Lena Horne. **R:** 2h, 6m.

Three Little Words (1950).
D: Richard Thorpe. **S:** Fred Astaire, Vera-Ellen, Red Skelton, Arlene Dahl, Keenan Wynn, Gloria DeHaven, Debbie Reynolds, Carleton Carpenter. **R:** 1h, 42m.

Three Smart Girls (1937).
D: Henry Koster. **S:** Deanna Durbin, Binnie Barnes, Alice Brady, Ray Milland, Barbara Read, Mischa Auer, Nan Grey, Charles Winninger. **R:** 1h, 24m.

Threepenny Opera, The (1931).
D: G W Pabst. **S:** Rudolph Forster, Lotte Lenya, Carola Neher, Reinhold Schunzel, Fritz Rasp, Valeska Gert. **R:** 1h, 52m.

Till the Clouds Roll By (1946).
D: Richard Whorf. **S:** Van Johnson, June Allyson, Lucille Bremer, Judy Garland, Kathryn Grayson, Van Heflin, Lena Horne, Tony Martin, Angela Lansbury, Dinah Shore, Frank Sinatra. **R:** 2h, 17m.

Tin Pan Alley (1940).
D: Walter Lang. **S:** Alice Faye, Betty Grable, Jack Oakie, John Payne, Esther Ralston, Allen Jenkins, the Nicholas Brothers, John Loder. **R:** 1h, 34m.

Toast of New Orleans, The (1950).
D: Norman Taurog. **S:** Mario Lanza, David Niven, Rita Moreno, J Carrol Naish. **R:** 1h, 37m.

Too Many Girls (1940).
D: George Abbott. **S:** Lucille Ball, Richard Carlson, Eddie Bracken, Ann Miller, Hal LeRoy, Desi Arnaz, Frances Langford. **R:** 1h, 25m.

Top Hat (1935).
D: Mark Sandrich. **S:** Fred Astaire, Ginger Rogers, Edward Everett Horton, Helen Broderick, Eric Blore, Erik Rhodes. **R:** 1h, 39m.

Top O' the Morning (1949).
D: David Miller. **S:** Bing Crosby, Barry Fitzgerald, Ann Blyth, Hume Cronin, Eileen Crowe. **R:** 1h, 40m.

Two Girls and a Sailor (1944).
D: Richard Thorpe. **S:** Van Johnson, June Allyson, Gloria DeHaven, Jose Iturbi, Jimmy Durante, Lena Horne, Donald Meek, Virginia O'Brien, Harry James, Xavier Cugat. **R:** 2h, 4m.

Two Sisters from Boston (1946).
D: Henry Koster. **S:** Kathryn Grayson, June Allyson, Lauritz Melchior, Jimmy Durante, Peter Lawford, Ben Blue. **R:** 1h, 52m.

Two Weeks with Love (1950).
D: Roy Rowland. **S:** Jane Powell, Ricardo Montalban, Louis Calhern, Ann Harding, Debbie Reynolds, Carleton Carpenter. **R:** 1h, 32m.

Unsinkable Molly Brown, The (1964).
D: Charles Walters. **S:** Debbie Reynolds, Harve Presnell, Ed Begley, Jack Kruschen, Hermione Baddeley. **R:** 2h, 8m.

Up in Arms (1944).
D: Elliott Nugent. **S:** Danny Kaye, Dana Andrews, Constance Dowling, Dinah Shore, Louis Calhern, Lyle Talbot, Elisha Cook Jr, Margaret Dumont. **R:** 1h, 46m.

Up in Central Park (1948).
D: William A Seiter. **S:** Deanna Durbin, Dick Haymes, Vincent Price, Albert Sharpe, Tom Powers. **R:** 1h, 28m.

Vagabond King, The (1956).
D: Michael Curtiz. **S:** Kathryn Grayson, Oreste, Rita Moreno, Cedric Hardwicke, Walter Hampden, Leslie Nielson. **R:** 1h, 26m.

Victor Victoria (1982).
D: Blake Edwards. **S:** Julie Andrews, James Garner, Robert Preston, Lesley Ann Warren, Alex Karras, John Rhys-Davies, Graham Stark. **R:** 2h, 13m.

Wabash Avenue (1950).
D: Henry Koster. **S:** Betty Grable, Victor Mature, Phil Harris, Reginald Gardiner, James Barton, Margaret Hamilton. **R:** 1h, 32m.

Waikiki Wedding (1937).
D: Frank Tuttle. **S:** Bing Crosby, Martha Raye, Shirley Ross, Bob Burns, Leif Erickson, Grady Sutton, Anthony Quinn. **R:** 1h, 29m.

Weekend in Havana (1941).
D: Walter Lang. **S:** Alice Faye, Carmen Miranda, John Payne, Cesar Romero, Cobina Wright Jr, George Barbier, Leonid Kinskey, Sheldon Leonard, Billy Gilbert. **R:** 1h, 20m.

West Side Story (1961).
D: Robert Wise, Jerome Robbins. S: Natalie Wood, Richard Beymer, George Chakiris, Rita Moreno, Russ Tamblyn. R: 2h, 31m.

When the Boys Meet the Girls (1965). D: Alvin Ganzer. S: Connie Francis, Harve Presnell, Herman's Hermits, Louis Armstrong, Liberace, Sue Ane Langdon, Fred Clark, Frank Faylen, Sam the Sham. R: 1h, 50m.

When You're in Love (1937).
D: Robert Riskin. S: Grace Moore, Cary Grant, Aline MacMahon, Thomas Mitchell, Emma Dunn. R: 1h, 44m.

Where Do We Go from Here? (1945).
D: Gregory Ratoff. S: Fred MacMurray, June Haver, Joan Leslie, Gene Sheldon, Anthony Quinn, Carlos Ramirez, Otto Preminger. R: 1h, 17m.

Where's Charley? (1952).
D: David Butler. S: Ray Bolger, Allyn McLerie, Robert Shackleton, Mary Germaine, Horace Cooper, Margaretta Scott. R: 1h, 37m.

Whoopee (1930).
D: Thornton Freeland. S: Eddie Cantor, Eleanor Hunt, Paul Gregory, John Rutherford, Ethel Shutta, Spencer Charters. R: 1h, 33m.

Wiz, The (1978).
D: Sidney Lumet. S: Diana Ross, Michael Jackson, Nipsey Russell, Ted Ross, Mabel King, Theresa Merritt, Thelma Carpenter, Lena Horne, Richard Pryor. R: 2h, 13m.

Wizard of Oz, The (1939).
D: Victor Fleming. S: Judy Garland, Frank Morgan, Bert Lahr, Jack Haley, Ray Bolger, Billie Burke, Margaret Hamilton, Charley Grapewin, Clara Blandick, The Singer Midgets. R: 1h, 41m.

Wonder Bar (1934).
D: Lloyd Bacon. S: Al Jolson, Kay Francis, Dolores Del Rio, Dick Powell, Ricardo Cortez, Louise Fazenda, Hal LeRoy, Guy Kibbee. R: 1h, 24m.

Words and Music (1948).
D: Norman Taurog. S: Mickey Rooney, Tom Drake, June Allyson, Ann Sothern, Judy Garland, Gene Kelly, Lena Horne, Cyd Charisse, Betty Garrett, Perry Como, Janet Leigh. R: 1h, 59m.

Yankee Doodle Dandy (1942).
D: Michael Curtiz. S: James Cagney, Joan Leslie, Walter Huston, Irene Manning, Rosemary DeCamp, Jeanne Cagney, S Z Sakall, Walter Catlett, Frances Langford, George Tobias. R: 2h, 6m.

Yellow Submarine, The (1968).
D: George Dunning. S: The Beatles.

Yoland and the Thief (1945).
D: Vincente Minnelli. S: Fred Astaire, Lucille Bremer, Frank Morgan, Mildred Natwick, Mary Nash. R: 1h, 48m.

You Were Never Lovelier (1942).
D: William A Seiter. S: Fred Astaire, Rita Hayworth, Adolphe Menjou, Leslie Brooks, Adele Mara, Xavier Cugat. R: 1h, 37m.

You'll Never Get Rich (1941).
D: Sidney Lanfield. S: Fred Astaire, Rita Hayworth, John Hubbard, Robert Benchley, Osa Massen, Frieda Inescort, Guinn Williams. R: 1h, 28m.

Ziegfeld Follies (1946).
D: Vincente Minnelli, S: William Powell, Judy Garland, Lucille Ball, Fred Astaire, Fanny Brice, Lena Horne, Red Skelton, Victor Moore, Virginia O'Brien, Cyd Charisse, Gene Kelly, Edward Arnold, Esther Williams. R: 1h, 50m.

Ziegfeld Girl (1941).
D: Robert Z Leonard. S: James Stewart, Lana turner, Judy Garland, Hedy Lamarr, Tony Martin, Jackie Cooper, Ian Hunter, Philip Dorn, Charles Winninger. R: 2h, 11m.

INDEX

Page numbers in italics refer to illustrations.

Academy Awards 41, 44, 51-2, 71, 77, 87, *88*, 90, 95, 100, 109, 146, 147, 150, 167, 192, 196, 199, 205, 230, 212, 226; for music 48, 58, 67-8, 95, 144, 145, 167, 205, 226
Alexander's Ragtime Band 58, *59*, 126
Alda, Robert 127, *128*
All That Jazz 231, 231, *234*, 234, *237*
Allen, Gracie 63, 130
Allen, Steve 137
Allyson, June 118, *119*, 129, 130, 133, *137*, 161, 173
Ameche, Don *58*, 58, 59, *60*, *113*, 118, *119*, 119, *121*, 126
American in Paris, An 91, 147, *150*, *151*
Anchors Aweigh 130, 130
And the Angels Sing 125
Andrews, Julie, *6*, *7*, 196, *199*, 199, *201*, *225*, 226-27, *227*, *229*
Anderson, Eddie 107, 122
Ann-Margret 195
Annie 9, 215, *216*
Annie Get Your Gun 175, 175-6
Arden, Eve 171, 215, 216, 225
Are You With It? 175
Arlen, Harold 93, 130, 158
Arlen, Richard *61*
Armstrong, Louis 108, 145
Arnold, Edward *29*, 29, *58*
Arthur, Beatrice 213
Artists and Models 63
Astaire, Fred *3*, *9*, *38*, 39-40, *40*, *41*, *44*, 44-51, *45*, *46*, *47*, *48*, 60-1, *63*, *67*, 99, 104, *105*, 107, *125*, 125-26, *134*, 139-42, *139*, *141*, *142*, *144*, 176, *185*, *186*, *202*, 203, *234*, *240*
At Long Last Love 226
Babes in Arms 98, 99, 101, *102*, 170
Bacon, Lloyd 27
Babes in Toyland 74, 74
Babes on Broadway 101, *102*, *103*
Bailey, Pearl 137, 179, 190
Balalaika 82, 83
Ball, Lucille 28, 125, 171, *172*, 172-73, *212*, *213*, 213
Band Wagon, The 40, 141-42, *142*, 176
Barkleys of Broadway, The 42, *51*, 51, 141
Barrymore, Lionel 122, 171
Baxter, Warner *26*, 26, *53*
Beals, Jennifer 234, *236*
Beatles, The *221*, 220-22
Because You're Mine 161, 161
Bee Gees 231
Beery, Wallace *162*, 162
Belafonte, Harry *179*, 179, *180*
Belle of New York, The 141
Bells Are Ringing 190, *191*
Bells of St Mary's 112, *113*
Bendix, William 122
Benny, Jack 17, *61*, 61, 63
Benny Goodman Story, The 137
Bergen, Edgar 90
Berkeley, Busby *3*, *24*, 25-31, 77, 99, 100, 101, 116, 121, 122, 146, 161, 193
Berlin, Irving 22, 46, 47, 58, 107, 125, 139, 141, 145, 165, 175-6
Bernstein, Leonard 146, 192
Best Foot Forward 118, 172
Beymer, Richard 192, *193*
Big Broadcast, The (series) 63, 67, *67*
Billy Rose's Jumbo 193, 193
Birth of the Blues, The 109
Bitter Sweet 78, *79*, 81
Blondell, Joan 16, 27, 28, 29, *31*, *35*, *37*, 108

Blossom Time 126
Blue, Ben *172*
Blue Skies 139, 142
Blue Skies 139, 142
Blyden, Larry 208
Blyth, Ann 164, 180, *181*
Boles, John *125*, 169, 170
Bolger, Ray *6, 86, 93, 95*, 93-5, 97, 118, 176
Bordoni, Irene 172
Borge, Victor 173
Born to Dance 63, 63, *65*
Boswell Sisters, The 63
Bowers, Kenny 125
Boy Friend, The 208
Boyd, Stephen *193*, 193
Boys From Syracuse, The 170
Bracken, Eddie 125, *129*, 129, 171
Brando, Marlon *168, 180*, 180
Brasselle, Keefe 137
Brazzi, Rossano *8, 186*, 190
Bremer, Lucille 125, 129
Brent, George 27
Brice, Fanny 16, 58
Bricusse, Leslie 201, 225-26
Brigadoon 176, 179, *179*
Bright Eyes 54, 54
Britton, Pamela 130
Broadway Melody, The 15, 15, 60; *of 1936* 61; *of 1938* 63, 96, *97*; *of 1940 9*, 104, *105*
Broadway Rhythm 16, 125
Broadway to Hollywood 72
Broadway Serenade 82, *83*
Brown, Joe E 162
Brown, Nacio Herb 61, 155
Bruce, Virginia 63
Brynner, Yul *2*, 182, *183, 185*
Buchanan, Jack *142*, 142
Buddy Holly Story, The 222
Buloff, Joseph *185*
Burke, Billie 125, 171
Burnett, Carol 216
Burns, George *48*, 63
Busey, Gary 222
Butterworth, Charles 74, *105*
Bye Bye Birdie 195, 195
Cabaret 9, 211, 211-12, *238*
Cabin in the Sky 95, 104, *107*
Caesar, Sid 214, 215
Cagney, James *28*, 28, 126-27, *127*, 137
Cairo 82
Calhern, Louis 175
Call Me Madam 175, 176
Calloway, Cab 63, 137
Camelot 9, 201-02, *201, 202*
Can-Can 190, *191*, 192
Cantor, Eddie 25, 28, *29*, 122, 169
Captain January 54, 54
Carefree 48, 51
Carmen Jones 179-80, *179, 180*
Caron, Leslie *91, 142*, 142, 147, *150*, 163-65, *164, 167*, 167
Carousel 8, 181-82, *182, 183*, 185
Caruso, Enrico 134
Casablanca 8
Caulfield, Joan *139*
Cavallero, Carmen 137
Centennial Summer 116, 118
Chakiris, George 192
Champion, Gower 144, 163
Champion, Marge 93, 144, 163
Channing, Stockard 214, 215
Dimples 54
Charisse, Cyd *2*, 99, 125, 133, *134, 142*, 142, 152, *155*, 155, 165, 176, *179, 185, 186*
Chasing Rainbows 16
Chevalier, Maurice 16, *17, 20*, 20, 21, 22, 24, 74, *77*, 165, *167*, 170, *191*, 192
Chocolate Soldier, The 83, 83
Churchill, Sarah 141
Clark, Petula *202*, 203, 226
Clooney, Rosemary *145*, 145
Coburn, Charles 173
Cohan, George M 171
Colbert, Claudette 21, 22
Cole, Nat 'King' 137
Colonna, Jerry 165
Comden, Betty 99, 145
Coney Island 116
Cooper, Jackie 22, 121
Como, Perry 133, *134*, 173
Cover Girl 126
Coward, Noel 81, 226
Crain, Jeanne *104*
Crane, Norma 208
Crawford, Joan 14, 17, *40*, 40, *41*, 601-, *63*
Crosby, Bing 63, 67-8, *67, 68, 69, 107*, 107, 108-09, *109, 110, 111, 112*, 122, 125, 127, 130, *130, 139*, 142, 144-6, *145, 146*
Cugat, Xavier 119-21, 130, 158, 162
Cummings, Robert *113*
Curly Top 54
Daddy Long Legs 142, 142
Dailey, Dan *138*, 138, *155*, 155, *165*, 165, 171
Dames 29, 29, *31*
Damn Yankees 186, 186
Damone, Vic *181*, 181
Damsel in Distress 48, 48
dancing 16, 39, 45, 48, 54, 63, 115, 125, 130, 137, 141, 146, 155, 185, 190, 207, 234; ballet 90, 133, 147, 150, 176, 181
Dancing Lady 40, 40, *41*, 60-61, *63*
Dandridge, Dorothy *179*, 179, *180, 190*, 190
Dangerous When Wet 158
Daniels, Bebe 26, 27
Darling Lili 226
Date With Judy, A 162, 162
Davis, Bette 29, 122, 125
Davies, Marion 17, 22, 67
Davis, Sammy, Jr 137, 165, *190*, 190
Day, Doris 137, 162, *163*, 171, *185*, 193, 193
Deep in My Heart 137
DeHaven, Gloria 125, 130, 134
Del Rio Dolores *44*, 45, 170
DeMille, Cecil B. 122
Desert Song, The 20, *170*
DeWolfe, Billy *175*
Diamond, Neil *222*, 222
Diamond Horseshoe 137-38
Dietz, Howard 142
Disney, Walt 93, 121
Dixie 127
Doctor Doolittle 225, 225-6
Dolly Sisters, The 115, 116
Don Juan 13
Donen, Stanley 152, 155
Dorsey, Tommy *101*, 129
Double or Nothing 67
Down Argentine Way 118
Down to Earth 162
Downey, Morton 16
Drake, Dona *109*
Drake, Tom *119*, 133
Drei von der Tankstelle, Die 84-5, *84, 85*
Dressler, Marie 17
Drew, Ellen *68*
DuBarry Was a Lady 172-3, *172*
Dunne, Irene *38*, 45, *61*, 169
Durante, Jimmy 22, 57, *58*, 118, 130, 162, *163*, 193
Durbin, Deanna *70, 71*, 71, 93, 96, 175
East Side of Heaven, The 108
Easter Parade 139, 139, *140*, 157, *240*
Eastwood, Clint 207
Easy to Love 159, 161
Eberle, Ray 129-30
Ebsen, Buddy *54*, 54, 61, *63*, 96, 97
Eddie Cantor Story, The 137
Eddy, Nelson 22, 40, *72*, 74, *75*, 77, 80-3, *80, 81, 82, 83*, 170, 173
Eddy Duchin Story, The 137
Edwards, Cliff 17
Eggar, Samantha 225
Elg, Taina *157*, 157
Ellington, Duke 108
Emperor Waltz, The 144
Etting, Ruth 28-9, 137
Errol, Leon 173
Erwin, Stuart *67*, 96
Evans, Madge *53, 69*
Ewell, Tom *59*
Fabray, Nanette *142*, 142
Fairbanks, Douglas, Jr. 20
Fashions of 1934 29
Faye, Alice 31, 36, *37*, 54, 57-8, *58, 59*, 115, 118, 119, *121*, 170
Felix, Seymour *88*
Fellows, Edith 67, *68, 69*
Ferrer, Jose 137
Ferrer, Mel 163-7, *164*
Fiddler on the Roof 208-09, *209*
Fields, Gracie 71
Fields, W C 63
Fifty Million Frenchmen 170
Finian's Rainbow 202, 202
Finney, Albert *216*
Firefly, The 81
First Love 70
Fitzgerald, Barry *112*, 144
Fitzgerald, Ella 137
Flashdance 234
Diamond, Neil
Fleet's In, The 129, 129
Fleming, Victor 95
Flower Drum Song 192, 192
Flying Down to Rio 42, 44, 45
Flying High 25
Foch, Nina 150
Follow the Fleet 43, 46, 47
Fontaine, Joan 48, 142, *161*, 161
Footlight Parade 3, 28, 28, *29*, 126
For Me and My Gal 116
For the First Time 161
Ford, John 52
Forty Second Street *8*, 8, 25-6, *26*, 36, 45, 60
Fosse, Bob *167*, 185, 206, 231, 234
Foster, Stephen 126
Foster, Susanna 126
Freed, Arthur 61, 95-6, 99, 101, 121, 155, 211
Frey, Leonard 208
Friml, Rudolf 20, 77, 81-2, 185
Fritsch, Willy *84, 85*
Froman, Jane 134, 137
Funny Face 142, *144*
Funny Girl, 2, 9, 58, 202, *205*, 205
Funny Lady 228, 228
Funny Thing Happened on the Way to the Forum, A 201
Gable, Clark 60, 96
Gang's All Here, The 31, 36-7, *36, 37*, 119
Garber, Victor 213
Gardner, Ava *91*, 162, *170*, 175
Garland, Judy *1, 6*, 8, 51, 71, *86, 93*, 93, *95*, 96-7, *96, 97, 98*, 99, *100, 101*, 101, *102, 103, 116*, 116, *118*, 118, 121, *122*, 122, *124, 125*, 125, 126, 129, 133, 138, *139, 141*, 141, 146-7, *147, 148, 157*, 157-8, 170, *171*, 171, 175, *240*; biography 96, 158
Garrett, Betty 133, 146, *147, 155, 167*
Gay Divorcee, The 42, 44, 45, 15, 170
Gaynor, Mitzi *8, 157*, 157, *165*, 165, *186, 189*, 190
Gentlemen Prefer Blondes 2, 176, 176
George White's Scandals 57, *58*, 61, 122
Gershe, Leonard 158
Gershwin, George 48, 82, 90, 101, 122, 125, 127, 142, 147, 150, 158, 162, 170, 190
Gershwin, Ira 48, 99, 101, 150

Gigi 165, *167*, 167
Gilbert and Sullivan 73
Gilford, Jack 201
Gillespie, Arnold 97
Gingold, Hermione 167, 214
Girl Crazy *101*, 101, *103*, 170
Girl of the Golden West, A *80*, 80
Gleason, James 138, *162*
Glenn Miller Story, The *137*, 137
Goddard, Paulette 104, *105*, 122
Godspell 8, 212-13
Going Hollywood 67
Going My Way 109, *112*, 112
Gold Diggers of 1933 *24*, 27-8, *27*
Gold Diggers of 1935 29-31, *31*, *33*
Gold Diggers of 1937 31, *35*
Good News 8, *173*, 173
Goodbye Mr Chips 226
Goodman, Benny 31, 137
Grable, Betty 31, 47, 58, 95, *113*, 113, 115-16, *115*, 118, *119*, 137-39, *138*; biography 115, 138-9
Grahame, Gloria 181
Granger, Farley 164
Grant, Cary 28, *126*, 127
Gray, Dolores, 135, *181*, 181
Grayson, Kathryn 73, *91*, 118, *119*, *125*, 125, 129, 130, *161*, 161, *162*, 162, 163, 169, *176*, 176
Grease *2*, *214*, *215*, 216-17, *216*, 225
Great Caruso, The *134*, 134, 161
Great Day 22
Great Victor Herbert, The 126
Great Waltz, The 81, 126
Great Ziegfeld, The 87, *88*, *90*, 90
Green, Adolph 99, 146
Green, Harry 20
Green, Martyn 73
Greenwood, Charlotte 25, 31
Grey, Joel 212, *238*
Grosse Liebe, Die 126
Guys and Dolls *168*, *180*, 180-81
Gypsy 192-3, *193*
Hagen, Jean 152, 155
Hair 215
Haley, Jack 54, 58, *86*, *93*, 93, *95*, 95, 96, 97, 173
Half a Sixpence 202
Halleluja 22
Hammerstein, Oscar, II 20, 77, 81, 90, 122, 152, 179, 181-2, 186, 190, 192, 198
Hamilton, Margaret 93, 95, *96*, 97
Handy, W C 137
Hans Christian Andersen 163
Harburg, E Y 93, 96, 99, 202
Hard Day's night, A *220*, *221*
Harris, Richard *201*, *202*, 201-02
Harrison, Rex *6*, *196*, 196, *225*
Hart, Lorenz 81, 101, 133, 186, 193
Hart, Moss 173
Harvey, Lilian *84*, *85*, 8405
Harvey Girls, The 118
Haver, June *115*, 116, 125
Havoc, June *58*, 138, 175, 192
Hayley, Bill 219
Haymes, Dick *104*, 175
Hayworth, Rita *2*, 104, *106*, 107, *126*, *162*, *185*, *186*, 186; biography 107
Hayward, Susan 122, 137
Hecht, Ben 90
Hello, Dolly! *7*, 206-07, *207*
Hello, Frisco, Hello *58*, 58
Help! *221*, 221
Henderson, Florence 208
Henie, Sonja 58-60, *60*
Hepburn, Audrey 142, *144*, *196*, 196, 198
Hepburn, Katharine 133
Herbert, Victor 74, 81, 126, 170
Here Comes the Waves *130*, 130
Here's to Romance 73
Herman, Jerry 207
High Society 145-6, *145*, *146*
High, Wide and Handsome *61*
Higher and Higher 173
Hilliard, Harriet 47
Hit the Deck 181
Holden, William 129
Holiday in Mexico 121
Holiday Inn *107*, 107
Holliday, Judy 190, *191*
Hollywood Calvalcade 58
Hollywood Revue of 1929, The 16-17, *17*, *19*, 20
Holm, Celeste 145
Honkey Tonk 16
Hope, Bob 63, 108, *109*, 122, 172
Hopkins, Miriam 21, 22
Horne, Lena 107, 108, 125, 129, 130, 133, 165, 171, 215
Horton, Edward Everett *37*, 46, 115
Howard, Ken 209
How to Succeed in Business Without Really Trying *201*, 201
Hunter, Tab *186*, 186
Hutton, Betty 125, *129*, 129, *130*, 130, *141*, 141, *175*, 175
I Dream Too Much 73
I Married an Angel *78*, *81*, 81
Iceland 60
In the Good Old Summertime *157*, 157, 212
Irene 170
It Happened in Brooklyn *162*, 162
It'a Always Fair Weather 95, *155*, 155
Iturbi, Jose 119, *125*, 130, 161
Jailhouse Rock *218*, *220*, 220
Jackson, Michael 215
Jahan, Marine 234
James, Harry 121, 130, 137
Jazz Singer, The 8, *10*, *13*, 13, 15; and remakes *222*, 222
Jessel, George 16
Jesus Christ, Sueprstar 8, *212*
Jewison, Norman 213
Johns, Glynis *226*, 226
Johnson, Van 129, *157*, 157, 161, 171, *179*
Jolson, Al 9, *10*, *13*, 13, *14*, 15, 29, 129, 128-9, 170
Jolson Sings Again 129
Jolson Story, The *128*, 128
Jones, Allan 81, 90, 96, 126, 169
Jones, Shirley *181*, 181, 182, *183*, 193-95, *195*
Jordan, Dorothy 41
Jourdan, Louis 165, *167*, 192
Jumbo 31
Jurgens, Curt 196
Just Around the Corner 57
Kahn, Madeline 226
Kane, Helen 20, 134
Karlweis, Oskar *84*, *85*
Kaye, Danny 25, 30, *145*, 145, 163
Kaye, Stubby 180, 190
Keaton, Buster 201
Keel, Howard *91*, 162, 163, 164, 165, *166*, 170, *175*, 175, *176*, 176, *181*
Keeler, Ruby *26*, 26, *27*, 27, *28*, 29, *31*
Kelly, Gene *2*, *9*, *91*, *93*, 99, *116*, 116, *125*, 125, *126*, 130, *131*, *132*, 133, 141, 146-50, *147*, *149*, *150*, *151*, *152*, 152, *154*, *155*, 155, 157, 157, 176, *179*, *252*
Kelly, Grace *145*, *146*, 145-6
Kendall, Kay *157*, 157
Kern, Jerome 48, 90, 116, 118, 122, 129, 162, 163
Kerr, Deborah *2*, *183*, *185*
Kerr, John 186
Kidd, Michael *155*, 155, 165
King, Carlotta 169
King, Charles 15
King and I, The *2*, 182, *183*, *185*, 185
Kinsky, Leonid *121*
Kirsten, Blanche 134
Kismet *181*, 181
Kiss Me Kate *176*, 176
Kissing Bandit, The 162
Kitt, Eartha 137
Knickerbocker Holiday 173
Kolmar, Bert 134
Kongress Tanzt, Der *84*, *85*
Korjus, Miliza 81
Kristofferson, Kris *228*, 228
Krupa, Gene 137
Ladd, Alan 122
Lady Be Good 122, 171-2, *171*
Lady in the Dark *173*, 173
Lahr, Bert 25, *93*, 93, *95*, 95, 97, 129, 164
Lake, Veronica 125
Lamas, Fernando 158, *171*
Lamarr, Hedy *121*, 121
Lamour, Dorothy 63, 108, 129
Lanchester, Elsa *75*
Lane, Burton 141, 165, 167, 202
Lane, Frankie 165
Langford, Frances 61, *63*, *107*, 171
Lansbury, Angela *118*
Lanza, Mario *134*, 134, *161*, 161, 180
Laurel and Hardy 73, *74*
Laurents, Arthur 192
Lawford, Peter *119*, 139, 161, *162*, 162, 173
Lee, Gypsy Rose 170, 192
Lee, Michele *201*
Lee, Peggy 144
Legrand, Michel 231
Lehar, Frank 74
Leigh, Janet 133, *167*, 195
Leonard, Sheldon 180
Lerner, Alan Jay 141, 165, 167, 176, 196, 201, 207
Leslie, Joan 107, *128*
Les Girls 155, *157*, 157
Lester, Mark *205*, 205
Lester, Richard 220, 221
Let It Be *221*, 222
Let's Dance 141
Let's Go Places 115
Levant, Oscar 142
Liebeswalzer *84*, 84
Lightner, Winnie 20
L'il Abner 190
Lili 163-4, *164*
Lillian Russell *58*, 58
Lillie, Beatrice 20
Lind, Jenny 73
Little Colonel, The *54*, 54
Little Miss Broadway *57*, 57
Little Miss Marker *52*, 52, 53
Little Nellie Kelly *171*, 171
Little Night Music, A 214
Little Princess, The 57
Littlest Rebel, The 54
Loesser, Frank 158, 163, 176, 180-81
Loewe, Frederick 176, 196, 201
London Town 126
Lorre, Peter *185*
Lost Horizon *226*
Lost in the Stars 213
Louisiana Purchase 172
Love, Bessie 15, 16
Love Me Or Leave Me 137
Love Me Tender 219, *220*
Love Me Tonight 74
Love Parade, The 16, *17*, *20*, 21, 74
Lovely to Look At 163
Loving You 219
Loy, Myrna 74, 87, *90*
Lubitsch, Ernst 16, 20-22, 74, 77, 157
Lullaby of Broadway 162, *163*
Luft, Lorna 225
Lund, John *145*

Lupino, Ida *61*
Lynde, Paul 195
Lynn, Diana 125
Lynn, Vera 126
McAvoy, May *13*
McCracken, Joan 173
McDonald, Jeanette 16, *17, 20*20, 21, *22*, 22, *72*, 74, *77*, 77, 80-82, *80, 82, 83*, 170
McDowall, Roddy 121
MacLaine, Shirley *191*, 192, *206*, 206
MacMurray, Fred 68, 116, 125
MacRae, Gordon 169, 171, *181*, 181, 182, *183*
MacCrea, Joel *57*
Mad About Music 71
Malden, Karl *193*
Mamoulian, Rouben 22, 74
Martin, Dean *191*
Martin, Mary *109*, 109, 126, 127
Martin, Steve *222, 225*
Martin, Tony 121, *122*, 129, 161, 170, 181
Martini, Nino 73
Marvin, Lee 207, *208*
Marx, Groucho 144
Mason, James 158
Massey, Ilona *82*, 83, 121
Mame 212, 213, 213
Man of La Mancha 212
March of Time, The 22
Mary Poppins *6, 225, 226*, 226
Mature, Victor 195
May Time 78, 80, 170
Meet Me in Las Vegas 165
Meet Me in St Louis 95, 116
Mein Herz Ruft nach Dir 85
Melchoir, Lauritz *119*, 161
Menjou, Adolphe *52*, 52, 53, *115*, 116
Mercer, Johnny 99, 118, 130, 141, 165
Meredith, Burgess 104, *105*
Merkel, Una *63*
Merman, Ethel 58, *165*, 165, 172, *175*, 176
Merry Widow, The 74, *77*, 77, *171*
Midler, Bette *222*, 222
Milland, Ray 122, 171
Miller, Ann 139, 146, *147*, 162, *164*, 164, 171, *176*, 176
Miller, Glenn 60
Miller, Marilyn *16*, 16
Million Dollar Mermaid 28, *158*
Mills Brothers, The 63
Minnelli, Liza *211, 212*, 212, *238*
Minelli, Vincente 99, 108, 116, 121, 129, 150, 167, 208, 212
Miranda, Carmen 31, *36*, 36, *37*, 118-19, *121, 162*, 178
Mr Music 144
Monroe, Marilyn *2*, 138, 164, *165, 175*, 176
Montalban, Ricardo 158, 162
Monte Carlo 21, 22
Monetevecchi, Liliane 165
Montgomery, George 116
Montiel, Serita *161*
Moon Over Miami 113
Moore, Grace 73, *75*
Moore, Melba 213
Moore, Victor 125, 172
Moorehead, Agnes 162
Moreno, Rita 185, 192
Morgan, Dennis 90, 122, 169
Morgan, Frank 22 *80*, 93, 95, 125, 175
Morgan, Helen 22
Morgan, Michele 173
Morris, Chester 20
Morse, Robert *201*, 202
Mostel, Zero 201
Mother Wore Tights 138, 138
Mowbray, Alan *29*
Munshin, Jules 146, *147, 185*
Murphey, George 57, 96, *116*, 125, *171*, 171
Music in the Air 170
Music Man, The 8, 193-5, *195*
My Blue Heaven 138
My Fair Lady 6, 9, *196*, 196, 198
My Lucky Star 59-60
My Man 16
My Sister Eileen 167
Nagy, Kathe, von *85*
Naish, J Carrol *119*
Nash, Ogden 82
Naughty Marietta *72*, 73, *75*, 77, 170
Neagle, Anna 171
Neff, Hildegard 196
Nelson, Gene *163*
Neptune's Daughter 158
Nero, Franco *201*
New Moon, The 78, 80, 170
Newhart, Bob 208
Newley, Anthony 199, 201
Newton-John, Olivia 214
Nicholson, Jack 208
Night and Day 126
Niven, David 77
Nixon, Marni 182, 192, 196, 198, 199
Novak, Kim *185*, 186
No, No, Nanette 20, 171
Oakie, Jack *20*, 20, *58*, 115, 138
O'Brien, Margaret *118*
O'Brien, Pat 25
O'Brien, Virginia 125, *171*
O'Connell, Helen 129
O'Connor, Donald *9*, 68, *152*, 152, 155, *163, 165*, 165, *175*, 175, 176
Oklahoma! 9, 63, *181*, 181, *182*
Oland, Warner 13, 20
Oliver! 9, *205*, 205
On A Clear Day You Can See Forever 208, 208
On The Town 9, 95, 146-7, *147*
One Hundred Men and a Girl 71, 71
One in a Million 58-9, *60*
One Night of Love 73, *75*
O'Toole, Peter 212, 226
Our Dancing Daughters 14
Our Little Girl 57
Out of This World 125
Paint Your Wagon 207-08, *208*
Pajama Game, The 185, 185-6
Pal Joey 185, 186, 186
Palmer, Peter 186
Palmy Days 25
Panama Hattie 172, 172
Paramount on Parade 20, *21*
Parker, Dorothy 81
Parks, Larry *128*, 128, 129, *162*
Patrick, Gail *61, 69*
Payne, John *58*, 60, *115*, 115, 119
Pearce, Alice 146
Pearson, Jessie *195*
Pennies From Heaven (1936) 67, *68, 69*
Pennies From Heaven (1981) *222*, 222, *225*, 225
Peters, Bernadette *222*
Peters, Brock 213
Peters, Susan 100
Pickford, Mary 21, 25, 51
Picon, Molly 208
Pidgeon, Walter *80*, 121, 181
Pigskin Parade 96
Pin-Up Girl 137
Pirate, The 146, *147*
Plummer, Christopher *7*, 199
Poitier, Sidney *190*, 190
Pons, Lily 73
Poor Little Rich Girl 54, *57*
Porgy and Bess 190, 190
Porter, Cole 40, 45, 63, 82, 99, 104, 127, 146, 157, 162, 172-3, 176, 192, 226
Powell, Dick 26, *27*, 27, 28, 29, *31, 35, 37*, 122, 170
Powell, Eleanor *9*, 57, 61, *63*, 63, *65, 67*, 90, 96, 104, 122, 125, 129, *171*, 171, *234*; biography 122
Powell, Jane 121, 141, 162, 164, 165, *166*, 181
Powell, William 29, 87, *90*
Power, Tyrone 58, *59*, 60, 137
Presley, Elvis 195, *218*, 219-20, *220*
Preston, Robert 193, *195*, 195, 213, 227
Previn, André 162
Price, Vincent 161
Pryor, Richard 215
Prowse, Juliet 192
Quinn, Aileen *216*
Ragland, 'Rags' *172*, 172
Rainer, Luise 81, 87
Raitt, John *185*, 185
Ray, Johnny *165*, 165
Raye, Martha 63, 67, 193
Rebecca of Sunnybrook Farm 57, 57
Red Hot and Blue 175
Redgrave, Vanessa 201-02, *201*
Reinking, Ann *231*
Reynolds, Burt *217*, 226
Reynolds, Debby *9, 93*, 134, *140*, 152, 152, 155, 181, *198*, 198
Rhapsody in Blue 127-8, *128*
Rhythm on the Range 67, *69, 109*
Rice, Florence *80*
Rigg, Diana 214
Ritchard, Cyril 202
Road pictures 108-09, *109, 110, 111*
Robbins, Jerome 192
Roberta 38, 45, 45-6, 170
Robeson, Paul 169
Robinson, Bill *54*, 54, *57*, 57, *108*
Rock Around the Clock 219
Rocky Horror Picture Show 213, 213-14
Rogers, Ginger *26*, 27, *28, 38*, 390-48, *41, 44, 46, 47*, 51, 141, *173*, 173; biography 41, 44
Rodgers, Richard 81, 101, 133, 181-82, 186, 190, 192, 193, 198
Romberg, Sigmund 20, 81-2, 82, 137, 170, 180
Roman Scandals 28-9, *29*
Romero, Cesar *53*, 116
Romey 85, 85
Rooney, Mickey 22, 96, *98*, 990101, *100, 101, 103*, 125, 133, 170, 171; biography 100-01
Rosalie 63, 82
Rose, The 222, 222
Rose Marie 77, 170; (1954) *79*, 164, 170
Rose of Washington Square 58
Rosita 21
Ross, Diana *215*, 215
Royal Wedding 3, 141, 141
Rubinstein, Arthur 133
Ruby, Harry 134
Ruggles, Charles 74
Rumann, Heinz 84
Russell, Jane *174*, 176
Russell, Rosalind 192, *193*
St Louis Blues 137
Sakal, S Z *157*, 157
Sally 16, 16
Sally, Irene and Mary 170
Saludos Amigos 121
San Francisco 82
San Juan, Olga 175
Sanders, George *175*, 176
Sandrich, Mark 46-7
Saturday Night Fever 8, 214, 215, *231*, 231
Say It With Songs 15
Scheider, Roy *234*
Scott, Randolph 44, *61*
Second Chorus 104, *105*
Selznick, David O 52
Serenade 161, 161
Seven Brides for Seven Brothers 165, 165, *166*
Seven Hills of Rome 161
1776 209

Shall We Dance 42, *47*, *48*
Shaw, Winifred 31
Shearer, Douglas 77
Ship Ahoy 129
Shore, Dinah 25, 129, 130
Show Boat 90, *91*, 162, 169, *170*
Show of Shows 20
Silk Stockings *185*, 186
Silvers, Phil *126*, 138, 173, 201
Simmons, Jean *168*, 180
Simms, Ginny 125
Sinatra, Frank 129, 130, *131*, 145, 146, *147*, 149, 162, 162, 173, *180*, 180, *185*, 186, *191*, 192
Sing You Sinners *68*
Singing Fool, The *14*, 15
Singin' in the Rain *2*, 8, *9*, 95, *152*, 152, *155*, 155, *252*
Skelton, Red 99, *121*, 122, 125, 126, 141, 158, 163, *171*, 171, *172*, 173
Sky's the Limit, The 107
Small Town Girl *164*, 164
Smith, Kate 63
Smiling Lieutenant, The 21-2, 171
Snow White and the Seven Dwarfs *8*, 90, 93
So Endete eine Liebe *84*
So This Is Love 73
Something for the Boys 173
Sondergaard, Gale 97
Sondheim, Stephen 192-3, 201, 214
Song of Love 133
Song of Norway 208
Sothern, Ann 20, 122, 125, 133, *171*, 171, *172*
Sound of Music, The *7*, 198-9, *199*, *201*
South Pacific *8*, 8, 130, *186*, 187, *189*, 190
Stallone, Slyvester 234
Star! *2*, *227*
Star is Born, A 8, 157-8, *157*; (1976) *227*, *228*, 228
Stars and Stripes Forever 134
State Fair (1945) *59*, *101*, *104*; (1962) 58
Staying Alive *232*, 234
Steele, Tommy *202*, 202
Stein, Jule 192, 205
Stevens, Rise *83*, 83
Stewart, James *63*, 77, 121, *137*, 137
Stop the World, I Want to Get Off 199, 201
Stormy Weather *108*, 108
Story of Vernon and Irene Castle, The *42*, *51*, 51
Stowaway 54, 57
Stowkowski, Leopold 71, 71
Streisand, Barbra *2*, *7*, 58, *205*, 205, *206*, 206, *207*, *208*, 208, 227-31, *227*, *228*, *233*
Strike Up the Band *100*, 101, *103*, 171
Stuart, Gloria *31*
Student Prince, The 180
Summer Stock *6*, 147, *148*
Sun Valley Serenade 60
Swanee River 126
Swanson, Gloria 170
Swarthout, Gladys 73
Sweet Charity *206*, 206
Sweethearts *79*, *80*, 81, 170
Sweet Rosie O'Grady *115*, 116
Swing Time *43*, *47*, 47-8
Take Me Out to the Ball Game 146, *149*
Taylor, Elizabeth 162, 214
Taylor, Robert 96
Tea For Two 171
Temple, Shirley 51-4, *51*, *52*, *53*, *54*, *57*, 57, 58, 96
Thank Your Lucky Stars 122, 130
That's Entertainment 8, 234
There's No Business Like Show Business *165*, 165
This is The Army *129*, 129
Thousands Cheer *124*, 125
Three Little Words *134*, 134, 141
Three Smart Girls 71, . . . *Grow Up* 70
Threepenny Opera, The 195-6, 211
Till the Clouds Roll By 129
Tilton, Martha 137
Tin Pan Alley 58, 115
Toast of New Orleans, The *161*, 161
Too Many Girls 171
Top Hat *41*, *43*, *46*, 46
Top o' the Morning 144
Topol, Chaim 208, *209*
Torme, Mel 173
Tracy, Arthur 63
Travolta, John *214*, 214, *215*, 215, *216*, *231*, 231, *232*, 234
Treacher, Arthur 122, 171, 226
Tucker, Sophie 16, 96
Tufts, Sonny 130
Tune, Tommy 208
Turner, Lana 100, 121-2, *171*, 173
Twiggy 208
Two Girls and a Sailor 130
Two Sisters From Boston 118, 161
Unsinkable Molly Brown, The *198*, 198
Up in Central Park 175
Vagabond King, The 20, 185
Vallee, Rudy 57, *58*, 201
Van, Bobby 164, 176
Van Dyke, Dick 195, *225*, 226
Van Dyke, W S 73
Verdon, Gwen *186*, 186
Vera-Ellen *132*, 133, *134*, 134, 141, 146, *175*, 176
Victor, Victoria 226-7
Vidor, King 22
Viktor und Viktoria *229*
Wabash Avenue 138
Walker, Nancy 125
Walker, Robert 133, 175
Warren, Harry 141
Waters, Ethel *107*, 107
Webb, Clifton 134
Wee Willie Winkie *53*
Weill, Kurt 9, 125, 173, 175, 195, 196, 213
We'll Meet Again 126
West Side Story 8, 9, *192*, 192, *193*
Whale, James 90, 169
Wharf, Richard 129
When My Baby Smiles at Me 138
Where Do We Go From Here? 9, 125
Where's Charley? 176
White Christmas *145*, 145
Whiteman, Paul 67, 101
Whoopee 25, 115
Williams, Esther 28, 100, *121*, 121, 125, 146, *149*, 158, 158-61, *159*
Wilson, Dooley 8
Wilson, Eileen 175
Wilson, Meredith 193, 198
With a Song in My Heart 134, 137
Wiz, The *215*, 215, *217*
Wizard of Oz, The *1*, *6*, 9, *86*, 93-7, *93*, *95*; making of 97
Wonder Bar 170
Wood, Natalie 144, 192, *193*
Words and Music 133, *134*
Wynn, Ed 226
Wynn, Keenan 176, 202
Yankee Doodle Dandy 126-7, *127*
Yellow Submarine, The 221-2, *221*
Yentl 231, *233*
You Were Never Lovelier 107
You'll Never Get Rich 104, 107
Youmans, Vincent 22, 180
Young, Robert *115*, 116, 122, *171*, 171
Zanuck, Darryl F 13, 25, 58, 115
Ziegfeld, Florenz 16, 20, 87, 90, 101
Ziegfeld Follies 125-6, *125*
Ziegfeld Girl 121-2

ACKNOWLEDGMENTS AND CREDITS

Acknowledgments
The author and publisher would like to thank the following people who have helped in the preparation of this book: Ron Callow, who designed it; Robin Sommer, who edited it; John K Crowley, who did the photo research; Cynthia Klein, who prepared the index.

Picture Credits
All photos from Jerry Ohlinger's Movie Materials Store, with the following exceptions:
Associated Press: 153.
Museum of Modern Art: 8 (bottom), 14, 16, 17 (top), 21, 24, 26, 27, 28 (bottom), 31, 32-33, 37, 42 (top right, center right), 43 (bottom right), 44 (top), 46 (bottom), 48 (bottom), 52, 53 (top), 54 (bottom), 55, 56, 59 (top left, bottom), 61, 62, 63, 64-65, 66, 67, 68, 68-69, 69, 71, 72, 77, 78 (top and second from top), 79 (top left and bottom), 88-89, 90, 91 (top), 94-95, 96, 100, 101, 102 (top right), 103 (top right), 104, 105, 107, 109 (top), 110 (top right, bottom right), 111, 112, 115 (center, bottom), 118 (bottom), 119 (top), 121, 122, 125 (top), 126, 127, 128, 134 (center, bottom), 137, 139, 140, 141 (top), 143, 144 (bottom), 145, 147, 150 (bottom), 155 (bottom), 156, 157 (top), 162 (top), 163 (top), 164, 165 (top), 167 (top), 171 (top left, bottom), 172, 173 (bottom), 174, 181 (top, bottom), 183, 185 (top), 186 (top), 190 (top), 191, 193 (top left), 194, 195, 201 (top left, bottom), 202, 206 (top), 207 (bottom), 209 (bottom), 213 (top), 215, 220 (top left, bottom), 222, 223, 234.
National Film Archives: 4, 8 (top left), 9 (bottom), 10, 15, 17 (bottom), 18-19, 29 (bottom), 30, 38, 42 (top right), 47 (top), 48 (top), 56, 75 (top), 76, 103 (top left, bottom right), 116-117, 136, 138, 165 (bottom), 168, 180 (bottom), 182 (top), 186 (bottom), 197, 206 (bottom), 208 (bottom), 212 (center), 225 (bottom right), 226, 228 (bottom), 237.